Cultivation and Marketing Practices of Sugarcane Farmers

Dr.D. Tamilselvi,

Assistant Professor,

PG & Research Department of Commerce,

Gobi Arts & Science College, Gobichettipalayam.

Published by

Cultivation and Marketing Practices of Sugarcane Farmers

ISBN 978-93-86176-99-8

Author

Dr.D. Tamilselvi

Bonfring

309, 2nd Floor, 5th Street Extension, Gandhipuram,

Coimbatore-641 012.

Tamilnadu, India.

E-mail: info@bonfring.org

Website: www.bonfring.org

Phone: 0422 4213231

Preface

Agriculture is the backbone of the Indian economy and it continues to be the most predominant sector of Indian economy. Now-a-days in the agricultural sector in India, cultivable land has been declined due to rapid urbanisation and industrialisation. Farmers' access to market is hampered by poor roads, rudimentary market infrastructure and excessive regulations and almost universal lack of good extension services are responsible factors.

In the field of agriculture, the role played by sugarcane is a vital one. Today, sugarcane cultivation and sugar industry stands as supporting pillars of Indian economy and contributes for seven per cent of the total value of agricultural output. In order to modernise the cultivation and marketing practices of sugarcane, it is necessary to identify the functioning of marketing channels.

Sugarcane occupies a prominent position as a cash and commercial crop. The major sugarcane producing countries are Brazil, India and Cuba. In India, the top sugarcane producing states are Uttar Pradesh, Maharashtra, Karnataka and Tamil Nadu. Tamil Nadu has registered with the highest yield in sugarcane production. In Erode district, sugarcane plays a pivotal role in the economy of the district and it is cultivated mainly under irrigated conditions. Erode district is the second highest among various districts of Tamil Nadu but the productivity of sugarcane in Erode district is far average level of overall districts of Tamil Nadu. The role of sugarcane cultivation in uplifting the rural masses and the rural economy through sugar industry cannot be ignored.

Sugarcane farmers follow different practices in different regions. The farmers have the option to sell the sugarcane or own crushing for produce of khandsari sugar. This book is primarily undertaken with a view to examine the cultivation and marketing practices of sugarcane farmers. Though sugarcane is grown in most of the districts in Tamil Nadu, this book confines to Erode district only as this district is one of the leading districts in sugarcane cultivation in the state. This book also focuses the cost of sugarcane cultivation. This book pertains to analyse the attitude of farmers towards the adoption of drip irrigation system in sugarcane cultivation.

The goal of this book is to identify the factors which motivate the farmers to market their sugarcane and khandsari sugar. This book further analyses the price spread along with the level of satisfaction of farmers about the functioning of sugarcane and khandsari sugar marketing channels. This book also analyses the problems of sugarcane farmers in cultivation and marketing. This book also covers the area, production and productivity of sugarcane at National, State and District level. It enables students to evaluate the performance of these practices, as well as gain an appreciation for marketing and its contribution to economic development.

Organisation of the Book

This book is organized in the following chapters.

Chapter I contains introduction, statement of the problem, review of literature, importance, objectives, hypotheses, operational definitions, scope, period, pilot study and pre-testing, methodology and tools, collection of data, tools used for analysis, limitations.

Chapter II examine the growth in area, production and productivity of sugarcane and export and import of sugar in India.

Chapter III deals with existing sugarcane practices have been highlighted. Further, factors influencing the farmers to cultivate the sugarcane, reasons for using a particular variety in sugarcane cultivation and cost & return analysis of sugarcane cultivation have been examined.

Chapter IV focuses on factors influencing the farmers to adopt drip irrigation system in sugarcane cultivation, satisfaction level of farmers, reasons for non-adoption of drip irrigation system and problems faced by the farmers in adoption of drip irrigation system in sugarcane cultivation.

Chapter V specifies, factors motivating the farmers to prefer marketing of sugarcane, production of khandsari sugar, to prefer the particular marketing channel of sugarcane and khandsari sugar, level of satisfaction of the farmers about the functioning of sugarcane and khandsari sugar marketing channels, marketing cost, marketing margin and price-spread of various identified channels in marketing of khandsari sugar have been examined.

Chapter VI examines the problems faced by the farmers in sugarcane cultivation, production of khandsari sugar and marketing of sugarcane & khandsari sugar.

Chapter VII has been made to bring together all the findings and conclusion and offers necessary suggestions for improving the cultivation and marketing of sugarcane in Erode district of Tamil Nadu.

Acknowledgement

First and foremost, I owe it all to **Almighty God** for granting me the wisdom, health and strength to undertake this work task and enabling me to its successful completion of this work.

I would like to express my gratitude to the many people who saw me through this book and all those who provided support, talked things over, read, wrote, offered comments, allowed me to quote their remarks and assisted in the editing, proofreading and design.

I would like to thank the management, principal, staffs and colleagues of our college for their encouragement and support to complete this work.

On a personal note, I would like to express my special thanks to my son S. Mohidhvishnu, my husband Mr.D. Sambathkumar and my family members for their patience, support and encouragement for publishing this book.

Finally, I thank the Bonfirng for publishing this book in a wonderful manner.

Dr.D. Tamilselvi

<table>
<tr><th>Chapter</th><th>Contents</th><th>Page No</th></tr>
</table>

CHAPTER I

INTRODUCTION AND DESIGN

Keywords

Sugarcane Scenario - Statement of the Problem - Review of Literature - Importance - Objectives - Hypotheses - Operational Definitions - Scope – Period - Methodology and Tools - Limitations.

1.1. Introduction

India is the seventh largest country at geographical level and second in population and twelfth largest country in economy wise. The economy of India is as diverse as it is large, with a number of major sectors including manufacturing industries, agriculture, textiles and handicrafts and services. Agriculture is a major component of the Indian economy. Mahatma Gandhi said "Indian economy lives in her villages" and many of the industries getting their raw material from agriculture sector. Agriculture, the predominant sector of the Indian economy, is the principal source of livelihood for more than 52 percent of the population though its contribution to the national GDP had declined to 13.9 percent due to the high growth in the industries and service sectors[1]. The importance of agriculture to the country is best summed up by this statement: "If agriculture survives, India survives". Agricultural sector is more useful to the economic development of the country either directly or indirectly.

"Agriculture is the backbone of the Indian Economy" said Mahatma Gandhi. Even today, as we entered the new millennium, the situation is still the same, with almost the entire economy being sustained by agriculture, which is the mainstay of the villages. The agricultural division plays an important role in the large scale employment to people. Large and fairly large farms employ workers to undertake various jobs relating to farming of crops and care of farm animals. In most of the countries of the world, agriculture still remains the biggest division responsible for the employing and feeding a large percentage of the population. Agriculture is also important from the viewpoint of assessing the standard of a country's development based on the capability of its farmers. Poorly trained farmers cannot apply the higher methods and new technologies.

The importance of science and technology in the development of agriculture is fairly clear from the words of Deng Xiaoping-The growth of agriculture depends primarily on policy and

---

[1] Raghavalu M.V., (2013), "Indian Agriculture: Performance and Challenge", Kisan World, Vol. 40, No. 5, May, Pp. 17-18.

1

next on science. There is neither any limit to developments in science and technology, nor to the role that they can play in the field of agricultural growth'. Even if agriculture frequently plays a contributory role in the 'Gross Domestic Product' of most countries, it nevertheless requires a substantial increase from both the local and the international community. Agriculture is conventionally based on bulk manufacturing. Harvesting is done once a season, most of the times and stocked and used later. In fact, some thinkers opine that people have begun to adopt 'batch processing' and 'stocking' in manufacturing, as a result of the practices from agricultural thinking. Before industrialization, people with the biggest stocks of food and other supplies were considered more stable and they were able to face challenges of nature without having to starve. So, important is the role of agriculture that new concepts keep 'cropping up' to give the traditional activity a modern turn. One such new idea the world is gibbering about these days is the importance of organic farming, drip method of irrigation, sugarcane sustainable initiative, adoption of new technology, etc.

Sugarcane

The history of sugar and sugarcane in India goes back to several thousand years BC. Indian mythology vouches for this since it contains some legends depicting the origin of sugarcane. The word 'sugar' is derived from the word Sarkara. Thus, it could be rightly said that India has been the original home for sugarcane as well as sugar manufacture.

Sugarcane provides the raw material mainly for the production of white sugar, jaggery [gur] and khandsari. It is also used for chewing and extraction of juice for beverage purpose. Sugarcane is a multi-product crop and has immense potential for diversification. Beside the production of sugar, green top of sugarcane is used as fodder for milk cattle, similarly molasses, a by-product of sugar processing is also used as a cattle feed. During the year 2012-2013, sugarcane used by factory for white sugar 73.90 per cent and khandsari sugar 14.80 per cent and seed, feed and chewing 11.30 per cent of the total production in India.[2]

Sugarcane and sugar beet are the main sources of sugar in Asia and Europe respectively. Sugarcane is grown primarily in the tropical and sub-tropical zones of the southern hemisphere; sugar beet is grown in the temperate zones of the northern hemisphere. During 1970s, sugarcane and sugar beet accounted for 60 per cent and 40 per cent respectively of the total sugar production in the world. However, during 1990s, the corresponding figures were 68 per cent and 32 per cent[3]. During the year 2012-2013, sugarcane accounted for 77 per cent

[2]Statistics, (2014), Indian Sugar the Complete Sugar Journal, Vol. 44, No. 6. April, p. 63.

[3] www.iisr.nic.in, retrieved on 17.10.2013

of the total sugar production in the world and sugar beet accounted for the rest. These figures amply demonstrate the growing importance of sugarcane in sugar production.

Sugarcane: World Scenario

At present, 115 countries of the world cultivate sugarcane for sugar production and produce about 133 million tonnes of sugar, which is three fourth of the total sugar production (169 million tonnes) of the world[4]. The major sugarcane producing countries are Brazil, India, China, Pakistan, USA, Australia, Thailand, Philippines, etc. India is the second largest producer of sugarcane in the world. Brazil is the major producer of sugarcane in the world.

Sugarcane: Indian Scenario

In India, sugarcane is the second largest crop in the country in terms of value next to rice and wheat. About 52 million sugarcane farmers and their dependents have been involved in sugarcane cultivation. In India, there are two distinct zones for sugarcane cultivation, tropical-south and subtropical north. Tropical regions are Maharashtra, Gujarat, Tamil Nadu, Andhra Pradesh and Karnataka. The Sub-Tropical regions are Uttar Pradesh, Bihar, Punjab and Haryana.

Sugarcane being a tropical crop finds favourable agro climatic conditions for its growth in this region i.e. higher yields. Growth after 1950's was more in this region and by 1994-1995 the sub-tropical region; sugarcane area was 65 per cent and production was 55 per cent of the total sugarcane produced. Now, the tropical region is already developed and reached near saturation level. The biggest state in this region- Maharashtra faces an acute problem of lack of water, which affects cultivation of sugarcane. The sub-tropical belt with fertile land, high water table and irrigation, appears to be the area for future growth. About 9 states produce 97 per cent of sugarcane and 5 states contributed to about 87 per cent of sugarcane produced in 1994-1995. Subtropical north comprising 60 per cent of total cane area contributes only 48 per cent to total cane and 37 per cent to total white sugar production in the country. The average cane productivity in subtropical north zone was 54.7 and 56.4 tonnes per hectare in comparison to 81.9 and 80.8 tonnes per hectare in tropical south zone (2009-2010 and 2010-2011 respectively)[5].

Sugarcane is grown by a large number of farmers its command area supply, marketing and payment to the farmers etc., have been regulated by various Acts and Sugarcane Control orders

---

[4]ibid

[5]ibid

promulgated and amended by the Government from time to time. Sugarcane development has received due importance both at the national level as well as at the state (province) levels. The rapid developments in sugarcane cultivation and sugar industry in the country have earned India a prestigious position among sugar producing nations in the world.

Sugar Production in India

Indian sugar production growth came up under structured and planned sugar programme. The demand, the production requirement, the capacity needed and cane production went through a planning process and close monitoring by the planners over the past 4 decades. Further, in order to achieve the set targets, the government has been setting up committees, task forces from time to time to make policy changes in consultation with industry, State agriculture Departments, etc., in areas such as cane and sugar pricing policy, levy price fixation, free sales/levy sugar ratio, etc. Also, the government has been closely monitoring the licencing policy. In India, sugarcane is also utilised for production of traditional sweeteners like gur and khandsari. The country produces a total of about 10 metric tonnes (9 metric tonnes gur and 1 metric tonne khandsari). This sector enjoys all the freedom. No controls, no restriction on cane prices, the sector can pay commercial price.[6]

Sugar Industry in India

Sugar industry is one of the agro-based industries in India and it is the second largest industry next to textile industry. About 0.4 million skilled and unskilled workers are employed by the industry and additional employment is also generated by the allied industries for the socio-economic development of the nation. During 2012-2013, there are 526 sugar mills operating in India with an aggregate installed capacity of 4125 metric tonnes. The total production of sugar at that time was only about 25140 thousand metric tonnes in India[7].

Sugar industry in Tamil Nadu plays a vital role in the rural development. At present, there are 46 sugar mills in Tamil Nadu consisting of 16 sugar mills in cooperative sector, 3 sugar mills in public sector and 27 sugar mills in the private sector. During 2012-2013, the total area used for sugarcane production 3.95 lakhs hectares, total sugarcane crushing capacity 213.95 lakhs metric tonnes with sugar production of 1958 lakhs metric tonnes and sugar recovery 9.15 per cent in Tamil Nadu.[8]

---

[6]Padmanabhan V., (2009), "Sugarcane and Sugar in India", Kisan World, Vol.36, No.5, May, Pp. 29-30.

[7]Statistics, (2014), op.cit., p. 2.

[8] Government of India, (2013), Ministry for agriculture, Policy Note, Demand No.5- Agriculture, Pp. 81-87.

Sugarcane: Tamil Nadu Scenario

Agriculture is the most predominant sector of the economy of Tamil Nadu, a state in India. 70 per cent of the state's population are engaged in agriculture and allied activities for their livelihood. Tamil Nadu has an area of 1.3 lakh km² with a gross cropped area of around 58.43 lakh hectares, of which the gross irrigated area is 33.09 lakh hectares which is 57 per cent and the balance 43 per cent of the area are under rain fed cultivation. Tamil Nadu is the homeland of Dr.M.S. Swaminathan, known as the "Father of the Green Revolution" in India. The state is historically known for its agriculture from ancient times. Tamil Nadu has been agro-climatic zones based on rainfall distribution, irrigation pattern, soil conditions, cropping pattern and other physical, ecological and social characteristics including administrative divisions.

Sugarcane is one of the traditional crops grown abundantly in the state of Tamil Nadu. The area under sugarcane cultivation is increasing year by year due to the increased demand in consumption of sugar and also demands from sugar mills as raw material. During the sugar season year 2012-2013, the sugarcane crop is cultivated in about 43 to 44 lakhs hectares in India whereas it is cultivated in 3.95 lakhs hectares in the state and the total estimated sugarcane production is 422.20 lakhs metric tonne[9]. The average productivity of sugarcane in India is 67 to 68 tonnes per hectare but Tamil Nadu is with the highest productivity of 100-106 tonnes per hectare compared to other states[10].

In Tamil Nadu, major sugarcane growing districts are Villupuram, Erode, Cuddalore, Tiruvannmalai, Vellore, Namakkal, Dharmapuri, Thanjavur, Perambalur, Salem, Pudukkottai, Theni, Coimbatore, Karur and Thiruvallur. Erode has the second highest productivity of sugarcane in the state.

Sugarcane Scenario in Erode District

Erode district is one of the important districts in Tamil Nadu and has an important role in the economic development of the state. Erode district is having a notable development in various fields viz., agriculture, textile products, trade, food products, etc. Erode is one among the Districts in Tamil Nadu where sugarcane is cultivated on a large scale. In Erode District, the total sugarcane production is 37,53,260 tonnes per annum. Abundance of labour force, availability of irrigation facilities and Government support, liberal loan facilities from bank etc.,

---

[9] ibid.

[10] Sivanappan R.K., (2009), "Sugarcane Cultivation with Drip Irrigation and Fertigation", Kisan World, Vol. 36, No. 2, March, p. 19.

are the factors which favoured for the large scale cultivation of sugarcane in this district. The average sugarcane yield in the district is 119 tonnes per hectare[11].

1.2.   Statement of the Problem

Sugarcane occupies a prominent position as a cash and commercial crop. The major sugarcane producing countries are Brazil, India and Cuba. In India, the top sugarcane producing states are Uttar Pradesh, Maharashtra, Karnataka and Tamil Nadu. Tamil Nadu has registered with the highest yield in sugarcane production. In Erode district, sugarcane plays a pivotal role in the economy of the district and it is cultivated mainly under irrigated conditions. It is a base for many agro industries in this district. In terms of the area and production per hectare, Erode district is the second highest among various districts of Tamil Nadu but the productivity of sugarcane in Erode district is far average level of overall districts of Tamil Nadu. The role of sugarcane cultivation in uplifting the rural masses and the rural economy through sugar industry cannot be ignored. This is the only crop which plays a very significant role in the rural area of this district. The favourable climate and soil conditions coupled with assured irrigation enable Erode district to emerge as one of the largest sugarcane growing belts of the state.

A steep rise in production cost and wide fluctuation in the prices of agricultural commodities are the two major factors affecting the income levels of farmers. The price elasticity of demand for these commodities raising steadily, their price instability is largely attributed to the changes in their production and the consequent changes in the market arrivals. The price instability is more pronounced in the case of commercial crops like groundnut, sunflower, chilly and sugarcane. The minimization of fluctuation in the prices of commodities over space and time through adequate processing, transportation, storage, government policies and other facilities not only stabilises the income of the farming community but also synchronizes the demand for and supply of farm products.

The State Government fixes State Advisory Prices for sugarcane per tonne which is above the Central Government's Minimum Statutory Price every year. The sugarcane farmers incur high input cost of labour and materials in sugarcane cultivation. They have the option of selling sugarcane to the sugar factories or to jaggery producers or producing khandsari sugar and selling in the market. If the sugarcane farmers are selling their sugarcane to sugar factory, they get delayed payments and incur the high cost of cutting charges. So, the farmers prefer to

---

[11] Season and crop report (2012-2013), (G- Return Fasli_1421), Government of Tamil Nadu, Directorate of Economics and Statistics.

supply their sugarcane to jaggery producers for reasonable price based on the conditions of jaggery market. At present, most of the sugarcane farmers are not ready to take risk for producing khandsari sugar due to high input cost, non-availability of trained labourer, lowerprice of khandsari sugar, problem in grading & analysing and also high marketing costs involved. In the view of said constraints, it is very much essential to look into the present position of sugarcane farmers, khandsari sugar and jaggery producers in Tamil Nadu. The farmers are losing their interest in sugarcane cultivation which ultimately affects the economy of the state and nation where sugarcane is considered as one of the important valuable crops of India. It is in this context, several pertinent questions are raised:

- What is the growth in area, production and productivity of sugarcane?
- What are the cultivation practices followed by the farmers?
- What is the cultivation cost incurred by the farmers?
- Why do farmers adopt drip irrigation system in cultivating sugarcane?
- What are the marketing practices followed by the sugarcane farmers?
- What are the problems of farmers in cultivation and marketing of sugarcane?

Hence, the present research is undertaken to cultivation and marketing practices of sugarcane farmer in Erode district of Tamil Nadu with an aim to improve the cultivation and marketing of sugarcane in the area.

1.3. Review of Literature

In any study, the review of previous studies is considered as important for getting a better understanding of the problem, objectives, the methodology followed and to identify the unexplored part of the field of study under consideration. In this regard, a review of some of the studies relating to the present study has been undertaken and presented in the following section.

Singh and Jagdish Lal[12](1992) analysed the sugarcane production targets and results revealed that the compound growth rate of sugarcane production in sub-tropical states were less than the tropical states. The contribution of area in increasing the output was more than the productivity. There is disparity in yield in different tropical and sub-tropical states. The sugarcane yield in tropical belt is generally higher 84.11 tonnes per hectare when compared to those in sub-tropical belt 50.4 tonnes per hectare. Further, it is found that Tamil Nadu has recorded the highest

---

[12] Singh G.B. and Jagdish Lal., (1992), "Sugarcane Production Targets and Strategies to Realise", Agricultural Situation in India,Vol. XLVI, No. 5, August, pp. 383-388.

average yield 104.8 tonnes per hectare followed by Maharashtra 86.1 tonnes per hectare as against the Punjab and Uttar Pradesh.

Singhet al.[13](1994) conducted a study to examine the annual compound growth rate of area, production and productivity of sugarcane by making use of an exponential equation. The results revealed that the acreage, production and productivity of sugarcane have increased with moderate year to year fluctuations in the different agro-economic regions and Uttar Pradesh as a whole except Bundel-Khand region of the State. The major factors significantly and positively influencing to sugarcane area are found that rainfall, gur price, competitive crop price and current year's price of sugarcane.

Baliyan et al.[14](1995) estimated that the cost of production of sugarcane (planted), sugarcane (ratoon) and sugarcane (planted+ratoon) shows the direct relationship with the size of farms. The profitability of the sugarcane (planted), sugarcane (ratoon) and sugarcane (planted+ratoon) increases with the increase in the size of the farm. Further, the study suggested that and more preferably to medium and large farms to allocate more acreage under sugarcane crop in their cropping pattern. However, there is a need for educating small farmers to adopt improved practices for the production of sugarcane and also to sell their produce to the appropriate purchasing agencies paying higher prices.

Jagdish Lal[15](1996) identified that there should be only one price regime fixed by the union government and that should permit premium for higher quality. An efficient marketing network is also called for, which requires direct contact between growers and the millers as prevailing in certain tropical states. Prompt payment of cane price will act as an incentive for raising cane supply to sugar factories. However, the problem of diversion could also be checked to some extent if the cane price announced by the government is made applicable to these industries.

Teggiet al.[16](1996) estimated the price-spread in marketing of jaggery and analyse the pace and pattern of jaggery prices and arrivals. The results noted that the decision to process

---

[13] Singh K.V., Sanjeev Kumar Malik and Jagdish Lal, (1994), "Inter-regional Trend Analysis of Sugarcane Acreage, Production and Productivity in Uttar Pradesh", Agricultural Situation in India, Vol. XLIX, No-2, May, Pp. 113-117.

[14] Baliyan S.P., Bhogal T.S., Rohal and Archna B.S., (1995), "Economics of Sugarcane Production in Muzaffarnagar District of Western Uttar Pradesh", Agricultural Situation In India, Vol. LII, No-6, September, Pp. 407-411.

[15] Jagdish Lal., (1996), "Improving the development Marketing and Supply of Sugarcane to Accelerate Sugar Productivity", Financing Agriculture, Vol. XXVIII, No. 4, October - December, Pp. 20-23.

[16] Teggi M.Y., Basavaraja H., Hiremath G.K. and Poddar R.S., (1996), "Marketing of Jaggery in Ghataprabha Command Area of Karnataka", The Bihar Journal of Agricultural Marketing, Vol. IV. No. 1, January- March, Pp. 51-55.

sugarcane into jaggery largely depended on the cane price offered by the sugar mills operating in the area and the prices of jaggery. The study also showed that the processors to crush cane into jaggery at times of attractive jaggery prices coupled with low prices offered for sugarcane by the sugar mills. Further, the study revealed that there was no significant seasonal pattern in the prices and arrivals of jaggery in Jamakhandi market. The price indices were generally higher during the months in which the indices of arrivals were low. Thus, the study showed an inverse relationship between prices and arrivals of jaggery in Mahalingpur market.

Ravi Kumar and Raju[17](1996) highlighted that the marketing of jaggery involves a number of middlemen and market functionaries between the producer and the final consumer. However, there is a large scope for improving the efficiency of jaggery marketing in this market. The study revealed that regulated market suffers from lack of good storage facilities for storing the jaggery during peak seasons. It is presently housed in a municipal market with an area of 2.71 acres, which is considered to be highly insufficient in view of the volume of business taking place in the yard. Hence, it is suggested that market committee could not provide sufficient storage facilities for want of space. The basic amenities and facilities expected from a market of this importance (second biggest market for jaggery in India) are also lacking. The credit facilities for marketing of jaggery also need to be strengthened, besides development of transport and other infrastructural facilities in the study area.

Pani and Dibakar Naik[18](1997) revealed that the growth rate of productivity is also negative in five districts which together contribute 32 per cent to state average production due to lack of suitable high yielding varieties and modern technology for increasing productivity in these districts. On average positive trends in area, production and productivity of sugarcane in Orissa and it's evident that the performance of the crop in the state is satisfactory compared to national level. Further, the study revealed that the growth rate in this state in respect of area, production and productivity are 0.69, 1.47 and 0.76 respectively. At national level, the growth rate of area, production and productivity are positive and significant. It implies that the growers of sugarcane at national level have adopted modern technology which has increased productivity significantly. Along with the significant rise in productivity, significant rise in area clearly indicates that there is dependable market support for sugarcane in India.

---

[17] Ravi Kumar K.N. and Raju V.T., (1996), "Marketing of Jaggery - A Case Study from Andhra Pradesh", The Indian Journal of Agricultural Marketing, Vol. (10), No.(3), September- December, Pp. 93-96.

[18] PantK.C. and Dibakar Naik, (1997), "Trends in Area, Production and Productivity of Sugarcane in Orissa in Comparison with National and Global Levels", Agricultural situation in India, Vol. LIII, No-10, January, Pp. 669-671.

Vijaya Kumar and Venkatachalam[19](1997) found that the annual growth rate of sugarcane area in Tamil Nadu is 2.44 per cent which is more than all India growth rate (1.37 per cent) and also significant at 1 per cent level of significance. Despite all difficulties, no other industry in the state of Tamil Nadu has developed as fast as the Sugar Industry. The Industry has indeed very bright prospects, as there is abundant supply of raw materials, cheap labour and huge local market. The Government is bound to continue on a long-term basis partial control and dual pricing system so that the interests of consumers one the one hand and that of industry are Protected and reconciled.

Jagdish Lal[20](1997) conducted a study to analyse the performance constraints and prospects of sugarcane production in India. The study concluded that the growth rates of sugarcane production were higher in tropical states when compared to sub-tropical states. The downward trend in certain states was because of switching over to marginal and waste lands for cane cultivation and problems of water stress. Sugarcane productivity performance up to seventies was better in tropics but its rate declined in the subsequent years. Further, the study suggests that an efficient management of ratoons, varieties, inputs, biotic and abiotic stress along with partial mechanization of sugarcane cultivation and effective dissemination of available technology are essential for achieving the sugarcane production targets by the end of this century.

Baliyan et al.[21](1998) analysed the costs and returns per hectare from sugarcane (planted) and sugarcane (ratoon) and to determine comparative profitability of sugarcane production with its main competing crops. For the purpose, a multistage stratified random sample was used, in which 90 cane growers of different size groups were randomly selected from four randomly selected villages in the two development blocks. The results concluded that, in case of sugarcane (planted) as well as in case of sugarcane (ratoon) also, the higher net returns were on medium and large farms which may be attributed to the higher yields and higher prices received by them. This indicates that these farmers are more efficient than small farmers. Therefore, there is a need of educating small farmers to adopt new practices and

---

[19] Vijaya Kumar A. and Venkatachalam A., (1997), "Growth Performance of Tamil Nadu Sugar Industry", Agricultural Situation in India, Vol. LIII, No-12, March, Pp. 819-821.

[20] Jagdish Lal., (1997), "Performance Constraints and Prospects of Sugarcane Production in India", Agricultural Situation in India, Vol. LIII, No-12, March, Pp. 833-839.

[21] Baliyan S.P., Bhogal T.S. and Archna, (1998), "A Study of Costs and Returns in Sugarcane Production vis-a-vis Its Competing Crops in Muzaffarnagar District, Western Uttar Pradesh", Agricultural Situation In India, Vol.LV, No. 4, July, Pp. 209-214.

advanced technologies of higher production and also to sell their produce to the agencies paying higher prices.

Patil et al.[22](1999) made an attempt to estimate the cost of planted sugarcane cultivation, costs in marketing of raw sugarcane, jaggery and the returns from sugarcane. It is found that regarding income and benefit cost ratio of sugarcane growers are presented the average quantity of sugarcane sold to factory was 108.44 tonnes per hectare. The gross income obtained by them was ₹ 87736.79 per hectare. Farm business income and family labour income worked out to ₹ 55670.45 and ₹ 50977.45 per hectare and net income realised by the farmers was ₹ 44395.51 as against total cost of ₹ 43341.28 while benefit cost ratio with cost was found to be 2.08. The jaggery producers of planted crop sold 110.50 quintals of jaggery per hectare at the rate of ₹ 592.30 per quintal. Thus, gross income obtained by them was ₹ 65449.15 per hectare. Farm business income, family labour income and net income worked out to ₹ 33382.81, ₹ 28689.81 and ₹ 20084.30 per hectare respectively, while the benefit cost ratio with cost of these farmers was 1.44.

Grover[23](1999) made a study to identify the various factors responsible for fluctuations in the price of sugar and other sweetening agents and to suggest measures that would help stabilise the prices of sugar and other sweetening agents and hence the sugar economy in the country. The sugarcane price was found to be positively and significantly influenced by the price of sugar and supply of sugar. The gur price was positively and significantly influenced by the price and sugarcane supply to the factories while it was negatively and significantly influenced by the production of sugarcane. The sugarcane supply to the factories was positively and significantly influenced by the price of sugarcane, production of sugarcane and installed crushing capacity of the factories. The sugar industry in the country is plagued by instability arising out of the variations in sugarcane production on the one hand and the presence of a more competitive gur and khandsari industry on the other. The higher gur price becomes the cause of diversion of sugarcane from sugar factories. The study suggested that any attempt to stabilise sugar price should not only seek or stabilise sugarcane production but also try to ensure that each industry whether gur, khandsari or sugar gets its due share.

---

[22] Patil S.M., Kunnal L.B. and Balappa Shivaraya, (1999), "Economics of Production and Marketing of Sugarcane in Karnataka", Agricultural Banker, Vol. 23, No. 1, January- March, Pp. 8-13.

[23] Grover K., (1999), "Sugar Price Model-A System Approach", The Indian Journal of Agricultural Marketing, 7 (2), 186-192

Ramasamy et al.[24](1999) examined the supply response of cane producers to price and non-price factors and discern out the decision process relating to allocation of cane between jaggery and white sugar production by Tamil Nadu farmers. To study the decision behaviour of farmers who grow cane factory supply and jaggery production, farm level data were collected by contacting 60 sugarcane growers in Erode district. It is found that allocation of sugarcane between supply to sugar mills and jaggery making has been an intractable problem for cane growers as several factors influence the decision. Most often jaggery production by the farmers offers higher profitability. Labour shortage pulls back the farmers from jaggery making and supply cane to factory. Production of jaggery also involves a bit of complex organisational efforts and also faces price risks. In view of these factors, experienced farmers handle jaggery production and marketing easily than less experienced farmers.

Murthy[25](1999) made a study to identify the marketing margin and marketing cost of sugarcane and sugar. This would facilitate ascertaining the share of price paid by the consumer to the sugarcane cultivating farmers. The cooperative sugar factories perform better than private sugar factories in terms of several growth indicators and physical performance variables, while opposite is the case with the profit earned. The reason for this is the relatively better financial management of the private sector. This profit motive has helped them realised the higher returns to the investment. The farmers registered with the private sugar factories incurred lesser cost of cultivation, those with the co-operative sugar factories were found to incurring more cost of production. He also found out that the cultivation of sugarcane is more economical in cultivation and more profitable in terms of returns when compared to other crops like paddy, tobacco, pulses, turmeric, cotton, ground-nut oil, palmoil etc. It is evident that cane growers are very much happy about the present cane marketing methods and Government's dual pricing policies.

Uttam Kumar Debet al.[26](1999) made a study to analyses growth and variability in sugarcane production. The results revealed that sugarcane area and production in Bangladesh has increased over time while the yield has decreased. There was no significant change in variability in sugarcane production, area and yield in succeeding periods in Bangladesh though

---

[24] Ramasamy C., Uma K. and ManimegalaiS., (1999), "An Analysis of Supply: Price Relationship in Sugarcane-Production in Tamil Nadu", The Indian Journal of Agricultural Marketing, Vol. (13), No. (1), January- April, pp. 15-23.

[25] Murthy P.S.R., (1999), "Economics of Sugarcane Cultivation in West Godavari District of Andhra Pradesh -A Review", Economic Affairs, Vol. 44, Qr. 3, September, Pp. 172-176.

[26] Uttam Kumar Deb, Gopal Krishna Bose and Madan Mohan Dey, (1999), "Growth and Variability in Sugarcane Production in Bangladesh", The Asian Economic Review, Vol.41, No.1, April, Pp. 152-165.

different regions showed a mixed pattern. The study concluded that researchers and policy makers of Bangladesh should develop a mechanism to increase sugarcane yield on a priority basis. Unless the declining trend in sugarcane yield can be reversed it would not be possible for Bangladesh to increase sugarcane production in future because it is unlikely to have an expansion in sugarcane area in future due to the land scarcity.

Padmanaban et al.[27](1999), the study found that contribution of crop pattern was the major factor that accounted for the growth of sugarcane output. The next major contribution of output is through yield increase. Therefore, the future efforts need to be focused towards stabilization and expansion of sugarcane area and increasing the yield level. For this aspect introduction of pest and disease resistant clones and varieties with higher recovery of sugar is needed. Moreover steps should be taken extensively to motivate the farmers to grow more sugarcane by making available subsidies, credit facilities and timely supply of agricultural inputs, such as good seed materials, fertilizer and chemicals, etc. Timely forecast of pest and disease incidence should be made available to the growers to take up sufficient steps needed to overcome the problems and tackle the situation. It is also necessary to increase the sugarcane production for meeting the increased demand and also for exports. The import of sugar should be cut down and Government policy towards sugarcane production may be suitably refined to motivate the farmers to increase sugarcane production.

Ahamed et al.[28](2001) conducted a study to analyses the variation in yield, cost & return of sugarcane under the spaced transplanting method and factors responsible for the variations. The study concluded that under STP method of sugarcane cultivation, variation in yield, cost and return is high within the expected yield group irrespective of different factors responsible for variations.

Sani et al.[29](2002) examined the cost benefit and major constraints of sugarcane production as well as the resource use efficiency. The result of this study showed that despite the low level of resource-use efficiency in small scale sugarcane production in the study area, it is still profitable to produce. It is evident from the result that profit can be increased through

---

[27] Padmanaban N.R., Sankaranarayanan K. and M. Chinnadurai, (1999), "Sugarcane Production in Tamil Nadu-A Decomposition Analysis", Agricultural Situation in India, Vol. LXI, No. 5, August, Pp. 339-343.

[28] Ahamed S., Khanam F., Hossin A.K.M.M and Saidur Rahman Md., (2001), "Studies on Variation in Yield, Cost and Return of Sugarcane under the Spaced Transplanting Method and Factors Responsible for the Variations in Bangladesh", Economic Affairs, Vol.46, Qr. 4, October-December, Pp. 210-214.

[29] Sani R.M., Kushwaha S., Abdullahi G. and Chandra Sen, (2002), "Economic Analysis of Small Scale Sugarcane Production in Bauchi State, Nigeria", Economic Affairs, Vol. 47, Qr. 1, January-March, Pp. 37-41.

efficient resource use. Also, the constraints identified to be affecting the business should be properly alleviated for increased production.

Naresh Nain et.al.[30](2002) found that the processing cost of sugarcane for manufacturing one quintal of sugar was found higher in co-operative sugar mill (₹193.50) in comparison to the private sugar mill (₹113.44). The higher processing efficiency in private sector may be attributed to lower fixed as well as overhead expenses and more quantity of sugarcane crushed. The irregularity in the distribution of sugarcane purchase indent delay in payments of sugarcane to the farmers (by co-operative sugar mill),delay in unloading, lack of transportation facilities etc., were the major problems reported by in selected respondents in the marketing of sugarcane to the sugar mills. Thus, there is a need to improve the operating efficiency of sugar mills especially in the co-operative sector to lower down the processing cost as well as to make them economically viable units. All the problems faced by the farmers needs to be attended by the sugar mills on priority basis for the development of sugar industry in the state.

Yousuf Ali et al.[31](2003) found that the mill authority cannot distribute enough money to the cane growers to produce large amount of cane because they do not have sufficient amount of capital that they can distribute among the farmers. For these reasons, middlemen come to the cane market. They offer money to the farmers and acquire money from the transactions between mill and cane growers. Regarding the existence of middlemen, farmers are losing returns from selling sugarcane to the mill. Government should take care of this situation to make both mill and growers profitable. By allocation sufficient amount of capital to the sugar mill, government can develop sugar industries in the country and farmers will also be encouraged to cultivate sugarcane in their lands to raise their economic conditions.

Archana Singh and Srivastava[32](2003) made a study growth and instability in sugarcane production. It estimated that compound growth rates in area, production and productivity was measured through co-efficient of variation analysis by using semi-log equations method. Further, it is found that growth rate the problem of instability in sugarcane production has engaged the attention of scientists and planners in the recent past. The production of sugar too in Uttar Pradesh recorded sharp fluctuations over time. The primary reason for the instability

---

[30] Naresh Nain, Khatkar R.K. and Singh V.K., (2002), "Role of Sugarcane processing Industry and Efficiency of Processing in Haryana", Indian Journal of Agricultural Marketing, Vol. 16, No. 1, January-April, Pp. 92-96.

[31] Yousuf Ali Md., Saidur Rahman Md. and S.A. Sadur, (2003), "A Study on Marketing of Sugarcane under the Zeal Bangla Sugarmill Area Jamalpur District,"Economic Affairs, Vol. 48, Qr. 1, March, Pp. 31-41.

[32] Archana Singh and Srivastava R.S.L.,(2003), "Growth and Instability in Sugarcane Production in Uttar Pradesh: A Regional Study", Indian journal of Agriculture Economics, Vol. 58 No. 2, April – June, Pp. 279-282.

in sugar production is the uncertainty in supply of raw material, i.e., sugarcane which has itself recorded wide fluctuations. The study revealed that the growth rate and instabilities in sugarcane production in different region.

Narayanamoorthy[33] (2004) analysed the impact assessment of drip irrigation under sugarcane cultivation using farm-level data from Maharashtra. Using a discounted cash flow technique, it was found that productivity was 23 per cent higher than that under the flood method of irrigation, with water saving of about 44 per cent per hectare and electricity saving of about 1059 kWh per hectare in short, drip investment in sugarcane cultivation remains economically viable even without subsidy.

Rao and Ravi Kumar[34] (2005) studied the marketing scenario of jaggery in India, Anakapalle regulated market in Andhra Pradesh was selected purposively as it ranks next to Muzaffarnagar market in Uttar Pradesh. The total marketing costs paid by the producer, exporter, wholesaler and retailers were higher in channel I (₹ 190.62 i.e. 18.85 per cent of consumers price) when compared to channel II (₹ 148, 96 i.e. 14.73 per cent of consumer's price). As the total marketing costs are lower in channel II, the producers' share in consumer's price is higher in channel II (85.27 per cent) when compared to channel I (81.15 per cent). Further, suggested that there is a greater need to improve the export competitiveness of jaggery in the international market, as the jaggery is found to competitive only in UAE and UK countries. Hence, selecting suitable variety of seed, improving processing efficiency, reducing cost of production of jaggery, encouraging farm level grading and storage facilities, improving transportation and market information network etc. should be given more attention.

Narayanamoorthy[35](2005) made an attempt to analyse the various economic advantages of drip method of irrigation in sugarcane cultivation by selecting a model farmer from Sivagangai district in Tamil Nadu. While the productivity gains due to drip method of irrigation is about 54 per cent (30 tonnes per acre), water saving due to DMI comes to about 58 per cent flood method of irrigation. Owing to less consumption of well water, the farmer is able to save about 1260 KWh/acre of electricity, which is used for fitting water from wells. Besides these advantages, the farmer could reduce the cost of cultivation to the tune of ₹ 3450 per acre particularly in operations like weeding, intercultural and irrigation cost (both labour and other

---

[33] Narayanamoorthy A., (2004), "Impact Assessment of Drip Irrigation in India: The Case of Sugarcane" Development Policy Review, Vol. No. 22, Issue 4, July, Pp. 443–462.

[34] RaoK.P.C. and Ravi Kumar K.N., (2005), "Production and Marketing Scenarios of Jaggery in India with Special Reference to Andhra Pradesh, Agricultural Marketing", Vol. XLVII, No. 4, January-March, Pp. 39-43.

[35] Narayanamoorthy A., (2005), "Economics of Drip Irrigation in Sugarcane Cultivation: Case Study of a Farmer from Tamil Nadu", Indian Journal of Agriculture Economics, Vol. 60, No. 2, April-June, Pp. 235-248.

costs). The benefit cost ratio varies from 1.98 to 2.02 under without subsidy condition and the same varies from 2.07 to 2.10 with subsidy (30 per cent) at different discount rates. Further, the results of net present worth indicate that the farmer can cover the entire capital cost of drip set from the income of the very first year itself even without subsidy. The study suggested that drip method of irrigation is economically viable even without subsidy in water intensive crops like sugarcane.

Panwar Sanjeev et al.[36](2006) conducted a study on forecasting the profitability of sugarcane farming in major states of India. This study is based on the data of cost of cultivation of sugarcane in different states of India for the period 1990–2001. Multiple regression models have become the methods of choice in the area of forecasting. In the study, the Holt's two-parameter Model is used (Exponential smoothing adjusted for trend).The results revealed that there was an increasing trend in sugarcane production in India.

Pawaret al.[37](2007) made a study to ascertain the share of major sugar export and import countries in world trade and sugar prices. It is found that India has less than 0.20 per cent share in world sugar trade while Brazil accounts for only about 10 to 13 per cent of world production and it has a share of over 23 per cent in world export. Brazil dominates the foreign market due to better quality and minimum per unit cost of production of sugar. In the world trade of export of sugar, India's share was 0.18 per cent and per kg price realized was ₹ 14.26. The Cuba, Australia, Thailand and France are the four major sugar exporting countries contributing each about 10 per cent of the total sugar export.

Sale and Lohar[38](2007) conducted a study to estimate per tonne cost of production of sugarcane, to per quintal cost of production and marketing of jaggery and to identify the problems faced by the sample farmers in respect of production and marketing of jaggery. Per tonne cost of cultivation of surusugarcane was estimated to ₹ 648.24. The per quintal cost of production of jaggery including marketing charges worked out to ₹ 982.16. Per quintal cost of marketing of jaggery was ₹ 58.67. The net profit per quintal and per hectare from jaggery production was worked out to the tune of ₹ 117.84 and ₹ 11219 respectively.

---

[36] Panwar Sanjeev, Kumar Anil, Kaul Sushila and Jaggi Namita, (2006), "Forecasting the profitability of sugarcane farming in major states of India", Agricultural Economics Research Review, Vol. 19, Pp. 207.

[37] Pawar P.P., Kale P.V. and Kaware S.S., (2007), "Changing World Sugar Scenario and Indian Export", Agricultural Situation in India, Vol. LXIII, No. 11, February, Pp. 639-646.

[38] Sale Y.C. and Lohar N.S., (2007), "Economics of Production and Marketing of Jaggery in Kolhapur district", Agricultural Marketing, Vol. XLIX, No. 4, January-March, Pp. 29-30.

Anjugam et al.[39](2007) found that the growth rates in area and production of sugarcane are positive during the post-liberalization period in India and Tamil Nadu. The study found that the productivity of sugarcane has shown a negative growth rate in India and Tamil Nadu, which might be due to monsoon failure during this period. The productivity of cane in the western zone of Tamil Nadu has shown a low but positive growth rate, may be due to change in the cropping pattern and better access to sugar mills and also found that the net income realized from jaggery production has been recorded as ₹ 14138, which is higher than that farm the cane produced for sugar factory. Delays in cutting of cane by the sugar factories and labour problems during harvesting season have been found as the major reasons for jaggery making. Further, it is found that non-remunerative prices, lack of government support in price policies and traditional technology have been identified as the major constraints in jaggery production. The study suggested that introduction of modern technologies, creation of infrastructure and formulation of appropriate price polices need to be encouraged to enhance jaggery production among the farmers to get remunerative price for their produce.

Ankur gaurav[40] et al.(2007) identified the various marketing channels being adopted by the sugarcane cultivators. The results of the study revealed that large farmers were observed to enjoy higher net returns than small farmers as the farmers supplied their sugarcane produce to the sugar mills, which was found to be paying higher prices to the farmers than what the traditional jaggery making units were paying. And also revealed that majority of the farmers (about 60 per cent) were supplying their sugarcane to the sugar mills irrespective of the land size category to which they belonged. The producer's share in consumer rupee was found to be 83.70 and 50.11 per cent in channel-I and channel-II, respectively. There is an urgent need for setting up of a sugar mill or khandsari unit in the una district as it holds the promise of vastly increasing the sugarcane cultivation along with providing employment hundreds of people on farm and non-farm sectors.

Jitender Singh et.al.[41](2007) conducted a study and it revealed that on an overall average, the percentage of marketable surplus of sugarcane was found increasing in the size of farms. Large farms had larger marketable surplus in the command area. Marketable surplus in

---

[39] Anjugam M., Govindarajan K., Kumar D and Suresh, (2007), "Value-addition of Sugarcane-A case of Jaggery Production", Agricultural Economics Research Review, Vol. 20, Pp. 606.

[40] Ankur Gaurav, Sushil Kumar and Sharma S.K., (2007), "An Analysis of Marketing Cost, Margins and Price Spread of Sugarcane, in Himachal Pradesh", Agricultural Marketing, Vol. L, No. 2, July- September, Pp. 14-16.

[41] Jitender Singh, Subash Chandra and Gvanprakas, (2007), "Economic aspects of Sugarcane Marketing in Faizabad, District of Eastern Uttar Pradesh", Agricultural Marketing, Vol. L, No. 1, April – June, Pp.21- 26.

outside area was slightly less than that in the command area. Marketed surplus of sugarcane in the command area was 538.99 quintal per farm of which the maximum i.e. 67.69 per cent was supplied to sugar factories and 32.31 per cent to the commercial gur processing units. The quantity of sugarcane supplied to sugar factory was larger on the large farms. In the outside area of sugar factories, total marketed surplus to only gur processing units due to lack of sugar factories. The marketing cost was ₹ 7.52 per quintal in the command area. The net price received by the sugarcane growers from the gur processing units in the outside area of sugar factories was ₹ 50.60 quintal and the average price paid by the gur-processing unit was ₹ 57.90 per quintal. The total marketing cost was ₹ 7.30 per quintal. On an average in the outside area of sugar factories. The production share was the highest i.e. 89.69 per cent in the command area against the lower i.e. 87.32 per cent in the outside area of sugar factories. The marketing efficiency of sugarcane was the highest in case of supply to sugar factories in the command area due to impact of sugar factories.

Bahgat et al.[42](2007) made a study to identify the production and marketing problems facing sugar cane growers in Qena governorate. The most important production problems perceived by focus groups of farmers and extension personnel were: spread of different kinds of weeds and insects, weak role of agricultural extension, shortage and high costs of fertilizers and labour, high costs of production, insecticides and irrigation. High costs and unsystematic cutting, shortage and high costs of transportation, delay of cutting and delivery of product to the factory, inaccurate weigh and low prices of the product were the most important marketing problems mentioned by farmers and extension personnel in Qena governorate.

Chockalingam and Nagarajan[43](2008) made a study and found that Namakkal is one among the districts in Tamil Nadu where sugarcane is cultivated in 9,476 hectares. This works out to 2.82 per cent of the total area under cultivation in Tamil Nadu. In Namakkal District, the total sugarcane Production is 13, 06,920 tonnes per annum, which is 5.34 per cent of the total production of Tamil Nadu. Abundance of labour force, availability of irrigation facilities and Government support, liberal loan facilities from bank etc., are the factors which favoured for the large scale cultivation of sugarcane in this district. The Government as a stakeholder is responsible to protect the interests of the primary stakeholders' viz., farmers. Hence it has to make concerted efforts with the help of agricultural department, Tamil Nadu Agricultural

---

[42] Bahgat M.Abdel-Maksoud & Amro B.E.A. and El-Sharabassy., (2007), "Production and Marketing Problems facing Sugar Cane Growers in Qena Governorate", African Crop Science Conference Proceedings, Pp. 1301-1306.

[43] ChockalingamS.M. and NagarajanP., (2008), "Sugarcane Cultivation in Namakkal District", Kisan World, Vol. 35, No. 11, November, Pp. 25-27.

University and also with coordination from the co-operative bank, commercial bank, sugar mills and voluntary agencies to mitigate the above said problems. Such integrated effort of Government would solve most of the problems. If these problems are solved or minimized not only the primary stakeholders viz., the sugarcane farmers but also all other stakeholders will enjoy the benefits and the rural economy would ultimately prosper.

Vijay Gorakh Patil[44](2009) conducted a study to examine the cost of cultivation of sugarcane. The study revealed that the cost of preparatory village 5.13 per cent, the cost of seed bed preparation 1.11 per cent, the cost of seed and sowing operation was 18.30 per cent, the cost of intercultural operation 7.76 per cent, irrigation labour charge 6.99 per cent, electricity charge 5.74 per cent, the cost of chemical fertilizers and FYM 18.97 per cent, the cost of plant protection 2.77 per cent, interest on investment 6.0 per cent, the cost of harvesting 11.09 per cent, the cost of land rent for 12 months 13.86 per cent, agricultural income tax 0.28 per cent and management charges for 12 months were 2.00 per cent. The total cost of production of sugarcane ₹ 802 per tonne.

Rajula Shanthy and Senthil Kumar[45](2010) conducted a study by using descriptive type of research design applying ex-post facto approach and the respondents were selected among drip laid farmers. Drip irrigation for sugarcane cultivation is a valuable technology and an essential foundation for the development of sustainable sugarcane cultivation. With the shrinking water resource, the available water has to be used judiciously. Drip irrigation is the product of trial and error and keen observation through various irrigation technologies. So it should be our endeavour to assess the feasibility of drip irrigation in sugarcane cultivation and utilize it along with other modern technologies.

Shinde et al.[46](2010) reported that total sugar production in the world during 2008-2009 was 153.27 million tonnes (raw value), out of which sugarcane and sugar beet contributed 121.54 (79.32 per cent) and 31.68 (20.68 per cent) million tonnes respectively. In India, during 2008-2009, sugarcane was planted on 44.08 lakh hectares with production of 2946.56 lakh tonnes, which produced million tonnes of sugar. It is estimated that, sugar output of India will rise to 18.50 million tonnes in 2009-2010. India's sugar output is expected to rise to over 24

---

[44] Vijay Gorakh Patil, (2009), "Marketing Analysis of Sugarcane Production in Shirpur Tahasil of Dhule District of Maharashtra", Financing Agriculture, Vol. 41, Issue. 4, July-August, Pp. 23-25.

[45] Rajula Shanthy T. and Senthil Kumar R., (2010), "Socio-Economic analysis of DripIrrigation in Sugarcane", Co operative Sugar, Vol. 41, No. 10, June, Pp. 41-44.

[46] Shinde S.H., Takalkar B.J. and Pawar B.H.,(2010), "Global Scenario of Sugar Production and Thrust area for enhancing Sugarcane Productivity in Maharashtra", Cooperative Sugar, Vol. 41, No. 10, June, Pp. 23-27.

million tonnes (by around 30 per cent as compared to 2009-2010) in season 2010-2011, mainly because of higher cane prices paid by the sugar mills to the sugarcane growers and thereby the area under sugarcane has been increased substantially.

Karpagam et.al.[47](2010) analysed the impact of drip irrigation on sugarcane cultivation through various efficiency indicators under farmers' field condition. They revealed that higher efficiency percentage (40.64) was observed in case of water use efficiency followed by input use efficiency (34.88 per cent), yield efficiency (24.98 per cent) labour and energy use efficiency indicators in drip irrigation system.

Amit Kumar Dwivedi[48](2010) examined the cost-return analysis, profitability and operational efficiency of Gur manufacturing units in the study area. The study revealed that units of medium and large sizes were able to cover their operating expenses with significant level of profit but small size units were earning a marginal profit. The profit earned by this category was very low as compared to other two sizes.

Deokate et al.[49](2010) made a study and it revealed that the jaggery processing units are profitable even if only own sugarcane is processed. Further, findings showed that more profitable when the jaggery processing unit prepares the jaggery of other's on rent basis. The most important two marketing channels were observed in the sale of jaggery viz., Channel-I: Producer-Commission agent-Wholesaler-Retailer-Consumer, Channel-II: Producer-Co-operative Sangh-Wholesaler-Retailer-Consumer. The producer's share in consumer's rupee and channel wise marketing efficiency index was highest in Channel-II.

Kumar Suresh and Palanisami[50](2010) studied the impact of drip irrigation on farming system in terms of cropping pattern, resources use and yield. The study found that the significant impact on resources saving cost of cultivation, yield of crops and farm profitability. Hence, the policy should be focused on promotion of drip irrigation in those regions where scarcity of water and labour is alarming and where shift towards wider-spaced crops is taking place.

---

[47] Karpagam C., Ravikumar Theodore V, Ravichandran and Murali P. (2010) "Impact of Drip irrigation in Sugarcane a field level enquiry", Cooperative Sugar, Vol. 41, No. 5, December, Pp. 51-53.

[48] Amit Kumar Dwivedi., (2010), "An Empirical study on Gur (Jaggery) Industry with special reference to Operational Efficiency & Profitability Measurement", IIMA, India Research and Publications, December, Pp.1-19.

[49] Deokate T.B., Tilekar S.N., Suryawanshi S.D., Jadav K.L. and Nikam A.V., "Economics of Production and Marketing of Jaggery in Maharashtra", Internal national Journal of Commerce and Business Management, 2 (2), Pp. 68-72, 2010.

[50] Kumar Suresh D. and Palanisami K., (2010), "Impact of Drip Irrigation on Farming System: Evidence from Southern India", Agricultural Economics Research Review, Vol. 23, Issue. 2, Pp. 265-272.

Malarkodi et al.[51](2010) found that sugarcane productivity was 126.66 tonne per hectare in safe and semi-critical areas while it was 123.72 tonne per hectare in critical and over exploited blocks in the western zone. The total cost of cultivation (variable cost) was ₹ 79272 per hectare in critical and over exploited blocks whereas it was only ₹ 75802 per hectare in safe and semi-critical blocks. Strategy to maintain or increase the current western zone cane production can be done by continuation of sugarcane production only in the safe and semi-critical blocks (13 blocks) and expansion of the sugarcane area in safe and semi-critical blocks, which presently has minimum area under sugarcane cultivation.

Rama Rao[52](2010) made an attempt to work-out costs and returns of sugarcane production, to identify the major marketing channels and problems of jaggery growers. Multistage sampling technique was adopted in selecting the sampling units at various levels during 2007-2008. Analytical tools like simple averages, Benefit Cost Ratio (BCR), Garrets Ranking Technique and Kendall's co-efficient of concordance (W) test were employed to achieve the objectives. The study revealed that cost of cultivation of sugarcane is the prime factor in the various value added products. Among the value added products sugar juice production was found more profitable, which needs further study of technical and financial feasibility on large scale.

Balamurugan and Vetriselvan[53](2010) found that 36.00 per cent of marginal farmers had low level of adoption on sugarcane technology, whereas only 47.50 per cent of small farmers had medium level of adoption. In case of big farmers, 58.75 per cent of them had high level of adoption. Out of ten technologies of sugarcane cultivation, the difference could be observed between the marginal, small and big farmers for adoption of four technologies viz., sett treatment, herbicide application, bio-fertilizer application and use of bio- control agents.

Rajesh kumar et al.[54](2010) made an attempt to analysed the annual linear and compound growth rates for the period 1996-1997 to 2003-2004 were estimated to measure the growth in cost of cultivation of sugarcane in different states of India. The highest growth rate was registered for Maharashtra (11.17 per cent) followed by Karnataka (9.51 per cent), Haryana (8.70

---

[51] Malarkodi M., Bharathi K. and Janakirani A., (2010), "Sustaining Sugarcane Production in Western Zone of Tamil Nadu", Agriculture Update, Vol.5, Issue 1&2, February & May, Pp. 99-102.

[52] Rama Rao I.V.V., (2010), "Economic Analysis of Value Addition in Sugarcane in North Coastal Zone of Andhra Pradesh", Indian Journal of Agricultural Marketing, Vol. 24, No.2, May-August, Pp. 41-49.

[53] Balamurugan V. and Vetriselvan M., (2010), "Extent of Adoption of Recommended Sugarcane-Technologies by the Different Categories of Sugarcane Growers", Agriculture Update, Vol.5, Issue 3&4, August-November, Pp. 292-295.

[54] Rajesh Kumar Hasan S.S., Bajpai P.K. and Singh S.N., (2010), "Economic analysis of Sugarcane Cultivation in different States of India", Indian Journal of Sugarcane Technology, Vol. No. 25 (1&2), Pp. 97-101.

per cent) and Uttar Pradesh (4.49 per cent). However, there was no significant change in cost of cultivation in Tamil Nadu and Andhra Pradesh. As far as in cost term, there was ₹ 5261 hectare per year increase in Maharashtra followed by Karnataka (₹ 3778 hectare per year), Haryana (₹ 3657 hectare per year) and Uttar Pradesh (₹ 1248 hectare per year). In case of value of sugarcane, there was 8.38 per cent growth in Haryana followed by 5.84 per cent in Karnataka and 4.74 per cent in Maharashtra per year.

Clainos Chidoko and Ledwin Chimwai[55](2011) made a study to identify and explain the economic challenges faced by sugar cane farmers. The study showed that while sugarcane industry is a critical sector to the economy, its productivity is going down. It was discovered that the low productivity is largely due to failure to plough out old cane, lack of equipment for operations, low prices paid for the harvested cane, high transport and haulage charges, limited training and unavailability of inputs. This is largely due to limited access to cheap finance and credit. The study recommended that farmers be given cheap finance and easily access credit using their crop as collateral security.

Murali and Balakrishnan[56](2011) found that in the recent past, labour scarcity coupled with high labour wage rate has greatly affected the irrigation and harvesting of sugarcane crop in time. It has reduced sugarcane area from 3.91 lakh ha in 2006-2007 to 3.14 lakh hectare in year 2009-2010 in Tamil Nadu. The study found that mechanical operations to be superior to manual operations in sugarcane cultivation. These have reduced cost of production and have enabled efficient utilization of resources with better work output. Further they concluded that it has become inevitable to use modern sugarcane machinery, which is now available in the country. Although its initial cost is very high, the advantages accrued in their use are many and suggested the use of drip irrigation and mechanical harvesters to mitigate the acute labour scarcity (farm operation and harvesting). It has also proposed to implement custom hiring system on co-operative basis/or owned and operated by the sugar factories for sugarcane harvesters in the state.

Arjinder kaur and Sukhjeet Saran[57](2011) found that climatic constraints for sugarcane cultivation in Punjab will continue to account for disparity in cane productivity and sugar

---

[55] Clainos Chidoko and Ledwin Chimwai, (2011), "Economic Challenges of Sugarcane Production in the Low yield of Zimbabwe" International Journal of Economics Research, 2(5), Pp. 1-13.

[56] Murali P. and Balakrishnan R. (2011), "Labour Scarcity and Selective Mechanization of Sugarcane Agriculture in Tamil Nadu", Agricultural Economics Research Review, Vol.24.

[57] Arjinder Kaur and Sukhjeet K. Saran., (2011), "Status and Constraints of Sugarcane Cultivation in Punjab", Indian Journal of Agricultural Marketing, Vol. 25, No. 1, January-April, Pp. 78-87.

recovery in this area. The constraints regarding the sugarcane cultivation were mainly related to the payment problems, absence of any sugar mill in the sub-division, the long waiting period for the disposal of cane besides harassment of the farmers by the staff of sugar mills. The long distance between sugarcane growers of the sub division and sugar mill has added to difficulties of sugarcane growers, which has led to decline in area under sugarcane.

Deokate et al.[58](2011) examined the cost-price relationship of different commodities affects the relative profitability and economic incentives to produce. The harvest prices of sugarcane were not sufficient to cover the increased prices of inputs and parity between prices of output and input was not favourable. Price-cost ratios of sugarcane, at MSP are less than unity during the period under study, except from 1995-1996 to 1999-2000, indicating thereby that the cost of production was more than output prices. The price cost ratio of sugarcane at FHP was more than unity for the entire period under study, indicating thereby that the growth in output prices is more than the cost of production.

Deokate and Yadav[59](2011) conducted a study to examine economics of jaggery production in Maharashtra. The study revealed that the total cost of jaggery processing was ₹ 7, 78,489. The cost of raw materials was the major item of variable cost accounting for 67.09 per cent of the total cost. Per quintal total cost incurred for own jaggery preparation including the cost of raw material (sugarcane) was worked out to ₹ 1436.29. Per quintal average price realized for jaggery was ₹ 1812.06 and thereby the net return obtained from own jaggery preparation was ₹ 375.77 per quintal. The per quintal profit earned from rent basis jaggery preparation was ₹ 122.42. The per unit total net returns from jaggery processing unit was ₹ 249,129. Further, the study concluded that the jaggery processing units are profitable.

Deokate et al.[60](2011) conducted a study on marketing of jaggery in western Maharashtra. It is concluded that higher quantity of jaggery was sold through Channel-I (Producer-Commission agent-Wholesaler-Retailer-Consumer) than Channel-II (Producer-Cooperative union-Wholesaler-Retailer-Consumer). The price received through Channel-II was more (₹ 1875.10) than of the price received through Channel-I (₹ 1785.05). It indicated that there is a need of formation of 'co-operatives' in the sale proceeds of jaggery for the benefit of the

---

[58] Deokate T.B., Shendage P.N., Jadhav K.L. and Nirgude R.R., (2011), "Input-Output Prices, their Parity and Income from Sugarcane in Maharashtra", Cooperative Sugar, Vol. 41, No. 5, January, Pp. 39-44.

[59] Deokate T.B. and Yadav J.P. (2011), "Economic review of Sugarcane by-product (jaggery) in Maharashtra", Cooperative Sugar, Vol. 41, No. 5, February, Pp. 47-50.

[60] T.D. Deokate, S.N. Tilekar, H.R. Shinde, S.D. Suryawanshi and S.D. Shinde, (2011), "Marketing Of Jaggery In Western Maharashtra", Indian Journal of Agricultural Marketing, Vol. 25, No-1, January-April, Pp.155-159.

producers. Commission and packaging charges, were major items of total marketing cost in both the Channels. The producers received comparatively better returns, i.e. 70.10 per cent of consumer price in Channel- II than in Channel-I (67.61 per cent). Higher marketing efficiency was noticed in Channel-II as compared to Channel-I. The marketing of jaggery involves a number of middlemen and market functionaries between the producers and the final consumers. Hence, there is need to establish large number of jaggery cooperative marketing unions for improving the producers' share in consumer's rupee from jaggery marketing.

Awaradi et al.[61](2011) made a study to analyse the cost and returns in sugarcane cultivation and to estimate the cost and returns of different categories of jaggery production units. A sample of 30 jaggery producers was selected randomly from six villages of Jamakhandi Taluk. Per tonne cost of cultivation of sugarcane was estimated to ₹ 877.15. The major items of cost of cultivation were human labour (27 per cent) followed by chemical fertilizers (17.24 per cent) and seed material (17.10 per cent). The per quintal cost of jaggery preparation is decline with an increase of crushing capacity. Thus, study indicated that production of jaggery is a profitable business.

Anitta Fanish et al.[62](2011) stated that micro-irrigation is introduced primarily to save water and increase the water use efficiency in agriculture. Reduction in water consumption due to drip method of irrigation over the surface method of irrigation varies from 30 to 70 per cent and productivity gain in the range of 20 to 90 per cent for different crops. By introducing drip irrigation, it is possible to increase the yield potential of crops by three fold with the same quantity of water. All these emphasize the need for water conservation and improvement in water-use efficiency to achieve "More Crop per Drop of water".

Rama Rao and Sunil Kumar Babu[63](2011) made an attempt to work-out costs and returns in value added products of Sugarcane viz., sugar, jaggery and sugarcane juice, in order to suggest the sugarcane growers, the profitable and sustained way to deal with sugarcane. Multistage sampling technique was adopted in selecting the sampling units at various levels during 2010-2011. The results revealed that cost of cultivation of sugarcane is the prime factor in the various value added products. Among the value added products, sugarcane juice

---

[61] Awaradi K.M., Biradar Patil A.P and Vaikunthe L.D., (2011), "Economic Analysis of Jaggery Production in Bagalkot", S.E. Golden Jubilee Year, Vol. (50), No. 4, June, Pp. 7-30.

[62] Anitta Fanish S., Muthukrishnan P. and Santhi P., (2011), "Effect of Drip Fertigation on Field Crops - a Review", Agricultural Reviews, Vol. 32, Issue: 1, March.

[63] Rama Rao I.V.Y and Sunil Kumar Babu G., (2011), "Value Addition in Sugarcane: A Critical Analysis of Various Consumables Produced in Andhra Pradesh", Indian Journal of Sugarcane Technology, Vol. No. 26 (1), Pp. 51-54.

production was found more profitable, which needs further study of technical and financial feasibility of keeping quality in order to produce on large scale.

Anwar Hussain and Naeem-ur-Rehman Khattak[64](2011) found that the socio-economic variables like capital employment, labour employment, marketing, credit and financing and sources of income were more closely related with sugarcane production. The major economic practices were preparation of land, water management, weed control, insecticides and making of black sugar (Gur). Main sugarcane varieties grown were 77/400, 44, Mardan-92, 48, 310 and 722082. Variety 77/400 was observed as the most profitable variety. The average per acre cost was calculated as ₹ 35450 for all varieties. The major cost elements were land rent, labour input, seed, manure, irrigation, land preparation, fertilizer and hand weeding and making of black sugar (Gur). The net revenue of variety-77/400, 44, Mardan-92, 48, 310 and 722082 were observed as ₹ 54550, 48550, 48550, 45550, 48550 and 45550, respectively. Sugarcane crop was characterized by increasing returns to scale. The study recommended that modern techniques should be adopted for making Gur. Awareness among sugarcane growers about improved varieties should be created.

Sunil Kumar Babu and Rama Rao[65](2011) made a study to identify the important factors influencing the input use efficiency in sugarcane production, The study examine the costs and returns in cultivation by using Benefit Cost Ratio (BCR) and Cobb-Douglas type of production function. It is found that total cost of cultivation per hectare in Sugarcane was ₹ 1, 72,288, ₹1, 19,945 and ₹ 1, 08,215 respectively in irrigated plant, irrigated ratoon and rainfed conditions. There was 62 per cent higher yield in irrigated condition vis-à-vis rainfed conditions. BCR on operating cost was highest (1.53) in irrigated ratoon followed by irrigated plant (1.41) and rainfed (1.36). Further revealed that the most important factors influencing production were labour availability and manures usage in both irrigated and rainfed conditions.

Krishna Priya and Bajpai[66](2011) conducted a study on computation of compound growth rate for sugarcane using the non-linear growth models. The results of the parameter estimated and goodness of fit measures indicated that among the three models Logistic model is

---

[64] Anwar Hussain and Naeem-ur-Rehman Khattak, (2011), "Economic analysis of Sugarcane Crop in Charsadda district", Journal of Agriculture Research, Vol. No. 49 (1), pp. 153-163.

[65] Sunil Kumar Babu G and Rama Rao I.V.Y., (2011), "Economics of Sugarcane Cultivation in Andhra Pradesh - under Irrigated and Rainfed Condition", Indian Journal of Sugarcane Technology, Vol. No. 26(2), pp. 30-32.

[66] Krishna Priya S.R. and Bajpai P.K., (2011), "Computation of Compound Growth rates for Sugarcane using Non-linear Growth Models", Indian Journal of Sugarcane Technology, Vol. No. 26 (2), pp. 33-39.

appropriate for the present study. The compound growth rates have been calculated for Logistic model and the results of compound growth rates for sugarcane production data is 2.96 per cent, for area and productivity of cane, the growth rates have been estimated as 1.73 per cent and 1.12 per cent respectively.

Mandla Dlamini and Micah Masuku[67](2012) made a study and the Cobb-Douglas production function was used to identify the factors affecting sugarcane productivity. The results indicated that farm size, labour, basal fertilizer and topdressing fertilizer were statistically significant ($p<0.05$) in influencing sugarcane productivity. The adjusted R^2 was 0.68 suggesting that 68per cent of the variation in sugarcane yield per hectare is explained by the explanatory variables. Farmers should take note to use labour according to the industry standards in order to get good yields. Basal fertilizer and top dressing fertilizer need to be applied in the recommended amounts. Good crop husbandry practices like timely weeding, fertilization, irrigation should be adopted to produce a good crop which will enhance productivity. Government and the private sector need to intensify the out grower technical services rendered to sugarcane farmers, so that they can improve the productivity of sugarcane farming.

Basavaraj Banakar et al.[68](2012) conducted a study to assess the export competitiveness of jaggery. The Nominal Protection Co-efficient (NPC) was found to be less than unity (0.57), which implies that jaggery is a good exportable product; hence there is competitive advantage for export of jaggery from India. Similarly Domestic resource cost (DRC) was found to be less than unity. All these ratios indicated comparative advantage in production and export of jaggery. Therefore, its export should be encouraged to earn foreign exchange.

Girei and Giroh[69](2012) conducted a study to analyse the productivity and resource use efficiency in sugarcane production by random selection of 120 out grower farmers. The study revealed that 40 percent of the respondents had farming experience of between 16-20 years with an average farming experience of 10 years and cultivated a mean farm size of 1.5 hectare.

---

[67] Mandla B. Dlamini and Micah B. Masuku, (2011), "Productivity of Smallholder Sugarcane Farmers in Swaziland: The Case of Komati Downstream Development Programme (KDDP) Farmers' Associations", Environment and Natural Resources Research, Vol. 2, No. 4.

[68] Basavaraj Banakar, Sandesh K C and N Ashoka, (2012), "Export Competitiveness of Sugarcane Jaggery in Karnataka - A Comparative Analysis", Indian Journal of Sugarcane Technology, Vol. No. 27 (10), Pp. 1-3.

[69] Girei A.A. and Giroh D.Y., (2012), "Analysis of the Factors affecting Sugarcane (Saccharum Officinarum) Production under the out growers scheme in Numan Local Government Area Adamawa State, Nigeria", Advances in Agriculture, Sciences and Engineering Research, Vol. 2 (5), May, Pp. 158-164.

The study identified inadequate and late allocation of farms and inadequate credit as the major constraints of sugarcane production and possible suggestions to overcome the identified constraints were made in the study.

Gomatee singh[70](2013) made an attempt to analyse the economics of sugarcane based farming system i.e. sugarcane cultivation by all the categories of farmers, cost benefit ratio from sugarcane cultivation, major products of sugarcane and their economy etc. Sugarcane is one of the major cash crop of India and most important crop of Uttar Pradesh, which not only support the economy of Uttar Pradesh but also the major crop which is the source of income of millions of farmers, whether marginal, small, medium or large.

Nazir et al.[71](2013) found that a majority (68 per cent) of the farmers faced moderate problem in sugarcane cultivation, while 8 percent low and 24 per cent serious problem in sugarcane cultivation. Correlation analysis indicated that among 13 selected characteristics of the farmers, education, credit availability, input availability, extension, media contact, training exposure and knowledge had significant negative relationship with their problem faced in sugarcane cultivation and the rest age, family size, land possession, annual family income, sugarcane cultivation area, organizational participation and innovativeness had no significant relationship with their problem faced in sugarcane cultivation. Further, it is observed that "high price of fertilizer and pesticide", "non-availability of fertilizer and pesticide in time" and "insect and pest attack of sugarcane" were the major three problems in sugarcane cultivation.

An overview of the studies reviewed above shows that most of the studies pertain to the cultivation of sugarcane and production of jaggery units. No study on farmers' attitude in adoption of drip irrigation system in sugarcane cultivation and production and marketing of khandsari sugar could be traced out. Moreover, not a single comprehensive study for sugarcane crops covering various aspects such as cost and returns, factors, satisfaction and problems in adoption of drip irrigation system in sugarcane cultivation, problems in sugarcane cultivation, marketing cost, price spread, marketing problems, satisfaction about the functioning of sugarcane and khandsari sugar marketing channels, growth in area, production and productivity of sugarcane in Tamil Nadu, India, World and also export and import of sugar in India in terms of volume and value. Therefore, the study differs from the earlier studies in respect of its scope, nature, contents and the area covered.

---

[70] Gomatee singh, (2013), "An Empirical study of Economics of Sugarcane Cultivation and Processing based Farming in Uttar Pradesh", Sky Journal of Agricultural Research, Vol. No. 2(1), January, Pp. 7-19.

[71] Nazir, Adnan , Jariko, Ghulam Ali and Junejo, Mumtaz Ali (2013), "Factors affecting Sugarcane Production in Pakistan", Pakistan Journal of Commerce and Social Sciences, Vol. 7, No. 1, January, Pp. 128-140.

1.4. Importance

This book is expected to be useful not only to the sugarcane farmers in the Erode District of Tamil Nadu but also to sugar factories, jaggery producers, traders, intermediaries in different places and Government policy makers. It is worth to mention that proper investigation into cost & returns of sugarcane farmers would through light on the economy of sugarcane cultivation and it would help to judge the profitability of farming. This could help the farmers in formulating suitable production strategies to improve the productivity of sugarcane and identifying the proper marketing channels. This book would help to identify the major problems faced by the farmers in cultivation and marketing of sugarcane and offer suggestions to solve their problems.

1.5. Objectives

The book has been written with the following specific objectives.

- To find out the growth in area, production and productivity of sugarcane.
- To identify the cultivation practices of sugarcane.
- To study the adoption of drip irrigation system in sugarcane cultivation.
- To analyse the marketing practices adopted by the sugarcane farmers.
- To examine the cultivation and marketing problems of sugarcane farmers.

1.6. Hypotheses

The following hypotheses have been framed based on the opinion of the farmers, discussion with research experts, review of past studies and researcher's own perception.

Ho_1 : There is no significant positive compound growth rate in area, production and productivity of sugarcane among the sugarcane producing countries in the world.

Ho_2 : There is no significant positive compound growth rate in area, production and productivity of sugarcane among the sugarcane producing states in India

Ho_3 : There is no significant positive compound growth rate in area, production and productivity of sugarcane among the sugarcane producing districts in the state.

Ho_4 : There is no significant positive compound growth rate in export and import of sugar in India.

Ho_5 : There is no significant association between the socio-economic characteristics of the farmers and their level of satisfaction about the adoption of drip irrigation system in sugarcane cultivation.

Ho_6 : There is no significant association between the socio-economic characteristics of the farmers and their level of satisfaction about the functioning of sugarcane and khandsari sugar marketing channels.

1.7.   Operational Definitions

Productivity

Productivity is a measure of the efficiency of production in the form of an average, expressing the total output of sugarcane divided by the total area of land used for the production of sugarcane.

Marketing Cost

The cost incurred from the point of production to the point of consumption is known as marketing cost.

Marketing Margin

Marketing margin involves the cost of moving the product from the point of production to the point of consumption and the profit of various market functionaries.

Price Spread

Price spread refers to the difference between the price paid for by the consumer and the price received by the producer for the same quantity of product. It consists of marketing cost and margin of the intermediaries.

Communality

Communality is the amount of variance, a variable shares with all other variables being considered. This is also the proportion of variance explained by the common factors.

Eigen Value

The Eigen value represents the total variance explained by each factor.

Factor Loadings

The loadings are simple considerations between the variables and the factor.

Planted Sugarcane

The sugarcane sets which are freshly used in a land is called as sugarcane planted crop.

Ratoon Sugarcane

It is a method of harvesting a crop which leaves the roots and the lower parts of the plant uncut to give the ratoon or the stubble crop.

Drip Emitters or Drippers

Drip irrigation is sometimes called trickle irrigation and involves dripping water onto the soil at very low rates (2-20 litres/hour) from a system of small diameter plastic pipes fitted with outlets called emitters or drippers.

1.8. Scope

This book is primarily undertaken with a view to examine the cultivation and marketing practices of sugarcane farmers in Erode district of Tamil Nadu. Though sugarcane is grown in most of the districts in Tamil Nadu, this book confines to Erode district only as this district is one of the leading districts in sugarcane cultivation in the state. This book also focuses the cost of sugarcane cultivation. This book pertains to analyse the attitude of farmers towards the adoption of drip irrigation system in sugarcane cultivation. This book further analyses the price spread along with the level of satisfaction of farmers about the functioning of sugarcane and khandsari sugar marketing channels. This book also analyses the problems of sugarcane farmers in cultivation and marketing. This book also covers the area, production and productivity of sugarcane at National, State and District level.

1.9. Period

The information collected includes both primary and secondary data. Required primary data have been collected from sugarcane farmers and intermediaries during the year 2011-2012 in Erode District of Tamil Nadu. The required secondary data have been collected from various sources like Co-operative Sugar Journal, websites of Sugarcane Breeding Institution of Coimbatore, Food and Agricultural Organisation, Cane info, Directorate of Economics and Statistics of Government of India, Season and Crop Report of Government of Tamil Nadu and District hand book of statistics for the period of ten years from 2003-2004 to 2012-2013 during the year 2013-2014.

1.10. Pilot Study and Pre Testing

The pilot study is conducted with a sample of 50 farmers during June 2011. In the pilot study, the interview schedule is pre-tested and then refined for use in the final study. On the basis of outcome of the pilot study, appropriate modifications have been made in the final interview schedule. Further, the findings of the pilot study enabled to frame hypotheses and design of the final study.

1.11. Methodology and Tools

Sampling Design

A multi-stage sampling technique is used in the present study. The study is conducted during the year 2011-2012 in Erode district of Tamil Nadu.

Stage I: Selection of District

The present study is confined to Erode District of Tamil Nadu. This district is purposively selected due to the aggressive involvement of farmers in agriculture and it stands second in area and production of sugarcane in Tamil Nadu during the year 2010-2011 (vide appendix iii).

Stage II: Selection of Taluks

Erode district comprises of five Taluks namely Bhavani, Erode, Gobichettipalayam, Perundurai and Sathyamangalam. Based on the information provided by the statistical department regarding the area under sugarcane cultivation for the year 2010-2011 (vide appendix iv), two taluks namely Bhavani and Gobichettipalayam are selected purposively as these taluks have the largest area under sugarcane cultivation.

Stage III: Selection of Sample Farmers

Farmers who are cultivating sugarcane for the past five years with minimum land holding of one acre are selected from the two taluks. The sample size is 600. The sample farmers are selected by using convenience sampling technique. Out of 600 farmers selected, it is found that 313 (52.17 per cent) farmers are supplying sugarcane to the factory, 72 (12.00 per cent) farmers are supplying sugarcane to the jaggery producers and remaining 215 (35.83 per cent) farmers are producing khandsari sugar themselves.

Selection of Intermediaries

For the purpose of analysing the marketing cost, data relating to marketing cost incurred by intermediaries are required. Required data have been obtained from 50 intermediaries in the area and they are selected by using convenience sampling technique.

Collection of Data

This study is an empirical research based on survey method. Both primary and secondary data have been used in this study. Required primary data have been collected with the pre-tested, well-structured and non-disguised interview schedules from the sugarcane farmers. Required secondary data have been collected from the Co-operative Sugar Journal, websites of

Sugarcane Breeding Institution of Coimbatore, Food and Agricultural Organisation, Cane info, Directorate of Economics and Statistics of Government of India, Season and Crop Report of Government of Tamil Nadu, District hand book of statistics and the records of Erode District Statistical Office.

The necessary data and information have also been collected from the libraries of Tamil Nadu Agricultural University, Bharathiar University, Coimbatore and Madurai Kamaraj University, Madurai. The data relating to the theoretical parts have been collected from various books, journals, magazines and websites.

Tools Used for Data Analysis

Data obtained from the field are analysed with the help of statistical package for social science (SPSS) latest version. The statistical tools such as Mean, Standard Deviation, Compound Growth Rate, Chi-Square test, F-test, Z-test, Cobb-Douglas Production Function, Factor Analysis, Multiple Regression Analysis, Logistic Regression Model, Discriminant Function Analysis, Simple Ranking Technique, Ranked Based Quotient (RBQ) Technique and Garrett Ranking Technique have been used.

Compound Growth Rate has been applied to find out growth in area, production and productivity of sugarcane and export and import of sugar in India.

Factor analysis (Principal components with application of varimax rotation) has been used to analyse the factors influencing the farmers to cultivate sugarcane, factors influencing the farmers to adopt the drip irrigation system in sugarcane cultivation and problems faced by the farmers in sugarcane cultivation. To evaluate the resource use efficiency in cultivation of sugarcane, Cobb-Douglas type of Production Function has been used.

Garrett Ranking Technique has been used to analyse the reasons for not following intercropping, Reasons for using a particular variety, the reasons for non-adoption of drip irrigation system in sugarcane cultivation and problems in adoption of drip irrigation system in sugarcane cultivation.

The influence of the various personal and socio-economic variables of the sugarcane farmers and satisfaction in the adoption of drip irrigation system in sugarcane cultivation is analysed with the help of Chi-square test, F-test, Z-test and Multiple Regression Analysis (stepwise model). The influence of the various personal and socio-economic variables of the sugarcane farmers and their level of satisfaction about the functioning of sugarcane and khandsari sugar marketing channels is analysed with the help of Logistic Regression Model.

Simple ranking technique has been used for the factors motivating the farmers to market their sugarcane and khandsari sugar channels.

Discriminant Function Analysis has been applied to analyse the problems in cultivation of sugarcane. A Rank Based Quotient (RBQ) technique has been applied to analyse the marketing problems in sugarcane and khandsari sugar marketing.

1.12. Limitations

This book has the following limitations:

1. The size of the sample is restricted to 600. Therefore, the limitations of a restricted sample size are applicable to the present study.
2. The book confines to the sugarcane farmers who are residing in Erode district of Tamil Nadu. Moreover, only Bhavani and Gobichettipalayam taluks have been considered for this book. Hence, general application of the results may be restricted only to similar socio-economic environment.
3.   As the secondary data collected from many sources, the gap in one source is filled by referring the other sources. There may be some discrepancies if the data are not correctly reported by the referred sources. Hence, any generalization needs in-depth analysis.
4. The farmers are not in the habit of maintaining the detailed periodical accounts regarding cost, return and marketing price in their sugarcane cultivation and marketing. Hence, the information from the memory of sugarcane farmers might be subjected to recall bias.
5. The data for the study have been collected exclusively by personal canvassing of interview schedule. The data so collected are subject to what may be called the error of response in some degree or other. Such errors of response are largely due to lack of awareness, improper maintenance of accounts and fear of revealing trade information of the farmers.
6. In some cases, the farmers failed to give their opinion categorically. In such situations, further questions are asked and logical conclusions are drawn based on their replies.

CHAPTER II

GROWTH IN AREA, PRODUCTION AND PRODUCTIVITY OF SUGARCANE

Keywords

Country-wise Growth in Area, Production and Productivity of Sugarcane - State-wise Growth in Area, Production and Productivity of Sugarcane – District-wise Growth in Area, Production and Productivity of Sugarcane - Export and Import of Sugar in India

2.1. Introduction

Sugarcane is one of the major cash crops of India which is the home land of sugarcane cultivation and sugar production. Sugarcane cultivation and development of sugar industry runs parallel to the growth of human civilisation and is as old as agriculture. In the present scenario too, sugarcane and sugar continue to be important for India's rural economy. About 6 million sugarcane farmers and large number of agricultural labourers are involved in sugarcane cultivation and ancillary activities, constituting 7.5 per cent of rural population. Besides, the industry provides employment to 5 lakh skilled and semi-skilled workers in rural areas.

India is one of the largest sugarcane producers in the world, producing around 300 million tonnes of cane per annum. India also happens to be the second largest sugar producing country (after Brazil), contributing 15 per cent to white crystal sugar production. Further, India is the only country that produces plantation white sugar unlike other countries that produce raw or refined sugar or both. "India is the largest consumer of sugar in the world and the Indian sugar industry is the second largest agro-industry located in rural India. With 526 operating sugar mills in different parts of the country, having a crushing capacity of 4125 tonnes per day, the Indian sugar industry has been a focal point for socio-economic development in the rural areas by mobilising rural resources, generating employment and higher income, transport and communication facilities. It also produces ethanol, an eco-friendly and renewable energy for blending with petrol. In India, sugarcane area and production are mainly concentrated in the states of Uttar Pradesh, Maharashtra, Tamil Nadu and Karnataka. Tamil Nadu is registered the highest yield in sugarcane production in India. Even though Uttar Pradesh is the largest producer of sugarcane in India, yield rate is lower when compared with all India average. In Tamil Nadu, sugarcane is cultivated mainly in irrigated condition; the area under sugarcane is increasing over years. The production of sugarcane is concentrated mainly in the districts of Villupuram, Cuddalore, Erode, Pudukotai, Nammakal, Salem, Trichy and Coimbatore. The yield rate is higher in Nammakal and Erode. The sugarcane is preferred by the farmers as it gives remunerative price to the farmers. Sugarcane is rotated with other crops and one or two ratooning is practiced in major parts of the State. An assessment of contribution of various components to the total output of sugarcane in these districts will be of immense significance to increase the production of sugarcane in the State.

This chapter deals with country-wise, state-wise and district-wise area used for sugarcane production, volume in sugarcane production and productivity of sugarcane and sugar export & import in India. For the purpose of analysis, Statistical tools such as Mean, Standard Deviation, Co-efficient of Variation and Compound Growth Rate have been used. Sugarcane growth is particularly measured based on trend. With the intention to find out the trend of sugarcane growth, the overall data set is divided into two groups namely, Period I and Period II. Period I - 2003-2004 to 2007-2008 and Period II-2008-2009 to 2012-2013.

In order to find the growth in Area, Production and Productivity of Sugarcane, the data for ten years being divided into three decades viz., 2003-2004 to 2007-2008 considered as Period I, 2008-2009 to 2012-2013 as Period II and 2003- 2004 to 2012-2013 as Overall Period.

2.2. Country-wise Growth in Area, Production and Productivity of Sugarcane

The Country-wise Growth in Area, Production and Productivity of Sugarcane are analysed with Mean, Standard Deviation, Co-efficient of Variation and Compound Growth Rate.

2.2.1. *Area Used for Sugarcane Production*

Table 2.1 presents the Country-wise area used for production of Sugarcane for the Period I, Period II and the Overall Period with Mean, Standard Deviation, Co-efficient of Variation and Compound Growth Rate.

Table 2.1: Country-wise Area Used for Sugarcane Production from 2003-2004 to 2012-2013

('000 hectares)

COUNTRIES	Period I			Period II			Overall Period		
	(2003-2004 to 2007-2008)			(2008-2009 to 2012-2013)			(2003-2004 to 2012-2013)		
	Mean	S.D	C.V	Mean	S.D	C.V	Mean	S.D	C.V
Argentina	287.40	5.13	1.78	350.00	3.54	1.01	318.70	33.25	10.43
Australia	428.00	13.17	3.08	364.80	40.25	11.03	396.40	43.66	11.01
Brazil	6041.80	689.13	11.41	8968.53	594.58	6.63	7505.17	1657.58	22.09
China	1435.60	93.39	6.51	1730.64	44.18	2.55	1583.12	170.07	10.74
Cuba	511.60	149.25	29.17	452.44	55.22	12.21	482.02	110.58	22.94
India	4270.80	492.08	11.52	4735.88	414.87	8.76	4503.34	494.16	10.97
Indonesia	373.60	29.60	7.92	437.15	14.60	3.34	405.37	40.07	9.89
Mexico	666.20	20.69	3.11	706.50	23.99	3.40	686.35	29.95	4.36
South Africa	403.60	44.07	10.92	296.80	25.19	8.49	350.20	65.68	18.75
Thailand	1054.80	66.63	6.32	1099.73	168.35	15.31	1077.27	123.00	11.42
USA	376.00	16.78	4.46	356.58	7.65	2.14	366.29	16.00	4.37

Source: www.fao.org, www.sugarcane.res.in. S.D-Standard Deviation, C.V-Co-efficient of Variation

Table 2.1 reveals that Brazil stands first in the area of sugarcane production during the Period I with the mean area of 6041.80 thousand hectares with the standard deviation of 689.13 and co-efficient of variation of 11.41 per cent. India has occupied the second position followed by China, Thailand, Mexico, Cuba, Australia, South Africa, USA, Indonesia and Argentina. Cuba has the highest co-efficient of variation of 29.17 per cent because of the highest variation in the area used for the production of sugarcane. During the Period II, Brazil occupied the first place with the mean area of 8968.53 thousand hectares with standard deviation of 594.58 and co-efficient of variation is 6.63 per cent followed by India, China, Thailand, Mexico, Cuba, Indonesia, USA, Argentina and South Africa. Thailand has the highest co-efficient of variation of 15.31 per cent than the other countries. In Overall Period, Brazil has maintained the first place with the mean area of 7505.17 thousand hectares with standard deviation of 1657.58 and co-efficient of variation is 22.09 per cent. India has second place with mean area of 4503.34 thousand hectares with standard deviation of 494.16 and co-efficient of variation is 10.97per cent followed by China, Thailand, Mexico, Cuba, Indonesia, Australia, USA, South Africa and Argentina. Cuba has recorded a highest co-efficient of variation of 22.94 per cent.

2.2.2. *Compound Growth Rate of Area Used for Sugarcane Production*

The compound growth rate of Country-wise area used for Sugarcane production for Period I, Period II and the Overall Period have been presented in Table 2.2.

Table 2.2: Compound Growth Rate of Country-wise Area Used for Sugarcane Production from 2003-2004 to 2012-2013

COUNTRIES	Period I			Period II			Overall Period		
	(2003-2004 to 2007-2008)			(2008-2009 to 2012-2013)			(2003-2004 to 2012-2013)		
	CGR	R^2 Value	't' Value	CGR	R^2 Value	't' Value	CGR	R^2 Value	't' Value
Argentina	-0.54	0.044	-0.372	-0.32	0.047	-0.388	7.01***	0.722	4.561
Australia	-2.07	0.221	-0.922	-10.36	0.436	-1.524	-7.05***	0.677	-4.095
Brazil	17.12***	0.950	7.616	9.58***	0.875	4.591	18.44***	0.960	13.810
China	5.05	0.289	1.105	1.38	0.137	0.692	7.61***	0.782	5.351
Cuba	-35.20***	0.937	-6.705	18.59***	0.898	5.156	-6.21	0.139	-1.136
India	4.13	0.057	0.429	2.97	0.050	0.398	4.63*	0.282	1.770
Indonesia	11.89***	0.929	6.299	4.04**	0.658	2.404	7.68***	0.911	9.034
Mexico	4.61***	0.984	13.930	4.55***	0.792	3.384	3.18***	0.887	7.941
South Africa	12.23	0.447	1.560	-2.19	0.031	-0.310	-9.07**	0.442	-2.517
Thailand	-7.73***	0.748	-2.986	19.34**	0.646	2.339	2.39	0.078	0.824
USA	-6.02***	0.931	-6.407	2.42**	0.603	2.133	-2.27***	0.496	-2.808

CGR-Compound Growth Rate, *** Significant at 1 per cent level, ** Significant at 5 per cent level, *Significant at 10 per cent level

Table 2.2 depicts that Brazil has positive and significant compound growth rate of area used for sugarcane production of 17.12 at 1 per cent level of significance with the R^2 value of 0.950 and 't' value of 7.616 followed by Indonesia (11.89 per cent) and Mexico (4.61 per cent). Cuba (-35.20 per cent), Thailand (-7.73 per cent) and USA (-6.02 per cent) have recorded negative compound growth rate of area used for the production of sugarcane at 1 per cent level of significance during the Period I.

South Africa (12.23 per cent), China (5.05 per cent) and India (4.13 per cent) have recorded positive and insignificant compound growth rate. Argentina (-0.54 per cent) and Australia (-2.07 per cent) have recorded negative and insignificant compound growth rate.

During the Period II, Thailand (19.34 per cent), Cuba (18.59 per cent), Brazil (9.58 per cent), Mexico (4.55 per cent), Indonesia (4.04 per cent) and USA (2.42 per cent) have recorded the statistically significant and positive compound growth rate at 1 per cent and 5 per cent level. India (2.97 per cent) and China (1.38 per cent) have recorded positive and insignificant compound growth rate. The Countries which have recorded negative and insignificant compound growth rate are Argentina (-0.32 per cent), South Africa (-2.19 per cent) and Australia (-10.36 per cent).

In Overall Period, the area used for the sugarcane production by Brazil (18.44 per cent), Indonesia (7.68 per cent), China (7.61 per cent), Argentina (7.01 per cent), India (4.63 per cent) and Mexico (3.18 per cent) have recorded positive and significant compound growth rate at 1 per cent and 10 per cent level of significance. Thailand (2.39 per cent) has recorded a positive and insignificant compound growth rate.

The countries which have recorded negative compound growth rate at 1 per cent level of significance are USA (-2.27 per cent), Australia (-7.05 per cent) and South Africa (-9.07 per cent). Cuba (-6.21 per cent) has negative and insignificant compound growth rate.

2.2.3. Volume of Sugarcane Production

Table 2.3 shows the country-wise volume of sugarcane production for the Period I, Period II and the Overall Period with Mean, Standard Deviation, Co-efficient of Variation and Compound Growth Rate.

Table 2.3: Country-Wise Sugarcane Production from 2003-2004 to 2012-2013

('000 Tonnes)

COUNTRIES	Period I			Period II			Overall Period		
	(2003-2004 to 2007-2008)			(2008-2009 to 2012-2013)			(2003-2004 to2012-2013)		
	Mean	S.D	C.V	Mean	S.D	C.V	Mean	S.D	C.V
Argentina	20560.00	2285.66	11.12	26106.00	2163.49	8.29	23333.00	3598.07	15.42
Australia	37261.60	642.37	1.72	29100.18	3338.59	11.47	33180.89	4862.07	14.65
Brazil	451026.00	63733.18	14.13	691826.79	35514.20	5.13	571426.40	135914.70	23.79
China	95518.20	7731.10	8.09	117837.84	6084.32	5.16	106678.02	13468.36	12.63
Cuba	16260.40	6486.88	39.89	14820.00	1914.94	12.92	15540.20	4572.54	29.42
India	277848.40	49127.92	17.68	323154.18	31672.78	9.80	300501.29	45702.43	15.21
Indonesia	27010.00	2198.41	8.14	25868.32	1066.54	4.12	26439.16	1736.55	6.57
Mexico	49639.80	2846.69	5.73	50340.61	715.26	1.42	49990.21	1991.34	3.98
South Africa	20270.80	773.59	3.82	18274.14	1846.70	10.11	19272.47	1699.73	8.82
Thailand	60955.00	12553.67	20.59	80315.33	14726.37	18.34	70635.17	16448.23	23.29
USA	27191.20	2389.70	8.79	26404.97	1424.32	5.39	26798.08	1900.37	7.09

Source: www.fao.org, www.sugarcane.res.in. S.D-Standard Deviation, C.V-Co-efficient of Variation

Table 2.3 indicates the quantity of sugarcane that has been produced by various countries. During the Period I, Brazil has the highest mean production of 451026.00 thousand tonnes with standard deviation of 63733.18 and co-efficient of variation of 14.13 per cent. India has second place with mean production of 277848.40 thousand tonnes with standard deviation of 49127.92 and co-efficient of variation of 17.68 per cent followed by China, Thailand, Mexico, Australia, USA, Indonesia, Argentina, South Africa and Cuba. Cuba has a highest co-efficient of variation of 39.89 per cent in Period I.

During the Period II, Brazil has retained the highest mean production of 691826.79 thousand tonnes with standard deviation of 35514.20 and co-efficient of variation of 5.13 per cent. Thailand has a highest co-efficient of variation of 18.34 per cent due to increase in the production of sugarcane from Period I to Period II. India has recorded a co-efficient of variation of 9.80 per cent.

In Overall Period, Brazil has attained the highest mean production of 571426.40 thousand tonnes with standard deviation of 135914.70 and co-efficient of variation of 23.79 per cent. India has second place with mean production of 300501.29 thousand tonnes with standard deviation of 45702.43 and co-efficient of variation of 15.21 per cent. Cuba has a highest co-efficient of variation of 29.42 per cent. India has recorded a co-efficient of variation of 15.21 per cent due to increase in production of sugarcane during the Period II.

2.2.4. *Compound Growth Rate of Volume of Sugarcane Production*

The compound growth rate of Country-wise volume of production of sugarcane for the Period I, Period II and the Overall Period have been given in Table 2.4.

Table 2.4: Compound Growth Rate of Country-wise Sugarcane Production from 2003-2004 to 2012-2013

COUNTRIES	Period I			Period II			Overall Period		
	(2003-2004 to 2007-2008)			(2008-2009 to 2012-2013)			(2003-2004 to 2012-2013)		
	CGR	R^2 Value	't' Value	CGR	R^2 Value	't' Value	CGR	R^2 Value	't' Value
Argentina	-2.34	0.024	-0.269	-8.47**	0.594	-2.093	7.30**	0.360	2.119
Australia	-1.84*	0.549	-1.910	-13.73***	0.755	-3.038	-10.26***	0.848	-6.672
Brazil	20.97***	0.920	5.873	3.20	0.176	0.802	19.53***	0.890	8.049
China	9.38**	0.595	2.101	-0.77	0.011	-0.179	8.73***	0.737	4.740
Cuba	-37.94***	0.715	-2.742	2.83	0.019	0.238	-6.57	0.105	-0.969
India	16.16	0.367	1.319	4.27	0.082	0.518	8.18**	0.441	2.511
Indonesia	3.56	0.087	0.534	-1.58	0.067	-0.464	-1.20	0.060	-0.713
Mexico	7.83***	0.778	3.243	-0.03	0.000	-0.027	1.45	0.214	1.474
South Africa	1.12	0.039	0.351	-4.83	0.111	-0.613	-4.12	0.361	-2.126
Thailand	-14.86	0.286	-1.097	23.21**	0.631	2.267	10.89	0.335	2.007
USA	-3.98	0.102	-0.583	4.26	0.279	1.079	-0.94	0.031	-0.509

CGR-Compound Growth Rate, *** Significant at 1 per cent level, ** Significant at 5 per cent level, *Significant at 10 per cent level

Table 2.4 indicates that during the Period I Brazil (20.97 per cent), China (9.38 per cent) and Mexico (7.83 per cent) have recorded positive and significant compound growth rate of sugarcane production at 1 per cent and 5 per cent level of significance. India (16.16 per cent), Indonesia (3.56 per cent) and South Africa (1.12 per cent) have recorded positive and insignificant compound growth rate of sugarcane production. Australia (-1.84 per cent) and

Cuba (-37.94 per cent) have recorded negative and significant compound growth rate at 10 and1 per cent level of significance. Argentina (-2.34 per cent), USA (-3.98 per cent) and Thailand (-14.86 per cent) have recorded negative and insignificant compound growth rate of sugarcane production.

During the Period II, Thailand has attained a highest compound growth rate of 23.21 percent with a significant level of 5 per cent. India (4.27 per cent), USA (4.26 per cent), Brazil (3.20 per cent) and Cuba (2.83 per cent) have recorded positive and insignificant compound growth in production of sugarcane. Argentina (-8.47 per cent) and Australia (-13.73 per cent) have recorded negative and significant compound growth rate at 1 and 5 per cent level of significance.

In Overall Period, Brazil has achieved a highest compound growth rate of 19.53 per cent with R^2 value of 0.890 and 't' value of 8.049. India has achieved a compound growth rate of 8.18 per cent with R^2 value of 0.441 and 't' value of 2.511 followed by China (8.73 per cent), Argentina (7.30 per cent) have recorded positive and significant compound growth rate at 1 percent and 5 per cent level. Thailand (10.89 per cent) and Mexico (1.45 per cent) have recorded positive and insignificant compound growth rate of production of sugarcane. Australia (-10.26 per cent) has recorded a negative and significant compound growth rate at 1 per cent level of significance.

2.2.5. *Productivity of Sugarcane*

Table 2.5 shows the Country-wise Productivity of Sugarcane for the Period I, Period II and the Overall Period with Mean, Standard Deviation, Co-efficient of variation and Compound Growth Rate.

Table 2.5: Country-wise Productivity of Sugarcane from 2003-2004 to 2012-2013

(Per hectare)

COUNTRIES	Period I			Period II			Overall Period		
	(2003-2004 to 2007-2008)			(2008-2009 to 2012-2013)			(2003-2004 to 2012-2013)		
	Mean	S.D	C.V	Mean	S.D	C.V	Mean	S.D	C.V
Argentina	71.60	8.79	12.28	74.49	5.45	7.31	73.04	7.06	9.67
Australia	87.20	2.68	3.08	79.89	3.95	4.94	83.55	5.00	5.98
Brazil	74.60	2.07	2.78	77.21	3.58	4.64	75.91	3.08	4.06
China	66.40	3.36	5.06	68.02	2.07	3.05	67.21	2.77	4.12
Cuba	31.40	6.23	19.84	32.98	5.26	15.94	32.19	5.50	17.08
India	65.20	5.22	8.00	68.23	2.14	3.14	66.72	4.08	6.12
Indonesia	72.80	5.97	8.21	59.32	3.01	5.08	66.06	8.39	12.70
Mexico	74.60	2.19	2.94	71.25	2.81	3.94	72.93	2.96	4.06
South Africa	50.80	7.05	13.88	61.47	2.10	3.42	56.14	7.46	13.29
Thailand	57.40	10.04	17.49	72.69	2.45	3.37	65.04	10.60	16.30
USA	72.40	5.32	7.35	73.97	3.41	4.61	73.18	4.29	5.87

Source: www.fao.org,www.sugarcane.res.in. S.D-Standard Deviation, C.V-Co-efficient of Variation

Table 2.5 exhibits that the highest productivity of sugarcane has been attained by Australia during the Period I with the mean value of 87.20 with standard deviation of 2.68 and co-efficient of variation of 3.08 per cent followed by Brazil, Mexico, Indonesia, USA, Argentina, China, India, Thailand, South Africa and Cuba. Cuba has recorded the highest co-efficient of variation of 19.84 per cent.

During the Period II, Australia has retained the highest productivity of sugarcane with the mean value of 79.89, with standard deviation of 3.95 and co-efficient of variation of 4.94 per cent followed by Brazil, Argentina, USA, Thailand, Mexico, India, China, South Africa, Indonesia and Cuba. Cuba has recorded a highest co-efficient of variation of 15.94 per cent.

In Overall Period, Australia also retained the highest productivity of sugarcane with the mean value of 83.55, with standard deviation of 5.00 and co-efficient of variation of 5.98 per cent followed by Brazil, USA, Argentina, Mexico, China, India, Indonesia, Thailand, South Africa and Cuba. Cuba has recorded a highest co-efficient of variation of 17.08 per cent. India has a recorded co-efficient of variation of 6.12 per cent due to decrease in the productivity of sugarcane.

2.2.6. *Compound Growth Rate of Productivity of Sugarcane*

The compound growth rate of country-wise productivity of sugarcane for Period I, Period II and the Overall Period have been shown in Table 2.6.

Table 2.6: Compound Growth Rate of Country-wise Productivity of Sugarcane from 2003-2004 to 2012-2013

COUNTRIES	Period I			Period II			Overall Period		
	(2003-2004 to 2007-2008)			(2008-2009 to 2012-2013)			(2003-2004 to 2012-2013)		
	CGR	R^2 Value	't' Value	CGR	R^2 Value	't' Value	CGR	R^2 Value	't' Value
Argentina	-1.57	0.009	-0.162	-7.99**	0.663	-2.429	0.30	0.002	0.121
Australia	0.05	0.000	0.018	-3.96	0.326	-1.205	-3.50***	0.602	-3.479
Brazil	3.42***	0.705	2.678	-5.67***	0.715	-2.740	0.88	0.081	0.839
China	4.57	0.384	1.367	-1.98	0.205	-0.880	1.17	0.140	1.139
Cuba	-4.39	0.020	-0.249	-12.98	0.372	-1.332	-0.24	0.000	-0.050
India	11.42***	0.888	4.873	1.18	0.064	0.452	3.16**	0.436	2.487
Indonesia	-7.10	0.351	-1.272	-5.75**	0.633	-2.277	-8.33***	0.824	-6.128
Mexico	2.56	0.340	1.243	1.18	0.568	0.452	-1.80**	0.347	-2.062
South Africa	-10.45	0.341	-1.245	-2.50	0.268	-1.047	5.38*	0.252	1.642
Thailand	-7.70	0.097	-0.568	3.52*	0.505	1.750	8.44**	0.361	2.127
USA	2.85	0.067	0.463	2.02	0.088	0.538	1.39	0.092	0.900

CGR-Compound Growth Rate, *** Significant at 1 per cent level, ** Significant at 5 per cent level, *Significant at 10 per cent level

Table 2.6 displays that India (11.42 per cent) has achieved highest productivity with R^2 and 't' value of 0.888 and 4.873 and Brazil (3.42 per cent) have positive and statistically significant at 1 per cent level of compound growth rate in productivity of sugarcane. China (4.57 per cent), USA (2.85 per cent), Mexico (2.56 per cent) and Australia (0.05 per cent) have recorded positive and insignificant compound growth rate. Argentina (-1.57 per cent), Cuba (-4.39 per cent), Indonesia (-7.10 per cent), Thailand (-7.70 per cent) and South Africa (-10.45 per cent) have recorded negative and insignificant compound growth rate during the Period I.

During the Period II, Thailand (3.52 per cent) has recorded a positive and significant compound growth rate at 10 per cent level of significance. USA (2.02 per cent), India (1.18 per cent) and Mexico (1.18 per cent) have recorded positive and insignificant compound growth rate. Argentina (-7.99 per cent), Brazil (-5.67 per cent) and Indonesia (-5.75 per cent) have recorded negative and statistically significant compound growth rate at 1 and 5 percent level of significance. In Overall Period, Thailand (8.44 per cent), South Africa (5.38 per cent) and India (3.16 per cent) have recorded positive and significant compound growth rate at 5 and 10 per cent level of significance for the productivity of sugarcane. Mexico (-1.80 per cent), Australia (-3.50 per cent) and Indonesia (-8.33 per cent) which are also have negative and significant compound growth rate at 1 and 5 per cent level for the productivity of sugarcane.

2.3. State-wise Growth in Area, Production and Productivity of Sugarcane

The State-wise area, production and productivity of Sugarcane are analysed with Mean, Standard Deviation, Co-efficient of Variation and Compound Growth Rate.

2.3.1. Area Used for Sugarcane Production

Table 2.7 presents the State-wise mean area used for Sugarcane production for Period I, Period II and the Overall Period with Standard Deviation and Co-efficient of Variation.

Table 2.7: State-wise Area Used for Sugarcane Production from 2003-2004 to 2012-2013

('000 hectares)

| STATES | Period I | | | Period II | | | Overall Period | | |
| | (2003-2004 to 2007-2008) | | | (2008-2009 to 2012-2013) | | | (2003-2004 to 2012-2013) | | |
	Mean	S.D	C.V	Mean	S.D	C.V	Mean	S.D	C.V
Andhra Pradesh	232.00	23.80	10.26	189.20	17.98	9.50	210.60	30.07	14.28
Bihar	109.60	11.76	10.73	186.40	66.98	35.94	148.00	60.78	41.07
Gujarat	199.00	15.05	7.56	193.80	24.86	12.83	196.40	19.57	9.96
Haryana	139.40	12.92	9.26	90.20	12.19	13.52	114.80	28.51	24.83
Karnataka	254.40	61.26	24.08	375.00	64.13	17.10	314.70	86.81	27.58
Maharashtra	682.00	361.13	52.95	889.60	120.52	13.55	785.80	276.38	35.17
Punjab	100.40	16.44	16.38	76.60	12.12	15.82	88.50	18.51	20.92
Tamil Nadu	300.40	84.41	28.10	331.80	40.22	12.12	316.10	64.49	20.40
Uttar Pradesh	2113.40	118.34	5.60	2112.00	88.99	4.21	2112.70	98.71	4.67
Uttarakhand	116.20	11.61	9.99	105.60	5.50	5.21	110.90	10.22	9.22

Source: Cooperative Sugar Journal, S.D-Standard Deviation, C.V-Co-efficient of Variation

Table 2.7 reveals that the area used for sugarcane production in the Period I, Uttar Pradesh stands first with mean area of 2113.40 thousand hectares with the standard deviation of 118.34 and co-efficient of variation of 5.60 per cent followed by Maharashtra (mean area

682.00), Tamil Nadu (mean area 300.40), Karnataka (mean area 254.40), Andhra Pradesh (mean area 232.00), Gujarat (mean area 199.00), Haryana (mean area 139.40), Uttarakhand (mean area 116.20), Bihar (mean area 109.60) and Punjab (mean area 100.40). Maharashtra is having the highest variability with co-efficient variation of 52.95 per cent in the area used for sugarcane production.

During the Period II, Uttar Pradesh has the mean area of 2112.00thousand hectares with standard deviation of 88.99 and co-efficient of variation of 4.21 per cent. Bihar has recorded the highest variability of co-efficient variation of 35.94 per cent due to increased area used for sugarcane production when compared to period I. Tamil Nadu is having fourth place in area used for sugarcane production with mean area of 331.80 thousand hectares with standard deviation of 40.22 and co-efficient of variation of 12.12 per cent due to decrease in area used for sugarcane production.

In growth of area used for sugarcane production for the overall period of ten years, Uttar Pradesh maintains the top position with mean area of 2112.70 thousand hectares with standard deviation of 98.71 and co-efficient of variation of 4.67 per cent followed by Maharashtra (mean area 785.80), Tamil Nadu (mean area 316.10), Karnataka (mean area 314.70), Andhra Pradesh (mean area 210.60), Gujarat (mean area 196.40), Bihar (mean area 148.00), Uttarakhand (mean area 110.90) and Punjab (mean area 88.50). Bihar has the highest variability of co-efficient of variation of 41.07 per cent in the area used for production of sugarcane.

2.3.2. *Compound Growth Rate of Area Used for Sugarcane Production*

The compound growth rate of state-wise area used for sugarcane production for the Period I, Period II and the Overall Period have been given in Table 2. 8.

Table 2.8: Compound Growth Rate of State-wise Area Used for Sugarcane Production from 2003-2004 to 2012-2013

| STATES | Period I | | | Period II | | | Overall Period | | |
| | (2003-2004 to 2007-2008) | | | (2008-2009 to 2012-2013) | | | (2003-2004 to 2012-2013) | | |
	CGR	R² Value	't' Value	CGR	R² Value	't' Value	CGR	R² Value	't' Value
Andhra Pradesh	13.84***	0.765	3.124	6.06	0.160	0.756	-4.71	0.195	-1.390
Bihar	7.57	0.244	0.983	63.62***	0.723	2.798	26.44***	0.690	4.224
Gujarat	10.80***	0.828	3.801	2.13	0.011	0.186	0.41	0.003	0.145
Haryana	-4.35	0.114	-0.623	14.71	0.478	1.657	-13.24***	0.533	-3.019
Karnataka	27.83	0.464	1.613	25.02***	0.709	2.703	21.67***	0.771	5.194
Maharashtra	98.66	0.435	1.521	17.47**	0.640	2.311	33.80**	0.463	2.628
Punjab	-1.88	0.001	-0.063	13.30***	0.278	10.96	-13.79*	0.296	-1.834
Tamil Nadu	49.08***	0.772	3.186	16.34***	0.787	3.329	15.18***	0.556	3.167
Uttar Pradesh	6.68	0.002	0.076	4.92**	0.599	2.119	18.91	0.101	0.947
Uttarakhand	1.38	0.001	0.059	4.07	0.258	1.022	1.09	0.060	0.213

CGR-Compound Growth Rate, ***Significant at 1 per cent level, ** Significant at 5 per cent level, *Significant at 10 per cent level

Table 2.8 depicts that Tamil Nadu (49.08 per cent), Gujarat (10.80 per cent) and Andhra Pradesh (13.84 percent) have recorded positive and significant compound growth rate at 1 per cent level of significance for area used for sugarcane production during the Period I. Maharashtra (98.66 per cent), Karnataka (27.83 per cent), Bihar (7.57 per cent), Uttar Pradesh (6.68 per cent) and Uttarakhand (1.38 per cent) have recorded positive and insignificant compound growth rate. Punjab (-1.88 per cent) and Haryana (-4.35 per cent) have recorded negative and insignificant compound growth rate for area used for sugarcane production.

During the Period II, Bihar has the highest compound growth rate of 63.62 per cent followed by Karnataka (25.02 per cent), Maharashtra (17.47per cent), Tamil Nadu (16.34 per cent), Punjab (13.30 per cent) and Uttar Pradesh (4.92 per cent) have recorded statistically significant and positive compound growth rate at 1and 5 per cent level.

In case of Overall Period, the area used for sugarcane production by Maharashtra has the highest positive and significant compound growth rate of 33.80 per cent with the R^2 value of 0.463 and 't' value of 2.628 followed by Bihar (26.44 per cent), Karnataka (21.67 per cent) and Tamil Nadu (15.18 per cent) which have positive and significant compound growth rate at 1 and 5 per cent level of significance. Haryana (-13.24 per cent) and Punjab (-13.79 per cent) have recorded negative and significant compound growth rate at 1 and 10 per cent level of significance.

2.3.3. Volume of Sugarcane Production

Table 2.9 depicts the state-wise volume of sugarcane production for the Period I, Period II and the Overall Period with Mean, Standard Deviation, Co-efficient of Variation and Compound Growth Rate.

Table 2.9: State-wise Sugarcane Production from 2003-2004 to 2012-2013

('000 Tonnes)

| STATES | Period I | | | Period II | | | Overall Period | | |
| | (2003-2004 to 2007-2008) | | | (2008-2009 to 2012-2013) | | | (2003-2004 to 2012-2013) | | |
	Mean	S.D	C.V	Mean	S.D	C.V	Mean	S.D	C.V
Andhra Pradesh	18090.60	2858.18	15.80	14864.40	1875.81	12.62	16477.50	2843.56	17.26
Bihar	4509.40	830.38	18.41	9279.60	3947.30	42.54	6894.50	3681.33	53.40
Gujarat	14527.80	1130.60	7.78	13434.00	1266.98	9.43	13980.90	1270.39	9.09
Haryana	8792.00	665.97	7.57	6191.20	1019.54	16.47	7491.60	1593.12	21.27
Karnataka	20693.60	6390.40	30.88	32895.00	6683.16	20.32	26794.30	8908.13	33.25
Maharashtra	50400.20	31147.87	61.80	70785.20	12554.31	17.74	60592.70	24832.94	40.98
Punjab	5872.00	831.79	14.17	4945.00	1145.22	23.16	5408.50	1062.59	19.65
Tamil Nadu	31070.80	10065.04	32.39	35519.80	4913.40	13.83	33295.30	7826.38	23.51
Uttar Pradesh	123110.80	7937.66	6.45	121212.00	8793.05	7.25	122161.40	7960.39	6.52
Uttarakhand	6802.40	801.81	11.79	6191.40	465.64	7.52	6496.90	696.99	10.73

Source: Cooperative Sugar Journal, S.D-Standard Deviation, C.V-Co-efficient of Variation

Table 2.9 reveals that Uttar Pradesh has registered with the highest mean production of 123110.80 thousand tonnes with the standard deviation of 7937.66 and co-efficient of variation of 6.45 per cent followed by Maharashtra (mean production 50400.20), Tamil Nadu (mean production 31070.80), Karnataka (mean production 20693.60), Andhra Pradesh (mean production 18090.60), Gujarat (mean production 14527.80), Haryana (mean production 8792.00), Uttarakhand (mean production 6802.40), Punjab (mean production 5872.00) and Bihar (mean production 4509.40). Maharashtra has recorded with the highest co efficient of variation of 61.80 per cent for the Period I in India.

During the Period II, Uttar Pradesh has again occupied the major share in the production of sugarcane with the mean value of 121212.00 thousand tonnes with the standard deviation of 8793.05 and the co-efficient of variation of 7.25 per cent. Production of sugarcane has increased in the selected states of Maharashtra, Tamil Nadu, Karnataka and Bihar during the Period II when compared to Period I. Bihar is having a highest variation with co-efficient of variation of 42.54 per cent in India.

Uttar Pradesh has been the major shareholder in the sugarcane production in India for the Overall Period of ten years with the mean production value of 122161.40 thousand tonnes with the standard deviation of 7960.39 and the co-efficient of variation of 6.52 per cent. Bihar has recorded the highest co-efficient of variation of 53.40 per cent due to high variation of production when compared to Period I to Period II.

2.3.4. *Compound Growth Rate of Volume of Sugarcane Production*

The Compound growth rate for state-wise volume of sugarcane production for Period I, Period II and the Overall Period have been given in Table 2.10.

Table 2.10: Compound Growth Rate of State-wise Sugarcane Production from 2003-2004 to 2012-2013

STATES	Period I (2003-2004 to 2007-2008)			Period II (2008-2009 to 2012-2013)			Overall Period (2003-2004 to 2012-2013)		
	CGR	R^2Value	't' Value	CGR	R^2 Value	't' Value	CGR	R^2 Value	't' Value
Andhra Pradesh	23.49***	0.847	4.083	9.16	0.197	0.858	-3.08	0.057	-0.697
Bihar	3.72	0.022	0.260	83.36***	0.729	2.844	35.44***	0.679	4.116
Gujarat	10.49***	0.720	2.777	-8.04	0.401	-1.418	-2.53	0.137	-1.128
Haryana	1.86	0.028	0.293	26.55***	0.973	10.460	-9.02*	0.307	-1.882
Karnataka	47.39***	0.758	3.063	22.74	0.428	1.497	27.19***	0.787	5.433
Maharashtra	140.93***	0.853	4.169	7.06	0.073	0.486	33.24***	0.525	2.976
Punjab	4.07	0.036	0.334	28.68**	0.572	2.002	-2.86	0.035	-0.536
Tamil Nadu	62.21***	0.844	4.029	19.25***	0.774	3.209	15.14***	0.458	2.602
Uttar Pradesh	7.69**	0.620	2.214	11.03***	0.959	8.377	1.62	0.103	0.961
Uttarakhand	-1.04	0.004	-0.107	10.77***	0.854	4.191	-2.04	0.067	-0.760

CGR-Compound Growth Rate, *** Significant at 1 per cent level, ** Significant at 5 per cent level, * Significant at 10 per cent level

Table 2.10 shows that during the Period I, Maharashtra (140.93 per cent), Tamil Nadu (62.21 per cent), Karnataka (47.39 per cent), Andhra Pradesh (23.49 per cent), Gujarat (10.49 per cent) and Uttar Pradesh (7.69 per cent) have recorded positive and significant compound growth rate of sugarcane production at 1 and 5 per cent level of significance. Punjab (4.07 per cent), Bihar (3.72 per cent) and Haryana (1.86 per cent) have recorded positive and insignificant compound growth rate. Uttarakhand has recorded a negative and insignificant compound growth rate (-1.04 per cent).

During the Period II, Bihar (83.36 per cent), Punjab (28.68 per cent), Haryana (26.55 per cent), Tamil Nadu (19.25 per cent), Uttar Pradesh (11.03 per cent) and Uttarakhand (10.77 per cent) have recorded positive and significant compound growth rate at 1 and 5 per cent level of significance. Gujarat (-8.04 per cent) has a negative and insignificant compound growth rate in the volume of sugarcane production.

In the Overall Period, Bihar has the highest positive and significant compound growth rate of 35.44 per cent with the R^2 value of 0.679 and 't' value of 4.116 followed by Maharashtra (33.24 per cent), Karnataka (27.19 per cent), Tamil Nadu (15.14 per cent) which have recorded positive significant compound growth rate at 1 and 5 per cent level. Uttar Pradesh (1.62 per cent) has recorded a positive and insignificant compound growth rate. All other states have a negative and insignificant compound growth rate.

2.3.5. *Productivity of Sugarcane*

Table 2.11 explains the state-wise productivity of sugarcane for the Period I, Period II and the Overall Period with Mean, Standard Deviation, Co-efficient of Variation and Compound Growth Rate.

Table 2.11: State-wise Productivity of Sugarcane from 2003-2004 to 2012-2013

(Per hectare)

STATES	Period I (2003-2004 to 2007-2008)			Period II (2008-2009 to 2012-2013)			Overall Period (2003-2004 to 2012-2013)		
	Mean	S.D	C.V	Mean	S.D	C.V	Mean	S.D	C.V
Andhra Pradesh	77.64	4.49	5.78	78.32	2.75	3.51	77.98	3.52	4.52
Bihar	41.10	3.80	9.24	48.52	4.28	8.82	44.81	5.46	12.19
Gujarat	72.98	1.08	1.48	69.86	7.27	10.40	71.42	5.17	7.23
Haryana	63.28	3.78	5.97	68.66	6.63	9.65	65.97	5.82	8.83
Karnataka	80.58	8.74	10.84	87.40	5.77	6.60	83.99	7.85	9.35
Maharashtra	70.90	9.86	13.91	79.60	8.83	11.09	75.25	9.94	13.22
Punjab	58.44	2.77	4.75	64.10	6.32	9.86	61.27	5.49	8.95
Tamil Nadu	102.02	6.16	6.04	105.58	4.90	4.64	103.80	5.57	5.37
Uttar Pradesh	58.24	2.03	3.49	57.36	3.05	5.31	57.80	2.48	4.30
Uttarakhand	58.60	4.65	7.94	58.66	3.77	6.43	58.63	3.99	6.81

Source: Cooperative Sugar Journal,   S.D-Standard Deviation, C.V-Co-efficient of Variation

Table 2.11 portrays that the highest productivity of sugarcane has been registered by Tamil Nadu during the Period I with the mean productivity value of 102.02 with the standard deviation of 6.16 and with the co-efficient of variation of 6.04 per cent followed by Karnataka, Andhra Pradesh, Gujarat, Maharashtra, Haryana, Uttarakhand, Punjab, Uttar Pradesh and Bihar. Maharashtra has the highest co-efficient of variation of 13.91 per cent and this may be due to the instability in area and production of sugarcane.

During the Period II, the highest mean productivity value of 105.58 has been recorded by Tamil Nadu with the standard deviation of 4.90 and the co-efficient of variation of 4.64 per cent. Maharashtra has the highest co-efficient of variation of 11.09 per cent due to increase in the productivity of sugarcane.

In Overall Period, Tamil Nadu has the highest productivity of sugarcane in India with mean productivity value of 103.80 with standard deviation of 5.57 and co-efficient of variation of 5.37 per cent followed by Karnataka, Andhra Pradesh, Maharashtra, Gujarat, Haryana, Punjab, Uttarakhand, Uttar Pradesh and Bihar. Maharashtra has the highest co-efficient of variation of 13.22 per cent when compared with Period I.

2.3.6. *Compound Growth Rate of Productivity of Sugarcane*

The compound growth rate of productivity of sugarcane for the Period I, Period II and the Overall Period have been listed in Table 2.12.

Table 2.12: Compound Growth Rate of State-wise Productivity of Sugarcane from 2003-2004 to 2012-2013

| STATES | Period I | | | Period II | | | Overall Period | | |
| | (2003-2004 to 2007-2008) | | | (2008-2009 to 2012-2013) | | | (2003-2004 to 2012-2013) | | |
	CGR	R² Value	't' Value	CGR	R² Value	't' Value	CGR	R² Value	't' Value
Andhra Pradesh	8.52***	0.942	6.975	2.84	0.296	1.123	1.68	0.231	1.552
Bihar	-3.13	0.055	-0.417	11.89***	0.737	2.898	7.01***	0.524	2.967
Gujarat	-0.22	0.010	-0.175	-9.98*	0.497	-1.720	-2.93*	0.282	-1.774
Haryana	6.72*	0.555	1.935	10.31	0.427	1.494	4.85**	0.481	2.721
Karnataka	15.29***	0.715	2.747	-1.82	0.036	-0.333	4.55**	0.346	2.059
Maharashtra	21.31***	0.853	4.172	-8.84	0.286	-1.096	5.50*	0.256	1.659
Punjab	5.39*	0.549	1.912	13.66***	0.808	3.548	5.46***	0.648	3.834
Tamil Nadu	8.57***	0.826	3.780	5.57**	0.639	2.307	2.91**	0.473	2.680
Uttar Pradesh	0.97	0.036	0.336	5.87*	0.515	1.786	0.25	0.006	0.215
Uttarakhand	-2.47	0.042	-0.363	6.45	0.413	1.452	0.52	0.009	0.274

CGR-Compound Growth Rate, *** Significant at 1 per cent level, ** Significant at 5 per cent level, *Significant at 10 per cent level

Table 2.12 shows that Maharashtra (21.31 per cent) has recorded a positive and significant compound growth rate in productivity of sugarcane at 1 per cent level of significance with R^2 value of 0.853 and 't' value of 4.172 followed by Karnataka (15.29 per cent), Tamil Nadu (8.57 per cent), Andhra Pradesh (8.52 per cent), Haryana (6.72 per cent) and Punjab (5.39 per cent) have recorded positive and significant compound growth rate at 1 and 5 per cent level of significance. Uttar Pradesh (0.97 per cent) has recorded a positive and insignificant compound growth rate. Gujarat (-0.22 per cent), Uttarakhand (-2.47 per cent) and Bihar (-3.13 per cent) have recorded negative and insignificant compound growth rate during the Period I.

During the Period II, Punjab (13.66 per cent), Bihar (11.89 per cent), Uttar Pradesh (5.87 per cent) and Tamil Nadu (5.57 per cent) have recorded positive and significant compound growth rate at 1, 5 and 10 per cent level of significance. Haryana (10.31 per cent), Uttarakhand (6.45 per cent) and Andhra Pradesh (2.84 per cent) have recorded positive and insignificant compound growth rate. Gujarat (-9.98 per cent) has recorded negative and significant compound growth rate at 10percent of significance. Karnataka (-1.82 per cent) and Maharashtra (-8.84 per cent) have recorded negative and insignificant compound growth rate.

In Overall Period, Bihar (7.01 per cent), Maharashtra (5.50 per cent), Punjab (5.46 per cent), Haryana (4.85 per cent) Karnataka (4.55 per cent) and Tamil Nadu (2.91 per cent) have recorded positive and significant compound growth rate at 1, 5 and 10 per cent level of significance. Gujarat (-2.93 per cent) has a negative and significant compound growth rate in the productivity of sugarcane.

2.4. District-wise Growth in Area, Production and Productivity of Sugarcane

The District-wise area, production and productivity of sugarcane are analysed with Mean, Standard Deviation, Co-efficient of Variation and Compound Growth Rate.

2.4.1. Area Used for Sugarcane Production

Table 2.13 represents the District-wise mean area used for sugarcane production for the Period I, Period II and the Overall Period.

Table 2.13: District-wise Area Used for Sugarcane Production from 2003-2004 to 2012-2013

(hectares)

DISTRICTS	Period I (2003-2004 to 2007-2008)			Period II (2008-2009 to 2012-2013)			Overall Period (2003-2004 to 2012-2013)		
	Mean	S.D	C.V	Mean	S.D	C.V	Mean	S.D	C.V
Coimbatore	9282.00	3216.88	34.66	6983.60	3036.88	43.49	8132.80	3188.36	39.20
Cuddalore	36155.80	4284.34	11.85	34951.80	5914.92	16.92	35553.80	4910.21	13.81
Dharmapuri	15945.00	8409.71	52.74	17363.60	1824.66	10.51	16654.30	5785.44	34.74
Erode	24938.00	8578.79	34.40	39766.80	3822.21	9.61	32352.40	10014.17	30.95
Karur	5982.40	3272.66	54.70	6553.00	853.69	13.03	6267.70	2274.75	36.29
Namakkal	10653.80	760.10	7.13	18359.00	2963.48	16.14	14506.40	4544.41	31.33
Perambalur	11080.80	1531.77	13.82	13745.80	5411.79	39.37	12413.30	4004.03	32.26
Pudukkottai	6144.60	898.34	14.62	8570.60	1339.95	15.63	7357.60	1670.78	22.71
Salem	7109.80	2456.62	34.55	11524.80	836.67	7.26	9317.30	2899.63	31.12
Thanjavur	11125.20	875.03	7.87	13818.00	3869.58	28.00	12471.60	3001.58	24.07
Theni	9396.20	2821.79	30.03	7228.00	1337.70	18.51	8312.10	2374.88	28.57
Thiruvallur	5401.60	1509.15	27.94	6440.40	1172.86	18.21	5921.00	1386.85	23.42
Tiruvannmalai	16964.20	7380.94	43.51	27033.80	2826.15	10.45	21999.00	7478.52	33.99
Vellore	19011.00	8067.69	42.44	18384.80	3369.26	18.33	18697.90	5837.98	31.22
Villupuram	36329.40	4005.61	11.03	56462.40	3438.75	6.09	46395.90	11179.47	24.10

Source: District Statistical Office Erode, S.D-Standard Deviation, C.V-Co-efficient of Variation

Table 2.13 reveals that Villupuram district stands first in the area of sugarcane production during the Period I with the mean area of 36329.40 hectares with the standard deviation of 4005.61 and co-efficient of variation of 11.03 per cent.

The second position has occupied by Cuddalore with the mean area of 36155.80 hectares with the standard deviation of 4284.34 and with the co-efficient of variation of 11.85 per cent. Erode district has occupied a third position with the mean area of 24938.00 hectares with the standard deviation of 8578.79 and with the co-efficient of variation of 34.40 per cent followed by Vellore, Tiruvannmalai, Dharmapuri, Thanjavur, Perambalur, Namakkal, Theni, Coimbatore, Salem, Pudukkottai, Karur, Thiruvallur district. Karur district has the highest co-efficient of variation of 54.70 per cent because of the highest variation in the area used for sugarcane production.

During the Period II, Villupuram again occupied the first place with the mean area of 56462.40 hectares with standard deviation of 3438.75 and co-efficient of variation of 6.09 per cent. Erode has occupied the second position with the mean area of 39766.80 hectares with the standard deviation of 3822.21 and co-efficient of variation of 9.61 per cent followed by Cuddalore, Tiruvannmalai, Vellore, Namakkal, Dharmapuri, Thanjavur, Perambalur, Salem, Pudukkottai, Theni, Coimbatore, Karur, Thiruvallur. Coimbatore has the highest co-efficient of variation of 43.49 per cent than the other districts.

In Overall Period, Villupuram district has maintained the first place with the mean area of 46395.90 hectares and Cuddalore stands at second place with the mean area of 35553.80 hectares.

Erode district has occupied the third position with the mean area of 32352.40 hectares with standard deviation of 10014.17 and co-efficient of variation of 30.95 per cent followed by Tiruvannmalai, Vellore, Dharmapuri, Namakkal, Thanjavur, Perambalur, Salem, Theni, Coimbatore, Pudukkottai, Karur, Thiruvallur. Coimbatore has recorded the highest co-efficient of variation of 39.20 per cent.

2.4.2. Compound Growth Rate of Area Used for Sugarcane Production

The compound growth rate for District-wise area used for sugarcane production for the Period I, Period II and Overall Period have been presented in Table 2.14.

Table 2.14: Compound Growth Rate of District-wise Area Used for Sugarcane Production from 2003-2004 to 2012-2013

DISTRICTS	Period I (2003-2004 to 2007-2008)			Period II (2008-2009 to 2012-2013)			Overall Period (2003-2004 to 2012-2013)		
	CGR	R² Value	't' Value	CGR	R² Value	't' Value	CGR	R² Value	't' Value
Coimbatore	-37.48***	0.803	-3.499	-54.31**	0.616	-2.192	-24.57***	0.451	-2.562
Cuddalore	-13.05**	0.605	-2.144	-19.20***	0.703	-2.664	-5.51*	0.268	-1.71
Dharmapuri	-53.38***	0.690	-2.581	8.58	0.271	1.056	-0.53	0.000	-0.044
Erode	-31.98*	0.484	-1.676	-11.47***	0.727	-2.826	12.62	0.171	1.284
Karur	-56.21***	0.767	-3.145	-13.93**	0.656	-2.394	-3.55	0.011	-0.296
Namakkal	-8.18**	0.648	-2.348	15.26	0.295	1.122	21.32***	0.673	4.057
Perambalur	-12.78	0.409	-1.440	-47.56**	0.611	-2.172	-5.06	0.030	-0.495
Pudukkottai	21.63***	0.855	4.198	-18.71***	0.812	-3.597	12.10***	0.442	2.519
Salem	-30.35*	0.512	-1.775	0.96	0.008	0.158	15.25*	0.261	1.680
Thanjavur	-1.99	0.029	-0.299	-31.67***	0.741	-2.933	1.59	0.008	0.255
Theni	-36.17***	0.920	-5.889	-19.77**	0.652	-2.371	-15.10***	0.601	-3.473
Thiruvallur	-34.94***	0.903	-5.278	-4.25	0.031	-0.310	1.24	0.004	0.178
Tiruvannmalai	-34.98	0.346	-1.259	-10.15*	0.503	-1.741	13.64	0.14	1.14
Vellore	-42.04***	0.816	-3.644	-14.24	0.330	-1.214	-7.37	0.111	-0.998
Villupuram	-5.31	0.107	-0.601	-5.45	0.414	-1.455	15.22***	0.557	3.173

CGR-Compound Growth Rate, *** Significant at 1 per cent level, ** Significant at 5 per cent level, *Significant at 10 per cent level

Table 2.14 represents that there is a positive and significant compound growth rate of area used for the production of sugarcane in Pudukkottai during the Period I (21.63 per cent) with the R^2 value of 0.855 and 't' value of 4.198. The negative and significant compound growth rate of area used for sugarcane production has been noted in Erode (- 31.98 per cent) with the R^2 value of 0.484 and 't' value of -1.676 followed by Coimbatore (-37.48 per cent), Cuddalore (-13.05 per cent), Dharmapuri (-53.38 per cent), Karur (-56.21 per cent) and Namakkal (-8.18 per cent), Theni (-36.17 per cent), Thiruvallur (-34.94 per cent), Vellore (-42.04 per cent). Perambalur (-12.78 per cent), Salem (-30.35 per cent), Thanjavur (-1.99 per cent), Tiruvannmalai (-34.98 per cent) and Villupuram (-5.31 per cent) have recorded negative and insignificant compound growth rate.

During the Period II, Namakkal (15.26 per cent) has recorded a positive and insignificant compound growth rate of area used for the production of sugarcane followed by Dharmapuri (8.58 per cent) and Salem (0.96 per cent). Coimbatore (-54.31 per cent) has recorded a negative and significant compound growth rate followed by Perambalur, Thanjavur, Theni, Cuddalore, Pudukkottai, Karur, Erode and Tiruvannmalai.

In Overall Period, the area used for sugarcane production by Namakkal (21.32 per cent), Salem (15.25 per cent), Pudukkottai (12.10 per cent) and Villupuram (15.22 per cent) have recorded positive and significant compound growth rate at 1 and 10 per cent level of significance. Tiruvannmalai (13.64 per cent), Erode (12.62 per cent), Thanjavur (1.59 per cent) and Thiruvallur (1.24 per cent) have recorded a positive and insignificant compound growth rate. Coimbatore (-24.57 per cent), Cuddalore (-5.51 per cent) and Theni (-15.10 per cent) have recorded negative and significant compound growth rate at 1 per cent level of significance.

Vellore (-7.37 per cent) and Karur (-3.55 per cent) have recorded negative and insignificant compound growth rate.

2.4.3. *Volume of Sugarcane Production*

Table 2.15 shows the District-wise volume of sugarcane production for the Period I, Period II and Overall Period with Mean, Standard Deviation, Co-efficient of Variation and Compound Growth Rate.

Table 2.15: District-wise Sugarcane Production from 2003-2004 to 2012-2013

(Tonnes)

| DISTRICTS | Period I | | | Period II | | | Overall Period | | |
| | (2003-2004 to 2007-2008) | | | (2008-2009 to 2012-2013) | | | (2003-2004 to 2012-2013) | | |
	Mean	S.D	C.V	Mean	S.D	C.V	Mean	S.D	C.V
Coimbatore	934568.80	379013.20	40.55	897067.80	455079.40	50.73	915818.30	395321.10	43.17
Cuddalore	4142605.00	403850.30	9.75	4035749.00	870849.10	21.58	4089177.00	642429.30	15.71
Dharmapuri	1286568.00	797907.80	62.02	1600714.00	325657.60	20.34	1443641.00	597918.40	41.42
Erode	3252983.00	1430775.00	43.98	4781726.00	947273.90	19.81	4017354.00	1399223.00	34.83
Karur	528695.80	341630.20	64.62	613038.60	103501.40	16.88	570867.20	242092.60	42.41
Namakkal	1382456.00	67809.46	4.90	2216119.00	1351043.00	60.96	1799287.00	1003170.00	55.75
Perambalur	1013883.00	246284.50	24.29	1482123.00	669311.50	45.16	1248003.00	535688.40	42.92
Pudukkottai	650084.20	159653.90	24.56	1114839.00	287304.70	25.77	882461.70	328654.90	37.24
Salem	699325.40	396662.30	56.72	1068887.00	164616.40	15.40	884106.00	346281.30	39.17
Thanjavur	1167034.00	122652.70	10.51	1516520.00	375256.60	24.74	1341777.00	321247.00	23.94
Theni	1114916.00	487140.10	43.69	908338.60	165594.40	18.23	1011627.00	359875.50	35.57
Thiruvallur	623141.20	225063.90	36.12	754972.80	226841.70	30.05	689057.00	224076.50	32.52
Tiruvannmalai	1150081.00	809244.80	70.36	2787114.00	421483.00	15.12	1968598.00	1055662.00	53.63
Vellore	1386158.00	556263.50	40.13	1652047.00	430237.20	26.04	1519102.00	489316.40	32.21
Villupuram	3885830.00	738744.70	19.01	6431847.00	1023562.00	15.91	5158838.00	1583919.00	30.70

Source: District Statistical Office Erode, S.D-Standard Deviation, C.V-Co-efficient of Variation

Table 2.15 describes the quantity of sugarcane that has been produced in various districts during the period I. Cuddalore has occupied the first place with the mean production of 4142605.00 tonnes, standard deviation of 403850.30 and co-efficient of variation of 9.75 per cent. Villupuram stands second position in the production of sugarcane with the mean production of 3885830.00 tonnes, standard deviation of 738744.70 and co-efficient of variation of 19.01 per cent. Erode has occupied a third position with the mean production of 3252983.00 tonnes with standard deviation of 1430775.00 and co-efficient of variation of 43.98 per cent followed by Vellore, Namakkal, Dharmapuri, Thanjavur, Tiruvannmalai, Theni, Perambalur, Coimbatore, Salem, Pudukkottai, Thiruvallur and Karur. Tiruvannmalai has recorded the highest co-efficient of variation of 70.36 per cent during the period I.

Erode district occupied second position in sugarcane production with a mean of 4781726.00 tonnes with a standard deviation of 947273.90 and co-efficient of variation of

19.81 per cent. Except Cuddalore, Theni and Coimbatore districts, the other districts have shown increased production of sugarcane. Namakkal district has recorded with the highest co-efficient of variation of 60.96 per cent during the Period II.

In Overall Period, Villupuram district has maintained the first place with the mean production of 5158838.00 tonnes and Cuddalore district stands at second place with the mean production of 4089177.00 tonnes. Erode district has occupied the third position with the mean production of 4017354.00 tonnes with standard deviation of 1399223.00 and co-efficient of variation of 34.83 per cent. Namakkal district has recorded the highest co-efficient of variation of 55.75 per cent due to instability of production.

2.4.4. *Compound Growth Rate of Volume of Sugarcane Production*

The compound growth rate for District-wise volume of sugarcane production for the Period I, Period II and the Overall Period have been given in Table 2.16.

Table 2.16: Compound Growth Rate of District-wise Sugarcane Production from 2003-2004 to 2012-2013

DISTRICTS	Period I			Period II			Overall Period		
	(2003-2004 to 2007-2008)			(2008-2009 to 2012-2013)			(2003-2004 to 2012-2013)		
	CGR	R^2 Value	't' Value	CGR	R^2 Value	't' Value	CGR	R^2 Value	't' Value
Coimbatore	-36.88**	0.631	-2.266	-62.82**	0.643	-2.326	-21.19	0.246	-1.617
Cuddalore	-8.33	0.358	-1.294	-15.20	0.278	-1.073	-4.37	0.136	-1.122
Dharmapuri	-58.83**	0.644	-2.330	-3.30	0.013	-0.199	2.87	0.004	0.187
Erode	-36.04	0.378	-1.350	-15.81	0.338	-1.237	8.89	0.067	0.757
Karur	-62.67***	0.763	-3.110	-14.36	0.453	-1.575	-1.61	0.001	-0.108
Namakkal	-5.38**	0.602	-2.131	-38.99	0.094	-0.560	-1.16	0.000	-0.059
Perambalur	-3.30	0.009	-0.170	-54.04***	0.692	-2.598	-0.30	0.000	-0.023
Pudukkottai	30.87***	0.716	2.747	-28.24***	0.703	-2.663	19.46**	0.413	2.370
Salem	-40.25	0.418	-1.468	-8.71	0.188	-0.835	12.07	0.101	0.948
Thanjavur	15.09***	0.903	5.280	-25.28*	0.500	-1.731	6.65	0.128	1.086
Theni	-43.15***	0.811	-3.583	-20.41***	0.729	-2.844	-13.58**	0.357	-2.109
Thiruvallur	-43.35***	0.932	-6.407	-7.02	0.035	-0.328	-0.05	0.000	-0.005
Tiruvannmalai	-24.21	0.036	-0.334	-9.59	0.210	-0.892	44.32*	0.275	1.741
Vellore	-36.73***	0.817	-3.662	-16.92	0.219	-0.918	-0.81	0.001	-0.097
Villupuram	-6.20	0.049	-0.392	-9.69	0.228	-0.942	17.10**	0.433	2.474

CGR-Compound Growth Rate, * Significant at 1 per cent level, ** Significant at 5 per cent level, ***Significant at 10 per cent level

It is noticeable from the Table 2.16 Pudukkottai district has attained the highest compound growth rate of 30.87 per cent with the R^2 value of 0.716 and 't' value of 2.747 and Thanjavur (15.09 per cent) with positive and significant at 1 per cent level of significance during the Period I. Karur (-62.67 per cent), Dharmapuri (-58.83 per cent), Thiruvallur (-43.35 per cent), Theni (-43.15 per cent), Coimbatore (-36.88 per cent), Vellore (-36.73 per cent) and Namakkal (-5.38 per cent) have recorded negative and significant compound growth rate at 1 and 5 per cent level.

During the Period II, Coimbatore (-62.82 per cent), Perambalur (-54.04 per cent) Pudukkottai (-28.24 per cent), Thanjavur (-25.28 per cent) and Theni (-20.41 per cent) have recorded negative and significant compound growth rate. The remaining districts have recorded negative and insignificant compound growth rate.

In Overall Period, Tiruvannmalai district has recorded with the highest compound growth rate of 44.32 per cent followed by Pudukkottai (19.46 per cent) and Villupuram (17.10 per cent) which have recorded positive and significant growth rate at 5 and 10 per cent level. Theni (-13.58 per cent) has recorded a negative and significant compound growth rate at 5 per cent level. Salem (12.07 per cent), Erode (8.89 per cent), Thanjavur (6.65 per cent) and Dharmapuri (2.87 per cent) have recorded positive and insignificant compound growth rate.

2.4.5. *Productivity of Sugarcane*

Table 2.17 exhibits the District-wise productivity of sugarcane for the Period I, Period II and the Overall Period with Mean, Standard Deviation, Co-efficient of Variation and Compound Growth Rate.

Table 2.17: District-wise Productivity of Sugarcane from 2003-2004 to 2012-2013

(Per hectare)

DISTRICTS	Period I			Period II			Overall Period		
	(2003-2004 to 2007-2008)			(2008-2009 to 2012-2013)			(2003-2004 to 2012-2013)		
	Mean	S.D	C.V	Mean	S.D	C.V	Mean	S.D	C.V
Coimbatore	100.07	13.49	13.48	121.99	19.54	16.02	111.03	19.60	17.65
Cuddalore	114.87	4.26	3.71	115.47	14.39	12.46	115.17	10.01	8.69
Dharmapuri	76.82	11.25	14.64	92.10	14.22	15.44	84.46	14.52	17.20
Erode	126.70	16.71	13.19	119.39	14.82	12.41	123.05	15.38	12.50
Karur	84.65	18.29	21.61	93.26	5.51	5.91	88.95	13.52	15.20
Namakkal	130.13	8.35	6.42	120.18	64.88	53.98	125.16	43.92	35.09
Perambalur	92.41	21.96	23.76	105.79	16.21	15.32	99.10	19.51	19.69
Pudukkottai	105.06	12.18	11.60	129.01	20.87	16.18	117.03	20.47	17.49
Salem	93.94	25.13	26.76	92.29	8.61	9.33	93.11	17.73	19.05
Thanjavur	105.40	13.45	12.76	111.03	13.84	12.46	108.21	13.20	12.20
Theni	117.25	28.62	24.41	127.10	19.01	14.96	122.17	23.49	19.22
Thiruvallur	113.11	12.82	11.33	115.78	14.06	12.15	114.45	12.76	11.15
Tiruvannmalai	66.37	34.93	52.64	102.97	9.21	8.95	84.67	30.86	36.45
Vellore	75.67	15.29	20.20	88.85	9.35	10.52	82.26	13.82	16.80
Villupuram	106.47	12.26	11.52	113.49	11.89	10.47	109.98	11.97	10.89

Source: District Statistical Office Erode, S.D-Standard Deviation, C.V-Co-efficient of Variation

Table 2.17 exhibits that the highest productivity of sugarcane has been attained by Namakkal during the Period I with the mean productivity value of 130.13 with the standard deviation of 8.35 and the co-efficient of variation of 6.42 per cent followed by Erode, Theni, Cuddalore, Thiruvallur, Villupuram, Thanjavur, Pudukkottai, Coimbatore, Salem, Perambalur, Karur, Dharmapuri, Vellore and Tiruvannmalai. Tiruvannmalai has recorded with the highest co-efficient of variation of 52.64 per cent and this may be due to the instability in area and production of sugarcane.

During the Period II, the highest mean productivity value of 129.01 has been recorded by Pudukkottai with the standard deviation of 20.87 and the co-efficient of variation of 16.18 per cent. Namakkal has the highest co-efficient of variation of 53.98 per cent due to increase in area used for production of sugarcane.

In Overall Period, Namakkal has the highest productivity of sugarcane in Tamil Nadu with the mean productivity value of 125.16 per cent with standard deviation of 43.92 and co-efficient of variation of 35.09 per cent. Erode district has second position in productivity of sugarcane with mean value of 123.05 with standard deviation of 15.38 and co-efficient of variation of 12.50 per cent followed by Theni, Pudukkottai, Cuddalore, Thiruvallur, Coimbatore, Villupuram, Thanjavur, Perambalur, Salem, Karur, Tiruvannmalai, Dharmapuri and Vellore. Tiruvannmalai has the highest co-efficient of variation of 36.45 per cent.

2.4.6. *Compound Growth Rate of District-wise Productivity of Sugarcane*

The compound growth rate for district-wise productivity of sugarcane for the Period I, Period II and the Overall Period have been shown in Table 2.18.

Table 2.18: Compound Growth Rate of District-wise Productivity of Sugarcane from 2003-2004 to 2012-2013

| DISTRICTS | Period I | | | Period II | | | Overall Period | | |
| | (2003-2004 to 2007-2008) | | | (2008-2009 to 2012-2013) | | | (2003-2004 to 2012-2013) | | |
	CGR	R^2 Value	't' Value	CGR	R^2 Value	't' Value	CGR	R^2 Value	't' Value
Coimbatore	0.95	0.002	0.083	-18.42***	0.679	-2.518	4.53	0.108	0.983
Cuddalore	5.43***	0.949	7.495	5.13	0.076	0.498	1.24	0.035	0.539
Dharmapuri	-11.68	0.319	-1.185	-10.85	0.249	-0.998	3.46	0.066	0.752
Erode	-5.97	0.096	-0.566	-5.08	0.081	-0.514	-3.36	0.125	-1.067
Karur	-14.76	0.267	-1.046	-0.41	0.002	-0.083	2.00	0.027	0.472
Namakkal	3.06	0.100	0.576	-47.07	0.156	-0.746	-18.55	0.125	-1.067
Perambalur	10.87	0.079	0.507	-12.25	0.323	-1.197	5.02	0.091	0.894
Pudukkottai	7.59	0.200	0.865	-11.92	0.269	-1.050	6.51	0.235	1.569
Salem	-14.22	0.162	-0.763	-9.78**	0.590	-2.077	-2.84	0.042	-0.592
Thanjavur	17.43***	0.770	3.170	9.41	0.278	1.075	5.00*	0.296	1.833
Theni	-10.93	0.105	-0.593	-0.68	0.001	-0.052	1.85	0.015	0.344
Thiruvallur	-12.94***	0.725	-2.811	-2.71	0.025	-0.275	-1.22	0.021	-0.419
Tiruvannmalai	16.56	0.017	0.229	0.78	0.004	0.104	27.04*	0.247	1.619
Vellore	9.16	0.065	0.457	-3.34	0.046	-0.382	7.03	0.207	1.444
Villupuram	-0.94	0.003	-0.093	-4.51	0.099	-0.573	1.62	0.037	0.551

CGR–Compound Growth Rate, *** Significant at 1 per cent level, ** Significant at 5 per cent level, *Significant at 10 per cent level

Table 2.18 exhibits that during the Period I, Thanjavur has attained the highest compound growth rate of 17.43 per cent with the R^2 value of 0.770 and 't' value of 3.170 and Cuddalore (5.43 per cent) have recorded positive and significant compound growth rate at 1 per cent level of significance. Thiruvallur (-12.94 per cent) has attained a negative and significant compound growth rate. Tiruvannmalai (16.56 per cent), Perambalur (10.87 per cent), Vellore (9.16 per cent), Pudukkottai (7.59 per cent), Namakkal (3.06 per cent) and Coimbatore (0.95 per cent) have recorded positive and statistically insignificant compound growth rate. Karur, Salem, Dharmapuri, Theni, Erode and Villupuram districts have recorded negative and insignificant compound growth rate.

During the Period II, Salem (-9.78 per cent) and Coimbatore (-18.42 per cent) have recorded negative and significant compound growth rate at 1 and 5 per cent level of significance. Thanjavur (9.41 per cent), Cuddalore (5.13 per cent) and Tiruvannmalai (0.78 per cent) have recorded positive and insignificant compound growth rate.

In Overall Period, Tiruvannmalai has attained the highest compound growth rate of 27.04 per cent with the R^2 value of 0.247 and 't' value of 1.619 and Thanjavur (5.00 per cent) which has recorded positive and significant compound growth rate at 10 per cent level. Vellore, Pudukkotai, Perambalur, Coimbatore, Dharmapuri, Karur, Theni, Villupuram and Cuddalore districts have recorded positive and insignificant compound growth rate. Namakkal, Erode, Salem and Thiruvallur districts have recorded negative and insignificant compound growth rate in the productivity of sugarcane.

2.5.   Export and Import of Sugar in India

Sugarcane is one of the major cash crops of India which is the home land of sugarcane cultivation and sugar production. Sugarcane as such is neither exported nor imported, however the sugar which is a main produce of sugarcane crop is exported and imported as per the Government policies. Even though India is one of the largest producers of sugar, its export is insignificant because of higher domestic consumption. Many a times, India has to import sugar to meet the increasing demand. In India, the total export of sugar is 4074.90 thousand tonnes with the value of ₹ 12973.73 crores and import of sugar is 119.66 thousand tonnes with the value of ₹ 374.67 crores, during the year 2011- 2012[72].

Table 2.19 describes the Growth in sugar export and import in India for the Period I, Period II and Overall Period with Mean, Standard Deviation, Co-efficient of Variation and Compound Growth Rate.

---

[72]Sugar Statistics, (2013), Cooperative Sugar Journal, Vol. 45(1), September, pp.117.

Table 2.19: Export and Import of Sugar in India from 2003-2004 to 2012-2013

| INDIA | Period I | | | Period II | | | Overall Period | | |
| | (2003-2004 to 2007-2008) | | | (2008-2009 to 2012-2013) | | | (2003-2004 to 2012-2013) | | |
	Mean	S.D	C.V	Mean	S.D	C.V	Mean	S.D	C.V
Export (in Volume)	986.36	733.71	134.44	3070.96	1793.38	171.25	2028.66	1695.78	119.63
Export (₹in Value)	1364.03	1164.26	117.16	6659.43	5070.56	131.34	4011.73	4451.81	90.12
Import (in Volume)	321.73	410.00	78.47	786.88	993.95	79.17	554.31	757.56	73.17
Import (₹in Value)	345.40	443.36	77.91	1928.89	2491.46	77.42	1137.15	1882.21	60.42

Source: Cooperative Sugar Journal, S.D-Standard Deviation, C.V-Co-efficient of Variation

Table 2.19 indicates that the mean value of sugar export in terms of volume is 986.36 thousand tonnes with standard deviation of 733.71 and co-efficient of variation of 134.44 per cent. The mean value of sugar export in terms of value is ₹ 1364.03 crores with standard deviation of 1164.26 and co-efficient variation of 117.16 per cent. The mean value of sugar import in terms of volume is 321.73 thousand tonnes with standard deviation of 410.00 and co-efficient variation of 78.47 per cent. The mean value of sugar import in terms of value is ₹ 345.40 crores with standard deviation of 443.36 and co-efficient variation of 77.91 per cent for the Period I.

During the Period II, the mean value of sugar export in terms of volume is 3070.96 thousand tonnes with standard deviation of 1793.38 and co-efficient of variation of 171.25 per cent. The mean value of sugar export in terms of value is ₹ 6659.43 crores with standard deviation of 5070.56 and co-efficient variation of 131.34 per cent. The mean value of sugar import in terms of volume is 786.88 thousand tonnes with standard deviation of 993.95 and co-efficient variation of 79.17 per cent. The mean value of sugar import in terms of value is ₹ 1928.89 crores with standard deviation of 2491.46 and co-efficient variation of 77.42 per cent.

In Overall Period, the mean value of sugar export in terms of volume is 2028.66 thousand tonnes with standard deviation of 1695.78 and co-efficient of variation of 119.63 per cent. The mean value of sugar export in terms of value is ₹ 4011.73 crores with standard deviation of 4451.81 and co-efficient variation of 90.12 per cent. The mean value of sugar import in terms of volume is 554.31 thousand tonnes with standard deviation of 757.56 and co-efficient variation of 73.17 per cent. The mean value of sugar import in terms of value is ₹ 1137.15 crores with standard deviation of 1882.21 and co-efficient of variation of 60.42 per cent.

2.5.1. *Compound Growth Rate of Export and Import of Sugar in India from 2003-2004 to 2012-2013*

The compound growth rate for export and import of sugar in India for the Period I, Period II and the Overall Period have been shown in Table 2.20.

Table 2.20: Compound Growth Rate of Export and Import of Sugar in India from 2003-2004 to 2012-2013

| INDIA | Period I | | | Period II | | | Overall Period | | |
| | (2003-2004 to 2007-2008) | | | (2008-2009 to 2012-2013) | | | (2003-2004 to 2012-2013) | | |
	CGR	R^2 Value	't' Value	CGR	R^2 Value	't' Value	CGR	R^2 Value	't' Value
Export (in Volume)	-0.14	0.031	-0.312	-0.03	0.001	-0.043	0.11	0.044	0.607
Export (₹ in Value)	0.04	0.002	0.083	0.26	0.045	0.374	0.23	0.178	1.317
Import (in Volume)	-0.53	0.098	-0.572	1.19	0.317	1.180	0.19	0.038	0.562
Import (₹ in Value)	-0.21	0.022	-0.257	1.18	0.365	1.314	0.34	0.150	1.186

CGR – Compound Growth Rate

Table 2.20 denotes that sugar export in terms of volume is -0.14 per cent negative compound growth rate in India with R^2 value of 0.031 and 't' value is -0.312. The sugar export in terms of value is 0.04 per cent positive compound growth rate in India with R^2 value of 0.002 and 't' value is 0.083. The sugar import in terms of volume is -0.53 per cent negative compound growth rate in India with R^2 value of 0.098 and 't' value is -0.572. The sugar import in terms of value is -0.21 per cent negative compound growth rate in India with R^2 value of 0.022 and 't' value is -0.257 at insignificant level for the Period I.

During the Period II, the sugar export in terms of volume is -0.03 per cent negative compound growth rate in India with R^2 value of 0.001 and 't' value is -0.043. The export of sugar in terms of value is 0.26 per cent positive compound growth rate in India with R^2 value of 0.045 and 't' value is 0.374. The sugar import in terms of volume is 1.19 per cent positive compound growth rate in India with R^2 value of 0.317 and 't' value is 1.180. The sugar import in terms of value is 1.18 per cent positive compound growth rate in India with R^2 value of 0.365 and 't' value is 1.314 at insignificant level.

In Overall Period, the sugar export in terms of volume is 0.11 per cent positive compound growth rate in India with R^2 value of 0.044 and 't' value is 0.607. The sugar export in terms of value is 0.23 per cent positive compound growth rate in India with R^2 value of 0.178 and 't' value is 1.317. The sugar import in terms of volume is 0.19 per cent positive compound growth rate in India with R^2 value of 0.038 and 't' value is 0.562. The sugar import in terms of value is 0.34 per cent positive compound growth rate in India with R^2 value of 0.150 and 't' value is 1.186 at insignificant level.

2.6. Summary

In this chapter, an attempt has been made to analyze growth in area, production and productivity of sugarcane in Country-wise, State-wise, District-wise and Sugar Export and Import in India. This study is based on the secondary data collected from various sources such as websites of Sugarcane Breeding Institution, Food and Agricultural Organisation Cooperative

Sugar Journal, Cane Info, Records of District Statistical office and Statistical year book published by Government of India.

From the analysis, it is found that India is in the second place in area used and production of sugarcane but the productivity of sugarcane in India is average among the countries. Compound growth rate is also revealed that Brazil, Indonesia, China, Argentina, India and Mexico have recorded positive and significant at 1 and 10 per cent level of significance in area used for sugarcane production. Brazil, China, India and Argentina have recorded positive and significant compound growth rate at 1 and 5 per cent level of significance in production of sugarcane. Thailand, South Africa and India have recorded positive and significant compound growth rate at 5 and 10 per cent level of significance in productivity of sugarcane in overall Period.

In State-wise analysis, it is found that Tamil Nadu is the first in productivity of sugarcane in India for all the period even though area used for sugarcane production and volume of sugarcane production in Tamil Nadu is in third place for the overall period. In Compound growth rate analysis, it is found that Bihar, Karnataka, Maharashtra and Tamil Nadu have positive and statistically significant at 1, 5 and 10 per cent level of significance in area used for sugarcane production, volume of sugarcane production and productivity of sugarcane for the period of ten years.

In District-wise analysis, it is found that Erode district stands third place in area used for sugarcane production, volume of sugarcane production but productivity of sugarcane is in second place for the period of ten years. Compound growth rate also exposed that Namakkal, Salem, Villupuram and Pudukkotai have recorded positive and statistically significant at 1 and 10 per cent level of significance in area used for sugarcane production for ten years. Tiruvannmalai, Pudukkotai and Villupuram have recorded positive and significant compound growth rate at 5 and 10 per cent level of significance in production of sugarcane. Tiruvannmalai and Thanjavur have recorded positive and significant compound growth rate at 1 per cent level of significance in productivity of sugarcane. Erode district has recorded positive and insignificant compound growth rate in area used for sugarcane production and volume of sugarcane production but the productivity of sugarcane has recorded negative and insignificant compound growth rate for the overall periods.

In India, the export and import of sugar, in terms of volume and value are increased during the Period II. Compound growth rate revealed that the sugar export and import in India in terms of volume and value are positive and insignificant in all periods.

CHAPTER III

CULTIVATION PRACTICES OF SUGARCANE FARMERS

Keywords

Sugarcane Cultivation Practices - Factors influencing the farmers to cultivate sugarcane - Intercropping in sugarcane cultivation - Sources of Finance - Sources of Purchasing Setts - Number of Setts used per acre - Varieties used in sugarcane cultivation - Cost and Returns from cultivation of sugarcane - Size of farms and Cost of Cultivation - Size of farms and Returns from cultivation of sugarcane - Cost and Returns from Production of Khandsari Sugar - Production Function Analysis.

3.1. Introduction

In India, more than 6 million farmers are engaged in sugarcane cultivation and the majority of them are small and marginal with very small land holdings between 0.5 and 5 hectares[73]. Sugarcane has provided a unique advantage for better land use through intercropping and increased input use efficiency. High value and remunerative crops like soya beans, onion, maize, vegetables, potato, oilseeds and pulses offer great scope for growing as intercrops and in further providing additional income and reducing risks. Monoculture of cane has resulted in substantial reduction in productivity. Sugarcane based cropping systems are generally 3-4 years duration. The plant crop of sugarcane is invariably followed by its ratoon crop. Mostly, one to two ratoons are taken in succession. However, the crop preceding sugarcane and succeeding its ratoon crop varies in different agro-climatic conditions.

Sugarcane provides juice which is utilized for making white sugar, khandsari sugar and jaggery (gur) and many by-products like bagasse, molasses and in making preserving various kinds of medicines like syrups, liquids and capsules etc. Green tops of the cane are a good source of fodder for cattle. Its remains are good manure in alkaline and saline soils. Sugarcane is grown to a large extent of the area in majority of the states. There are a number of varieties that are grown in India depending on the suitability of the soil. The area, output and yield in sugarcane cultivation is subjected to change in response to the policies of the government and also the conditions of cultivation.

The economy of the farmers as well as prosperity of the state is highly influenced by the earnings from this crop enterprise. Now-a-days, sugarcane farming is becoming gradually

---

[73]www.iisr.nic.in, op.cit., p.3.

commercialised in Tamil Nadu. The commercial farmers' chief concern is to secure a satisfactory margin between the cost and selling price of his produce. Sugarcane occupies an important place in the economy of the farmers as well as state, the farmers are more interested in determining optimum allocation of their land and other sources between sugarcane and its competing crops on the basis of cost and return analysis to maximise their income from the limited sources. Therefore, it seems worthwhile to analyse the comparative profitability of sugarcane and its competing crops in an area. The sugarcane farmers in this zone alter their decision to supply of sugarcane to factory or jaggery producers or produce of khandsari sugar based on the prevailing prices of sugarcane and khandsari sugar prices.

Keeping in view of the above ideas, this chapter focuses on the existing cultivation practices of sugarcane, factors influencing the farmers to cultivate sugarcane and cost and returns in sugarcane cultivation. This study is based on primary data collected through interview schedule from 600 farmers, who are cultivating sugarcane. For the purpose of analysis, statistical tools such as factor analysis, Garrett ranking technique and production function analysis have been applied.

3.2. Sugarcane Cultivation Practices

Sugarcane is a long term crop, which occupies the land for 10 to 14 months from planting to harvest and also multi ratooning crop. So the farmers, once cultivate sugarcane cannot change their crop due to inadequate finance. Sugarcane is one of the most important commercial multi ratoon crops grown in Tamil Nadu, wherever irrigation facility available. Sugarcane cultivation by the farmer is influenced by the size of the land holding, suitability of soil, climate conditions, the variety of setts used, applying of fertilizers and ratoon management practices. Farmers follow different practices in different regions. Following are the essential requisites for cultivation of sugarcane.

3.2.1. *Climate*

Sugarcane is produced primarily for its vegetative growth to extract juice. The crop grows well in tropical and sub-tropical climates between latitudes 35°N to 35°S. Warm and humid climate is favourable for its growth, a temperature range of 30 to 40°C with annual rainfall ranging between 70 cm and 150 cm is the best for its successful cultivation. Higher temperature like 50°C stops its growth and very low temperature below 20°C slows down its growth. In both cases quality and quantity of juice deteriorates. Warm long days produce plants with more tillers, juice and high sucrose contents.

3.2.2. Soil

Sugarcane crop can be grown on a wide range of soils like sandy-loam, clay-loam, loam or black cotton laterites, reddish or brown soil. It can be grown even on soil with pH 6.5 to 7.5. The principal characteristics of the soils suitable for sugarcane cultivation are that it must possess high contents of organic matter and is well drained. Therefore, heavy clay soil with proper drainage or light soils with irrigation facilities are also favourable for sugarcane crop.

3.2.3. Land Preparation

The preparation of the field for sugarcane crop a number of ploughings are given with a country plough, clods are broken and stubbles are removed. This is followed by deep-ploughing with tractor or mould-board-plough and planking. Finally, 2 or 3 harrowing are given to bring the seed-bed into fine tilth. After sowing, ridges are made to divide the field into convenient size beds for irrigation and drainage.

3.2.4. Varieties

Sugarcane crop is grown in a wide range of soil fertility and climatic conditions. Accordingly, there are a number of varieties to suit these conditions and ratoon nature selecting the varieties for getting higher cane productivity. Some of the important recommended varieties under three seasons are: Early Season: Co 86032, Co 91017, Co 94012, Co 0323 & Co C24, Mid-Season: Co 86032, Co 92012, Co V92102 & Co 95020 and Late Season: Co 86032.

3.2.5. Selection of Stem Cuttings

Sugarcane crop is propagated by stem-cutting. The upper-half-portion of the plant has buds of high viability and is best for producing new crop. Cane setts of two or three nodes, bearing 3 or 4 vegetative buds are made from the healthy, free from insect pests and diseases. About 15,000 setts are required for one acre.

3.2.6. Sett Treatment

Cane-seed-setts are wet and sugary, therefore, while in the soil, before sprouting into new plant, these are mostly damaged by insects (termites) and fungus. To avoid these losses, the setts, before planting, are dipped into 0.5 per cent Agallol (3 per cent), or 0.25 per cent Aretan or Tafasan (6 per cent) for 2-3 hours.

3.2.7. Method of Sowing

Efficient care and precautions should be taken while selecting the cuttings, treating it with chemicals at the time of planting. Sugarcane crop is sown by various methods depending upon the field. There are three methods for sowing namely Flat, Furrow, Trench.

Flat Planting

Flat planting method is mostly common in intensive sugarcane growing areas where soil-moisture is available in plenty. Setts are kept in shallow (8-10 cm) deep furrows at 75 cm apart. On an average, one viable bud per ten centimetre length in each furrow is planted (i.e. one sett per feet). The field is heavily planked. This method of sowing is popular in North India.

Furrow Planting

Furrow planting method is mostly common under low soil moisture condition. After sowing irrigation is immediately given. Setts are kept deep (10-15 cm) furrows, at 90 cm apart. On an average, a 3 budded sett per feet length is planted. Furrows are covered with 5-6 cm soil and irrigation in furrows is applied.

Trench Method

Trench method of sowing sugarcane is mostly used in areas where strong winds and rainy season cause lodging of the cane i.e. in coastal areas where crop grows tall. Furrows are not made, but in place of these only trench 25 cm deep at 90 cm distance in line are made by manual labour. Fertilizers and insecticides are mixed with soil and trenches are again filled with soil, keeping one sett/trench at the depth of 5 cm. irrigation is applied only on successful sprouting.

3.2.8. Season and Planting

Sugarcane is produced mainly in the main season (December-May) in the entire State. In parts of Tiruchirapalli, Perambalur, Karur, Salem, Namakkal and Coimbatore districts, it is also raised during the special season (June-September). The selection of season is one of the vital for achieving the targeted sugarcane productivity. The early season is most important to attain higher productivity. The season varies from field to field, irrigation source and crop rotation etc., There are three seasons followed in sugarcane crop, Early: December-January, Mid: February-March, Late: April-May. Special Season: June-July, Early season varieties are suitable for special seasons.

3.2.9. Time of Planting

The best time of planting the sugarcane setts for spring crop is the period when the atmospheric temperature records an average of 25°C. Therefore, it is the time of sowing in Erode District of Tamil Nadu i.e. December-January. The crop can be sown round the year.

Crop planted before winter season gives less sprouting and tillers due to cold weather during early sprouting stage.

3.2.10. Irrigation

In sugarcane crop cultivation, irrigation is essential to increase sucrose contents and vegetative growth. It depends upon the suitability of soil, weather conditions and irrigation practice. The irrigation schedule is very important. The irrigation should be applied once in a week or once in 10 days intervals.

3.2.11. Manures and Fertilizers Application

The method and time of fertilizer application are important for yield improvement. Farmyard manure is added one month before planting at the rate of 10-12 tonnes of well decomposed manure, to improve the soil texture and water holding capacity. Chemical fertilizers are employed based on the recommendation of the soil test. For general purpose, 300 kg nitrogen, 80 kg phosphorus, 80 kg potash and 80 kg calcium per hectare are applied. Half dose of nitrogen and full dose of other fertilizers are placed in furrows below or on the side of cane-sets, at the time of sowing as a basal dose. The rest of the nitrogen is applied in two split doses as topdressing during plant growth period. The application of fertilizer at the early stage of plant growth is advantageous and increases the sucrose contents in the juice.

3.2.12. Detrashing

The detrashing is one of the important cultural practices in sugarcane removal of dry cane leaves at the age of 6-7 months to reduce the pest incidence and good aeration, better sunlight in the fields. The dried trashes kept in the furrows to maintain the soil moisture and arresting of weed growth also.

3.2.13. Earthing

Earthing up is most important to sugarcane crop. Soil between the furrows of canes, is taken with the help of spade and applied to the sides of the plants. This earthing up is advantageous in many ways: (i) acts as weeding, (ii) mixes the top dress fertilizers well in the soil, (iii) support the plant, to save them from lodging, (iv) help the bud to leaf freely and (v) makes watering and drainage easy.

3.2.14. Tying the Plants

Sugarcane is 6-7 feet tall growing plant. Winds and heavy rains usually make it to fall down on the ground. This lodging spoils both yield and quality of the juice. To avoid such losses, plants are frequently (2 or 3 times) tied with sugarcane leaves in groups, to make the group of plants strong enough to face high winds and rains.

3.2.15. Harvesting and Yield

Sugarcane is a cash crop and after harvesting it is used in making khandsari sugar, jaggery or white sugar. Therefore, harvesting at the right stage of maturity is an important consideration. Experienced farmers judge the maturity by process of withering leaves or by taste of the cane juice. But to facilitate the judgment, a hand-sugar refractometer is used. The juice from the central portion of the stalk having reading 17-18 by the refractometer is suitable for, harvesting for sugar factory. In North Indian condition the crop matures in early December and maintains its juice quality till March. Harvesting is done with the help of sickle. Stalks are cut at ground level, leaves are stripped off and green top is cut. The canes are tied in bundle and carried to the factory for sugar or jaggery producers. The average yield of cane is 40-45 tonnes per acre, but under scientific management it may yield about 80-85 tonnes per acre. Ratoon crop gives lower yields than fresh crops.

3.2.16. Trash Mulching

Mulch the ridges uniformly with cane trash to a thickness of 10 cm within a week after planting. It helps to tide over drought, conserves moisture, reduce weed population and minimise shoot borer incidence. Mulch the field with trash after 21 days of planting in heavy soil and wetland conditions. Avoid trash mulching in areas where incidence of termites is noticed.

3.2.17. Ratooning

Sugarcane is a perennial crop i.e. it does not require fresh planting year after year. The crop of the second year and the subsequent years is called ratoon. Ratoon refers to subsequent harvesting taken from the cane stubble after first harvesting. Cultivation practices for ratoon crop includes all the practices as applied to main crop except land preparation and planting setts. Based upon practical experience, the growers can decide to keep the ratoon for 2-3 years. In sugarcane ratoon occupy a sizable proportion of the total area under cane cultivation, up to 50 per cent of cane area in sub-tropical states like Uttar Pradesh. Ratoons are poorly managed in India. The main advantage of ratoon lies in its early maturity, lower cost of cultivation and high sugar recovery during early period of crushing. The contribution of ratoon yield to total cane production is around 30 per cent since the yields are reduced due to several factors like variety, soil, irrigation, poor ratoon management. The main problem in keeping the ratoon is the accumulation of insect pests and diseases which deteriorate yield and quality of the juice. It never recommends keeping ratoon of diseased crop. The crop which is to be kept as ratoon is harvested in January after dismantling the ridges at ground level.

3.2.18. Ratoon Crop Management

Management of the field after harvest of the plant crop complete the following operations within 10 days of harvest of plant crop to obtain a better establishment and uniform sprouting of shoots.

- Remove the trash from the field. Do not burn it. Irrigate the field copiously.
- Follow stubble shaving with sharp spades to a depth of 4-6 cm along the ridges at proper moisture.
- Work with cooper plough along with sides of the ridges to break the compaction.
- The gap areas in the ratoon sugarcane crop should be filled within 30 days of stubble shaving. The sprouted cane stubbles taken from the same field is the best material for full establishment. The next best method is gap filling with seedlings raised in polybags.
- Apply basal dose of organic manure and super phosphate as recommended for plant crop.

3.3. Factors Influencing the Farmers to Cultivate Sugarcane

The farmers are influenced by a number of factors to cultivate sugarcane. The factors that influence farmers have been identified from the reviews and queries answered by the farmers in the pilot study conducted. The influencing factors are; one year crop, to get a lump sum amount, multiratoon system, minimum labour requirement, fixed price, less and easy maintenance, high profitability, high and assured yield, minimum risk, availability of water facility, suitability of land and soil, easy to market, provision of fertilizer by sugar factory, availability of machinery, easy to adopt drip irrigation, less pest and disease problem, long term practice, familiar in the sugarcane cultivation, favourable climate conditions and availability of crushing machineries. The farmers have been required to assess each factor on its own significance. The factors influencing the farmers to cultivate sugarcane are narrated with the help of factor analysis. The purpose of factor analysis is to find a method of summarizing the information contained in a number of original variables into a smaller set of new composite dimensions (factors) with minimum loss of information. That is, the factor analysis tries to identify and define the underlying dimensions in the original variables.

Factor analysis has many alternative algorithms that can be applied. The method applied here is the principal components analysis. The primary decision at each stage of factor analysis is to decide how many factors are to be extracted from the data. The sample rule of thumb normally used, says that all factors with an Eigen value of 1 or more should be extracted.

Before applying factor analysis, it is decided to use Bartlett's test and Kaiser-Meyer-Olkin (KMO) Measure. Bartlett's test of sphericity is a test statistic used to examine the hypothesis that the variables are uncorrelated in the population. In other words, the population correlation matrix is an identity matrix, whereby each variable correlates perfectly with itself (r = 1) but has no correlation with the other variables (r = 0). The Kaiser-Meyer-Olkin (KMO) measure of sampling adequacy is an index used to examine the appropriateness of factor analysis. High values (between 0.5 and 1.0) indicate that factor analysis is appropriate. Values below 0.5 imply that factor analysis may not be appropriate[74]. Details of the findings are shown in Table 3.1.

Table 3.1: KMO and Bartlett's Test

Kaiser-Meyer-Olkin Measure of Sampling Adequacy.		0.561
Bartlett's Test of Sphericity	Approx. Chi-Square	2407.214
	Sig.	0.000

Table 3.1 reveals that the measured value of Kaiser-Meyer-Olkin measure of sampling adequacy is 0.561 which is greater than 0.50. So, that ensures the appropriateness of sampling. Hence, it is decided to apply the Factor Analysis.

3.3.1. *Principal Component Analysis*

The principal component analysis has been used to extract the factors since the objective is to summarise most of the original information in a minimum number of factors for production purpose. A principle component analyse is a factor model used to transform a set of correlated factors into a set of uncorrelated factors. So, that the factors are unrelated and the variables selected for each factor are related. The variances extracted by the factors are called Eigen values.

3.3.2. *Rotated Component Matrix*

The rotated factor matrix is used to assign variables to factors and to interpret factors. This matrix should be viewed column wise for each column (factor) the variables which have high

---

[74] Naresh, Malhotra and Sathyabugan Desh (2009), Marketing Research - and Applied Orientation, Pearson Education, New Delhi, Pp. 610 - 635.

(close to 1) loading should be identified and a combined meaning for the factor found. This leads to a phrase which is the name given to the factor. The score of the variable leading to factors which influence the farmers in sugarcane cultivation have been included for the factor analysis. The rotated component matrixes for the influencing variables are given in Table 3.2.

Table 3.2: Factors Influencing the Farmers to Cultivate Sugarcane-rotated Component Matrix

Variables	Component					
	1	2	3	4	5	6
One year crop	**0.896**	-0.203	0.014	-0.031	-0.082	0.247
Multi ratoon system	**0.888**	0.143	-0.055	-0.016	-0.170	0.064
High and assured yield	**0.628**	0.073	0.444	0.029	0.287	0.348
Less pest and disease problem	**-0.793**	0.105	-0.074	0.009	0.056	0.328
To get lump sum amount	-0.198	**0.911**	0.036	-0.019	-0.072	0.084
High profitability	-0.034	**0.598**	0.415	-0.101	-0.401	-0.074
Fixed price	0.118	**-0.809**	-0.067	-0.133	-0.058	0.096
Minimum risk	-0.002	0.293	**0.816**	0.071	-0.201	0.145
Minimum labour requirement	-0.353	-0.374	**0.761**	-0.082	-0.073	0.063
Less and easy maintenance	0.384	0.036	**0.549**	-0.011	-0.015	0.477
Provision of fertilizer by sugar factory	0.067	0.377	-0.011	**0.810**	0.015	-0.056
Long term practice	-0.196	-0.033	0.152	**0.652**	0.478	-0.022
Familiar in the sugarcane cultivation	-0.635	-0.043	0.033	**-0.511**	0.338	-0.015
Easy to market	-0.023	0.281	0.142	**-0.798**	-0.099	-0.019
Suitability of land and soil	-0.280	0.093	0.046	0.072	**0.869**	-0.201
Availability of water facility	-0.255	0.093	0.003	0.117	**0.838**	-0.263
Favourable climate conditions	0.187	-0.068	-0.048	-0.473	**0.703**	-0.090
Easy to adopt drip irrigation	0.023	0.051	0.261	0.120	-0.318	**0.780**
Availability of crushing machineries	0.213	0.169	-0.091	-0.284	-0.037	**0.771**
Availability of cultivation machineries	0.090	0.489	-0.133	0.141	-0.069	**-0.695**

Extraction Method: Principal Component Analysis.

Rotation Method: Varimax with Kaiser Normalization

The factor analysis narrated the twenty variables into six factors namely Crop Orientation factor, Economic factor, Maintenance factor, General factor, Natural factor and Technology factor. The highly correlated variable of the Crop orientation factor is 'One year crop'. It has the factor loading of 0.896. The variable 'To get lump sum amount' is the highly correlated variable of the Economic factor since it has the highest factor loading of 0.911. 'Minimum risk' variable of the Maintenance factor has the highest factor loading of 0.816. In General factor, the variable 'Provision of fertilizer by sugar factory' has the highest factor loading of 0.810. The highly correlated variable of the Natural factor is 'Suitability of Land and Soil' which has the factor loading of 0.869. Regarding the Technology factor, higher correlation is noticed in the case of variable 'Easy to adopt Drip irrigation', since it has the highest factor loading of 0.780. The number of variables in each factor, Eigen value and the per cent of variation explained by each factor are presented in Table 3.3.

Table 3.3: Factors Influencing the Farmers to Cultivate Sugarcane - Principal Component Analysis

S. No.	Factors	No. of variables	Eigen value	Per cent of Variation explained	Cumulative per cent of Variation explained
1	Crop orientation factor	4	4.171	20.857	20.857
2	Economic factor	3	4.147	20.733	41.589
3	Maintenance factor	3	2.071	10.354	51.943
4	General factor	4	2.070	10.352	62.296
5	Natural factor	3	2.055	10.276	72.571
6	Technology factor	3	1.342	6.710	79.281

The most important factors influencing the farmers to cultivate sugarcane are 'Crop orientation factor' and 'Economic factor' since their Eigen values are 4.171 and 4.147 respectively. The Crop orientation factor consists of four variables with the variation explained by 20.857 per cent. The Economic factor consists of three variables with the variation explained by 20.733 per cent. The third and fourth factors are 'Maintenance factor' and 'General factor' since their respective Eigen values are 2.071 and 2.070. These two factors consists of three and four variables respectively and the per cent of variation explained by these two factors are 10.354 and 10.352 respectively. The fifth and sixth factors are 'Natural factor' and 'Technology factor' since their respective Eigen values are 2.055 and 1.342. These two factors consists of three variables and the per cent of variation explained by these two factors are 10.276 and 6.710 respectively. It is concluded that 'crop orientation factor' is highly influencing the farmers to cultivate sugarcane.

3.4. Intercropping in Sugarcane Cultivation

Sugarcane is cultivated with wider row spacing and the space between the cane rows is left vacant for initial 90-100 days. The weeds dominate this space and compete with the main crop which requires frequent manual weeding or application chemicals. So, the farmers to avoid weed and get additional income they prefer intercropping with Soybeans, Onion, Maize, Black gram etc. Table 3.4 shows the distribution of farmers based on intercrop cultivation practice.

Table 3.4: Intercropping in Sugarcane Cultivation

Intercropping in sugarcane cultivation	Number of Farmers	Percent
Following	46	7.67
Not following	554	92.33
Total	**600**	**100.00**

Source: Primary Data

Table 3.4 exposes that 92.33 per cent of the farmers are not cultivating intercrops in sugarcane cultivation where as 7.67 per cent of the farmers are cultivating intercrops in sugarcane cultivation. Hence, it is concluded that majority of the farmers (92.33 per cent) are not cultivating intercrops in sugarcane cultivation.

3.4.1. *Reasons for Not Following Intercropping*

There are many risks and problems involved in intercropping in sugarcane cultivation. The reasons for not following intercropping are less return and yield, high input price, inadequate water facility, lack of capital, spread of disease to main crop, requirement of high labour. For the purpose of analysis, Garret Ranking Technique has been applied with the following formula

$$\text{Per cent position} = \frac{100\,(Rij - 0.5)}{Nj}$$

Where,

Rij= Rank given for the the ith factor by the jth farmers

Nj= Number of factors ranked by jth farmers

By referring the Garrett Ranking Table, the percentage position estimated is converted into scores. Accordingly, scale values as per Garret ranking technique for first to six ranks are: 77.00, 63.30, 54.15, 46.85, 36.70 and 23.00 respectively. The percentage position of each rank is made into score by referring factors and summed up for assigning rank. Table 3.5 shows the results of Garrett ranking technique on reasons for not following intercropping in sugarcane cultivation.

Table 3.5: Reasons for Not Following Intercropping in Sugarcane Cultivation- Garrett Ranking Technique

S. No	Reasons	Rank	I	II	III	IV	V	VI	Total score	Mean score	Rank
		Score Value (x)	77.00	63.30	54.15	46.85	36.70	23.00			
1	Less return and yield	F	11	98	116	115	98	116	554	45.10	IV
		FX	847.00	6203.40	6281.40	5387.75	3596.60	2668.00	24984.20		
2	High input price	F	230	91	118	80	15	20	554	62.49	I
		FX	17710.00	5760.30	6389.70	3748.00	550.50	460.00	34618.50		
3	Inadequate water facility	F	88	91	172	102	87	14	554	54.41	III
		FX	6776.00	5760.30	9313.80	4778.70	3192.90	322.00	30143.70		
4	High lack of capital	F	70	19	30	118	230	87	554	43.66	V
		FX	5390.00	1202.70	1624.50	5528.30	8441.00	2001.00	24187.50		
5	Spread of disease to main crop	F	34	34	20	60	94	312	554	34.82	VI
		FX	2618.00	2152.20	1083.00	2811.00	3449.80	7176.00	19290.00		
6	Requirement of high labour	F	121	221	98	79	30	5	554	60.52	II
		FX	9317.00	13989.30	5306.70	3701.15	1101.00	115.00	33530.20		

Source: Primary Data

Table 3.5 it is found that the 'High input price' is identified as the most important reason for not following intercropping in sugarcane cultivation with the highest mean score value of 62.49, 'Requirement of high labour' (60.52) is selected as the second most important reason for not following intercropping, The third rank has been given to the factor' Inadequate water facility' (54.41), 'Spread of disease to main crop' has got the least mean score (34.82) among the six factors listed. Hence, it is concluded that as per the Garrett ranking technique, 'High input price' is identified as the most significant reason for not following intercropping in sugarcane cultivation.

3.5. Sources of Finance

Generally, the major problem faced by the farmers is insufficient finance. So that farmers are mobilising short term loans from friends & relatives, Banks, cooperative societies and local money lenders. Sometimes, the farmers depend factory for getting advance money for cultivating sugarcane. For the purpose of analysis, the sources of finance are classified into three i.e. Own fund, borrowed fund and both. The details of sources of finance for farmers cultivating sugarcane are shown in Table 3.6.

Table 3.6: Sources of Finance

Sources of Finance	Number of Farmers	Percent
Own Fund	165	27.50
Borrowed Fund	304	50.67
Both	131	21.83
Total	**600**	**100.00**

Source: Primary Data

Table 3.6 depicts that 50.67 per cent of the farmers used to borrowed fund, 27.50 per cent of the farmers used their own fund whereas 21.83 per cent of the farmers used the fund from both sources of finance for sugarcane cultivation.

3.6. Sources of Purchasing Setts

Generally, Setts are used from own plant. But most of the farmers purchased setts from factory to which they supply sugarcane. Remaining farmers have used setts from own plant or purchased from village traders. Table 3.7 shows the sources of purchasing setts for cultivation of sugarcane.

Table 3.7: Sources of Purchasing Setts

Sources of purchasing setts	Number of Farmers	Percent
Factory	344	57.33
Village traders	151	25.17
Own source	105	17.50
Total	**600**	**100.00**

Source: Primary Data

Table 3.7 indicates that 57.33 per cent of farmers are purchasing setts from factory, 25.17 per cent of farmers are purchasing setts from village traders and 17.50 percent of farmers used own source for cultivation of sugarcane. Hence, it is concluded that majority of the farmers (57.33 per cent) are purchasing setts from factory.

3.7. Number of Setts Used Per Acre

Sugarcane is mainly cultivated with two budded setts. Table 3.8 shows the distribution of farmers on the basis of number of setts used per acre.

Table 3.8: Number of Setts Used Per Acre

Number of Setts	Number of Farmers	Per cent
Upto 20000	325	54.17
20001-25000	258	43.00
Above 25000	17	2.83
Total	**600**	**100.00**

Source: Primary Data

Table 3.8 explains that 54.17 per cent of the farmers use upto 20000 setts per acre for sugarcane cultivation. 20001-25000 setts use by 43.00 per cent of the farmers and only 2.83 per cent of the farmers use above 25000 setts per acre for sugarcane cultivation. Hence, it is concluded that majority of the farmers (54.17 per cent) use upto 20000 setts per acre for sugarcane cultivation.

3.8. Varieties Used in Sugarcane Cultivation

The predominant variety Co 86032 is mainly used by majority of the farmers. This variety is moderately resistant to red rot & smut diseases, tolerant to drought, water logging conditions, erect cane, good yielder and good ratoon. The following are the sugarcane varieties used in cultivation such as Co 86032, Co 99006, CoSi 95071, Co 86249, CoG 93076 and CoV 94102. Table 3.9 shows the distribution of farmers according to sugarcane varieties used.

Table 3.9: Varieties Used in Sugarcane Cultivation

Sugarcane Varieties	Number of Farmers	Percent
Co 86032	562	93.67
Other varieties	38	6.33
Total	**600**	**100.00**

Source: Primary Data

Table 3.9 indicates that 93.67 percent of the farmers cultivate Co 86032 variety in sugarcane cultivation where as 6.33 per cent of the farmers cultivate other varieties in sugarcane cultivation. Hence, it is concluded that majority of the farmers (93.67 per cent) cultivate Co 86032 variety in sugarcane cultivation.

3.8.1. Reasons for Using a Particular Variety

In the present study, majority of the farmers (93.67 per cent) are used Co 86032 variety. An attempt is made to study the reasons for using a particular variety of sugarcane. Based on the pilot study, the reasons for using a particular variety are; Good quality setts, High yielding,

Own setts, Resistance to pest, disease and drought, Increase in growth, Suitability of Area, Provision of setts by factory, Seasonal suitability, High sugar content, Easy availability, Less maturity period, Less maintenance (detrashing) and Good ratoon. To identify the major reasons for using a particular variety, Garrett ranking technique has been applied. Scale values as per Garrett ranking technique for first to thirteen ranks are: 84.09, 73.05, 67.12, 62.14, 57.81, 53.83, 50.00, 46.17, 42.19, 37.86, 32.88, 26.50 and 15.91 respectively. The percentage position of each rank is made into score by referring factors and summed up for assigning rank. The results of the analysis are shown in Table 3.10.

Table 3.10: Reasons for Using a Particular Variety in Sugarcane Cultivation-Garrett Ranking Technique

S. No	Reasons	Rank	I	II	III	IV	V	VI	VII	VIII	IX	X	XI	XII	XIII	Total score	Mean score	Rank
		Score value (x)	84.09	73.05	67.12	62.14	57.81	53.83	50.00	46.17	42.19	37.86	32.88	26.50	15.91			
1	Good quality setts	F	11	16	25	13	19	62	64	65	41	54	90	70	70	600	41.53	XI
		FX	924.99	1168.80	1678.00	807.82	1098.39	3337.46	3200.00	3001.05	1729.79	2044.44	2959.20	1855.00	1113.70	24918.64		
2	High yielding	F	150	99	70	68	76	44	44	14	11	3	7	10	4	600	65.86	I
		FX	12613.50	7231.95	4698.40	4225.52	4393.56	2368.52	2200.00	646.38	464.09	113.58	230.16	265.00	63.64	39514.30		
3	Own setts	F	13	6	20	12	6	24	42	75	48	64	80	93	117	600	37.04	XII
		FX	1093.17	438.30	1342.40	745.68	346.86	1291.92	2100.00	3462.75	2025.12	2423.04	2630.40	2464.50	1861.47	22225.61		
4	Resistance to pest, disease and drought	F	22	26	47	25	19	61	60	68	53	58	57	64	40	600	46.03	VII
		FX	1849.98	1899.30	3154.64	1553.50	1098.39	3283.63	3000.00	3139.56	2236.07	2195.88	1874.16	1696.00	636.40	27617.51		
5	Increase in growth	F	125	114	71	65	40	35	37	54	3	10	5	6	35	600	62.61	II
		FX	10511.25	8327.70	4765.52	4039.10	2312.4	1884.05	1850.00	2493.18	126.57	378.60	164.40	159.00	556.85	37568.62		
6	Suitability of area	F	45	60	32	67	78	12	40	55	66	87	12	34	12	600	52.90	V
		FX	3784.05	4383.00	2147.84	4163.38	4509.18	645.96	2000.00	2539.35	2784.54	3293.82	394.56	901.00	190.92	31737.60		
7	Provision of setts by factory	F	18	8	17	2	5	11	44	90	115	47	78	75	90	600	38.69	XI
		FX	1513.62	584.40	1141.04	124.28	289.05	592.13	2200.00	4155.30	4851.85	1779.42	2564.64	1987.50	1431.90	23215.13		
8	Seasonal suitability	F	29	34	60	52	61	41	61	16	57	80	41	40	28	600	49.98	VI
		FX	2438.61	2483.70	4027.20	3231.28	3526.41	2207.03	3050.00	738.72	2404.83	3028.80	1348.08	1060.00	445.48	29990.14		
9	High sugar content	F	22	24	30	64	75	99	30	41	18	54	59	51	33	600	48.79	VII
		FX	1849.98	1753.20	2013.60	3976.96	4335.75	5329.17	1500.00	1892.97	759.42	2044.44	1939.92	1351.50	525.03	29271.94		
10	Easy availability	F	54	73	32	91	88	74	31	18	24	21	61	17	16	600	56.08	IV
		FX	4540.86	5332.65	2147.84	5654.74	5087.28	3983.42	1550.00	831.06	1012.56	795.06	2005.68	450.50	254.56	33646.21		
11	Less maturity period	F	22	24	27	43	36	56	30	47	54	48	59	64	90	600	43.36	X
		FX	1849.98	1753.20	1812.24	2672.02	2081.16	3014.48	1500.00	2169.99	2278.26	1817.28	1939.92	1696.00	1431.90	26016.43		
12	Less maintenance (detrashing)	F	11	28	42	44	37	52	70	28	37	67	48	73	63	600	44.78	IX
		FX	924.99	2045.40	2819.04	2734.16	2138.97	2799.16	3500.00	1292.76	1561.03	2536.62	1578.24	1934.50	1002.33	26867.20		
13	Good ratoon	F	78	88	127	54	60	29	47	29	73	7	3	3	2	600	61.90	III
		FX	6559.02	6428.40	8524.24	3355.56	3468.60	1561.07	2350.00	1338.93	3079.87	265.02	98.64	79.50	31.82	37140.67		

Source: Primary data

Table 3.10 clearly specifies that 'High yielding' variety is identified as the most significant reason for using a particular variety in sugarcane cultivation with maximum mean score

(65.86). 'Increase in growth' (62.61) is stands as the second. The third reason is 'Good ratoon' (61.90). 'Own setts' has got the least mean score value (37.04) among the thirteen factors listed.

Hence, it may be concluded that as per the Garrett ranking technique 'High yielding' variety is identified as the most significant reason for using a particular variety in sugarcane cultivation.

3.9. Cost and Returns from Cultivation of Sugarcane

The cost of cultivation varies from one type of farmers to another and even among the same type of farmers.

It varies from farmer to farmer in different areas. The size of the land holdings, the variety of sugarcane cultivated, application of manure & fertilizer and the method of cultivation followed are the major determinants of the cost of cultivation of sugarcane. Costs influence the immediate return to the farmers and the profitability of the venture over the long run.

Hence, an attempt has been made to study the average cost of cultivation, significant difference in cost incurred by farmers having different size of land holding in sugarcane cultivation.

In order to find out the costs and returns in the sugarcane cultivation, cost has been classified into three i.e. Cost A, Cost B and Cost C.

Cost A includes the expenses on Land Preparation, Sowing, Manuring &Fertilizer Application, Irrigation Operation, Intercultural Operation and Plant Protection Measures.

Cost B includes Setts, Manure and fertilizer and Plant protection.

Cost C includes Land revenue, Land rent, Depreciation on implements and Interest on working capital @ 12%. For the purpose of analysis, the sugarcane cultivating farmers have been divided into three groups as small farms (with less than 2.5 acres), medium farms (holding between 2.5 and 5 acres) and large farms (holding above 5 acres).

Table 3.11 indicates the cost per acre incurred by the farmers of different size farms and aggregate cost incurred in cultivation of sugarcane.

Table 3.11: Cost of Sugarcane Cultivation for Different Size of Farms

(in rupees per acre)

S. No.	PARTICULARS	PLANTED SUGARCANE				RATOON SUGARCANE			
		SMALL	MEDIUM	LARGE	ALL	SMALL	MEDIUM	LARGE	ALL
1	OPERATIONAL COST – A								
	Land Preparation	3870.00	4550.81	5120.00	4739.44	6116.67	6699.19	6756.15	6663.73
	Sowing	1653.33	1781.94	1821.54	1786.48	0.00	0.00	0.00	0.00
	Manure &Fertilizer Application	463.33	586.29	798.46	670.42	923.33	1144.35	1527.69	1296.48
	Irrigation Operation	7566.67	7714.52	8838.46	8213.38	7733.33	7874.19	8466.15	8130.28
	Intercultural Operation	7033.33	7524.19	7830.77	7612.68	7100.00	7705.65	7750.00	7661.97
	Plant Protection Measures	296.67	363.71	460.77	401.06	393.33	399.19	421.54	408.80
	TOTAL OPERATIONAL COST (A)	20883.33	22521.46	24870.00	23423.46	22266.66	23822.57	24921.53	24161.26
2	MATERIAL COST-B								
	Setts	8330.00	8837.90	9021.54	8868.31	0.00	0.00	0.00	0.00
	Manure and fertilizer	9766.67	11443.55	11892.31	11471.83	10533.33	11895.16	11786.92	11701.76
	Plant protection	746.67	847.58	961.54	889.08	746.67	847.58	957.69	887.32
	TOTAL MATERIAL COST (B)	18843.34	21129.03	21875.39	21229.22	11280.00	12742.74	12744.61	12589.08
3	OTHER COST - C								
	Land revenue	20.33	28.55	37.23	31.65	20.33	28.55	37.23	31.65
	Land rent	13600.00	14629.03	15815.38	15063.38	12866.67	14629.03	15815.38	14985.92
	Depreciation on implements	1200.00	1896.77	2353.85	2032.39	1200.00	1896.77	2353.85	2032.39
	Interest on working capital @ 12%	4767.20	5238.06	5609.45	5358.32	4025.60	4387.84	4519.94	4410.04
	TOTAL OTHER COST (C)	19587.53	21792.41	23815.91	22485.75	18112.60	20942.19	22726.40	21460.01
4	TOTAL COST = D (A+B+C)	59314.20	65442.90	70560.58	67138.43	51659.26	57507.50	60392.54	58210.35

Source: Primary data

Table 3.11 reveals that the cost of cultivation per acre in planted sugarcane for small, medium and large farms is ₹ 59,314.20, ₹ 65,442.90 and ₹ 70,560.58 respectively. The cost of cultivation per acre in ratoon sugarcane for small farms is ₹ 51,659.26, for medium farms is ₹ 57,507.50 and large farms is ₹ 60,392.54. The values indicate that the cost of cultivation per acre varies due to size of land. The operational cost is the more in the case of large farms due to more intercultural operation and amounts spent on land preparation, sowing and manure &fertilizers application for the plant and ratoon crop. Material cost incurred by large farms is high due to more amount spent for setts and manure& fertilizers. Due to less cost of depreciation and interest on working capital, the other cost is less in case of small farms than that of medium and large farms. Total cost incurred by the small farms is comparatively lower than that of medium and large size farms for the planted sugarcane and ratoon sugarcane due to family labour involved in the field.

3.10. Size of Farms and Cost of Cultivation

To test the significant difference in average total cost for sugarcane cultivation per acre for the planted sugarcane and ratoon sugarcane and individual cost incurred for sugarcane cultivation per acre by the three sizes of farms, viz., Small, Medium and Large, ANOVA has been applied. Further, to find out which size of farms has incurred higher cost among the three sizes Post-Hoc test has been applied.

3.10.1. Average Total Cost of Cultivation for Planted Sugarcane

The mean scores of the three sizes of farms, viz., Small, Medium and Large regarding average total cost incurred per acre for cultivation of planted sugarcane are presented in Table 3.12.

Table 3.12: Average Total Cost of Cultivation of Planted Sugarcane for Different Size of Farms

Size of farms	Number of farmers	Mean	Std. Deviation
Small	63	5.93	3099.78
Medium	262	6.54	3367.54
Large	275	6.04	4326.66
Total	600	6.25	4614.35

Table 3.12 shows that the mean score of the medium farms (6.54) is more than the other two sizes of farms. Hence, to test the significance of the difference in the mean scores of the different sizes of farms based on their average total cost of cultivation for planted sugarcane, the analysis of variance has been applied. The results of ANOVA are presented in Table 3.13.

Table 3.13: Average Total Cost of Cultivation of Planted Sugarcane for Different Size of Farms-
ANOVA

Variation	Sum of Squares	Degrees of freedom	Mean Square	F- Value	Result
Between Groups	9.778	2	4.889	33.571	Significant @ 5 per cent level
Within Groups	2.024	597	1.456		
Total	3.002	599			

Table 3.13 shows that the calculated value of 'F' (33.571) is greater than the table value (2.99). Hence, the hypothesis is not accepted. It indicates that there is a significant difference in the average total cost incurred per acre for cultivation of planted sugarcane among the three sizes of farms. To find out which category of farmers has incurred average total cost greater than the others, the Post-Hoc test has been applied. The results of the post hoc test are shown in Table 3.14.

Table 3.14: Average Total Cost of Cultivation of Planted Sugarcane for Different Size of Farms–
Multiple Comparisons

Land Holding(I)	Land Holding(J)	Mean Difference (I-J)	Std.Error
Small	Medium	-6128.69	1.09
	Large	-1078.35	1.09
Medium	Small	6128.69*	1.09
	Large	5050.34*	6.77
Large	Small	1078.35	1.09
	Medium	-5050.34*	6.77

* Significant at 5% level

Table 3.14 shows that the average total cost incurred per acre for cultivation of planted sugarcane crop by medium farms is more than that of the small and the large farms.

3.10.2. Average Total Cost of Cultivation for Ratoon Sugarcane

The mean scores of the three sizes of farms, viz., Small, Medium and Large regarding average total cost incurred per acre for cultivation of ratoon sugarcane are presented in Table 3.15.

Table 3.15: Average Total Cost of Cultivation of Ratoon Sugarcane for Different Size of Farms

Size of farms	No. of farmers	Mean	Std. Deviation
Small	63	5.17	3327.88
Medium	262	5.75	3886.43
Large	275	6.04	4326.66
Total	**600**	**5.82**	**4807.20**

Table 3.15 shows that the mean score of the large farms (6.04) is more than the other two sizes of farms. Hence, to test the significance of the difference in the mean scores of the different size of farms for the average total cost of cultivation for ratoon sugarcane, the analysis of variance has been applied. The results of ANOVA are presented in Table 3.16

Table 3.16: Average Total Cost of Cultivation of Ratoon Sugarcne for Different Size of Farms-
ANOVA

Variation	Sum of Squares	Degrees of freedom	Mean Square	F- Value	Result
Between Groups	9.839	2	4.920	30.065	Significant @
Within Groups	2.274	597	1.636		5 per cent level
Total	**3.258**	**599**			

Table 3.16 shows that the calculated value of 'F' (30.065) is greater than the table value (2.99). Hence, the hypothesis is not accepted. It indicates that there is a significant difference in the average total cost incurred per acre for cultivation of ratoon sugarcane among the three sizes of farms. To find out which category of farms has incurred average total cost greater than the others, the Post-Hoc test has been applied. The results of the post hoc test are shown in Table 3.17.

Table 3.17: Average Total Cost of Cultivation of Ratoon Sugarcane for Different Size of Farms–
Multiple Comparisons

Land Holding(I)	Land Holding(J)	Mean Difference (I-J)	Std. Error
Small	Medium	-5848.25*	1.16
	Large	-8733.29*	1.15
Medium	Small	5848.25*	1.16
	Large	-2885.04*	7.18
Large	Small	8733.29*	1.15
	Medium	2885.04*	7.18

* Significant at 5% level

Table 3.17 expresses that the average total cost incurred per acre for cultivation of ratoon sugarcane by large farms is more than that of the small and the medium farms.

3.11. Size of Farms and Returns from Cultivation of Sugarcane

In sugarcane cultivation, Gross return denotes the sum of the value realised by the farmers by way of the sale of sugarcane. Net return denotes the income realized by the farmers by the sale of sugarcane after deducting the cultivation cost. In the present study, out of 600 farmers, 385 farmers market their sugarcane. In this, 313 farmers (81.30 per cent) market their sugarcane to sugar factory and 72 farmers (18.70 per cent) jaggery producers. In this part, return from sugarcane cultivation is analysed only with the data collected from 385 farmers. Details of the findings are showninTable3.18.

Table 3.18: Returns from Cultivation of Sugarcane for Different Size of Farms

(in rupees per acre)

S. No.	Particulars	PLANTED SUGARCANE				RATOON SUGARCANE			
		Small	Medium	Large	All	Small	Medium	Large	All
A	Yieldof Sugarcane (In tonne)	47.00	48.07	48.08	47.92	41.85	43.44	44.49	43.64
	Gross Return (₹peracre)	110155.00	109208.04	111069.18	110100.05	97115.77	98633.29	101783.24	99697.25
B	Total Operational Cost	20492.30	21921.50	23495.90	22357.47	22015.40	23275.60	24568.90	23621.43
C	Total Material Cost	19107.70	22178.00	22393.20	21826.92	11207.70	13453.70	13731.10	13245.60
D	Other Cost	19426.20	21431.80	23828.60	22119.82	17814.80	20547.40	22917.90	21120.86
E	Total Cost E (B+C+D)	59026.20	65531.30	69717.80	66304.22	51037.90	57276.70	61217.90	57987.89
F	Net Returns (A - E)	51128.80	43676.70	41351.40	43795.80	46077.90	41356.60	40565.30	41709.40

Table 3.18 clearly specify that the Gross return per acre from planted sugarcane for all farms is ₹ 110100.05 whereas the Gross return per acre from sugarcane cultivation for small, medium and large farms is ₹ 110155.00, ₹ 109208.04 and ₹ 111069.18 respectively. The Net return per acre from planted sugarcane for small farms is ₹ 51128.80, for medium farms is ₹ 43676.70 and for large farms is ₹ 41351.40.

The Gross return per acre from ratoon sugarcane for all farms is ₹ 99697.25 whereas the Gross return per acre from sugarcane cultivation for small, medium and large farms is ₹ 97115.77, ₹ 98633.29 and ₹ 101783.24 respectively. The Net return per acre from ratoon sugarcane for small farms is ₹ 46077.90, for medium farms is ₹ 41356.60 and for large farms are ₹ 40565.30.

Hence, it is concluded that the Net return per acre from planted and ratoon sugarcane for small farms is ₹ 51128.80 and ₹ 46077.90 respectively which is higher than other farms.

3.11.1. *Size of Farms and Returns from Cultivation of Sugarcane for Planted Sugarcane*

In order to test whether there exists any significant difference in returns from the cultivation of planted sugarcane per acre by the three sizes of farms, viz., Small, Medium and Large farms, ANOVA has been applied. Then to find out which group of farms has earned higher return among the three groups, Post hoc test has been applied. The mean scores of the three sizes of farms, viz., Small, Medium and Large farms, regarding returns from cultivation of planted sugarcane per acre are presented in Table 3.19.

Table 3.19: Returns from Cultivation of Planted Sugarcane for Different Size of Farms

Size of farms	No. of farmers	Mean	Std. Deviation
Small	55	2.79	7097.709
Medium	173	2.25	7703.021
Large	157	2.10	9820.037
Total	385	2.27	8760.978

Table 3.19 reveals that the mean score of the small farms (2.79) is more than the other two sizes of farms. Hence, to test the significance of the difference in mean scores of the different size of the farms for the returns from cultivation of planted sugarcane, the analysis of variance has been applied. The results of ANOVA are presented in Table 3.20.

Table 3.20: Returns from Cultivation of Planted Sugarcane for Different Size of Farms - ANOVA

Variation	Sum of Squares	Degrees of freedom	Mean Square	F- Value	Result
Between Groups	4.583	2	2.292	3.127	
Within Groups	6.450	382	7.329		Significant @ 5 per cent level
Total	6.908	384			

Table 3.20 shows that the calculated value of 'F' (3.127) is greater than the table value (2.99). Hence, the hypothesis is not accepted. It indicates that there is a significant difference in the returns from the cultivation of planted sugarcane among the Small, Medium and Large farms. To find out which category of farms has earned returns from cultivation of planted sugarcane greater than that of others, the Post-Hoc test has been applied. The results of the post hoc test are shown in Table 3.21.

Table 3.21: Returns from Cultivation of Planted Sugarcane for Different Size of Farms - Multiple

Comparisons

Land holding (I)	Land holding (J)	Mean difference(I-J)	Std.Error
Small	Medium	5416.14*	2724.95
	Large	6884.99*	2760.18
Medium	Small	-5416.14*	2724.95
	Large	1468.85	1941.24
Large	Small	-6884.99*	2760.18
	Medium	-1468.85	1941.24

*Significant at 5 % level

Table 3.21 depicts that the returns from cultivation of planted sugarcane differ significantly among the three sizes of farms. For small farms, return from cultivation of planted sugarcane per acre is more than that of the medium and large farms. Further, it is concluded that the returns from cultivation of planted sugarcane varies with the size of land holdings.

3.11.2. Size of Farms and Returns from Cultivation of Ratoon Sugarcane

In order to test whether there exists any significant difference in returns from the cultivation of ratoon sugarcane per acre by the three sizes of farms, viz., Small, Medium and Large farms ANOVA has been applied. Then to find out which group of farms has earned higher return among the three groups, Post hoc test has been applied. The mean scores of all the three size of farms, viz., Small, Medium and Large regarding returns from cultivation of ratoon sugarcane per acre are presented in Table 3.22.

Table 3.22: Returns from Cultivation of Ratoon Sugarcane for Different Size of Farms

Size of farms	No. of farmers	Mean	Std. Deviation
Small	55	2.56	11230.440
Medium	173	2.04	9597.010
Large	157	1.87	8729.088
Total	**385**	**2.05**	**9659.820**

Table 3.22 reveals that the mean score of the small farms (2.56) is more than the other two sizes of farms. Hence, to test the significance of the difference in mean scores of the different size of the farms for the returns from cultivation of ratoon sugarcane, the analysis of variance has been applied. The results of ANOVA are presented in Table 3.23.

Table 3.23: Returns from Cultivation of Ratoon Sugarcane for Different Size of Farms - ANOVA

Variation	Sum of Squares	Degrees of freedom	Mean Square	F- Value	Result
Between Groups	4.574	2	2.287	2.535	
Within Groups	7.941	382	9.023		Significant @ 5 per cent level
Total	**8.398**	**384**			

Table 3.23 shows that the calculated value of 'F' (2.535) is greater than the table value (2.99). Hence, the hypothesis is not accepted. It indicates that there is a significant difference in the returns from the cultivation of ratoon sugarcane among the Small, Medium and Large farms. To find out which category of farms has earned returns from cultivation of ratoon sugarcane greater than that of others, the Post-Hoc test has been applied. The results of the post hoc test are shown in Table 3.24.

Table 3.24: Returns from Cultivation of Ratoon Sugarcane for Different Size of Farms - Multiple Comparisons

Land holding (I)	Land holding (J)	Mean difference (I-J)	Std.Error
Small	Medium	5147.52	3023.57
	Large	6895.24*	3062.67
Medium	Small	-5147.52	3023.57
	Large	1747.72	2153.98
Large	Small	-6895.24*	3062.67
	Medium	-1747.72	2153.98

*Significant at 5 % level

Table 3.24 depicts that the returns from cultivation of ratoon sugarcane differ significantly among the three sizes of farms. For small farms, return from cultivation of ratoon sugarcane per acre is more than that of the medium and large farms. Further, it is concluded that the returns from cultivation of ratoon sugarcane varies with the size of land holdings.

3.12. Cost and Returns from Production of Khandsari Sugar

In the study, out of 600 farmers, 215 farmers produce of khandsari sugar on their own, instead of marketing sugarcane. Gross return denotes the sum of the value realised by the farmers by way of the sale of khandsari sugar. Net return denotes the income realised by the farmers by the sale of khandsari sugar after deducting the cultivation cost of sugarcane and production cost of khandsari sugar. Details of the findings are shown in Table 3.25.

Table 3.25: Cost and Returns from Production of Khandsari Sugar for Different Size of Farms

(in rupees per acre)

	Particulars	SIZE OF FARMS							
		PLANTED SUGARCANE				RATOON SUGARCANE			
		Small	Medium	Large	All	Small	Medium	Large	All
A	Yield of Khandsari Sugar (in adasal per acre)	63.00	59.57	57.57	58.61	58.50	53.00	54.39	53.98
	Gross Return (₹ per acre)	183825.00	178431.00	172022.00	175124.00	169988.00	156862.00	154259.00	155948.00
B	Cost of Cultivation of Sugarcane (per acre)	61186.00	65270.30	71675.90	68626.90	55698.00	57958.30	59302.00	58607.30
C	Labour cost for production of khandsari sugar	36225.00	34636.53	35211.10	35032.55	33637.50	30815.71	33267.06	32266.51
D	Rental charges for production of khandsari sugar	9450.00	11205.10	10486.22	10744.77	8775.00	9969.05	9907.27	9896.41
E	Chemical & Other cost for production of khandsari sugar	1890.00	2411.22	2302.86	2332.82	1755.00	2145.24	2175.71	2148.63
F	Total Cost F (B+C+D+E)	108751.00	113523.16	119676.08	116737.04	99865.50	100888.30	104652.04	102918.85
G	Net Returns (A - F)	75074.00	64907.84	52345.92	58386.96	70122.50	55973.70	49606.96	53029.15

Source: Primary Data

Table 3.25 indicates that Gross return from production of khandsari sugar in planted sugarcane for all farms is ₹ 175124.00 per acre whereas the Gross return per acre from sugarcane cultivation for small, medium and large farms is ₹ 183825.00, ₹ 178431.00 and ₹ 172022.00 respectively. The Net return per acre from production of khandsari sugar for Small farms is ₹ 75074.00, for Medium farms is ₹ 64907.84 and for large farms is ₹ 52345.92 respectively.

The Gross return per acre from sugarcane cultivation in ratoon sugarcane for all farms is ₹ 155948.00 whereas the Gross return per acre from sugarcane cultivation in ratoon sugarcane for Small, Medium and Large farms is ₹ 169988.00, ₹ 156862.00 and ₹ 154259.00 respectively. The Net return per acre from cultivation of sugarcane for ratoon sugarcane for Small farms is ₹ 70122.50, for Medium farms is ₹ 55973.70 and for large farms is ₹ 49606.96 respectively. Hence, it is concluded that the Net return per acre from production of khandsari sugar in planted and ratoon sugarcane for Small farms ₹ 75074.00 and ₹ 70122.50 is higher than other farms.

3.12.1. Size of Farms and Returns from Khandsari Sugar in Planted Sugarcane

In order to test whether there exists any significant difference in return from the khandsari sugar for planted sugarcane per acre by the three sizes of farms, viz., Small, Medium and Large farms, ANOVA has been applied. Then to find out which group of farms has earned higher return among the three groups, Post hoc test has been applied. The mean scores of the three sizes of farms, viz., small, medium and large farms regarding returns from khandsari sugar in planted sugarcane per acre are presented in Table 3.26.

Table 3.26: Returns from Khandsari Sugar in Planted Sugarcane for Different Size of Farms

Size of farms	No. of farmers	Mean	Std. Deviation
Small	9	70313.00	9145.719
Medium	89	61076.76	20861.608
Large	117	48482.91	16795.001
Total	215	54524.70	19404.059

Table 3.26 reveals that the mean score of the small farms (70313.00) is more than the other two sizes of farms. Hence, to test the significance of the difference in mean scores of the different size of the farms for the returns from khandsari sugar for planted sugarcane, the analysis of variance has been applied. The results of ANOVA are presented in Table 3.27.

Table 3.27: Returns from Khandsari Sugar in Planted Sugarcane Crop for Different Size of Farms - ANOVA

Variation	Sum of Squares	Degrees of freedom	Mean Square	F- Value	Result
Between Groups	2422150750.703	2	1.211	3.544	Significant @ 5 per cent level
Within Groups	16403723804.836	213	3.417		
Total	18825874555.539	215			

Table 3.27 shows that the calculated value of 'F' (3.544) is greater than the table value (2.99). Hence, the hypothesis is not accepted. It indicates that there is a significant difference in the returns from the khandsari sugar for planted sugarcane among the Small, Medium and Large farms. To find out which category of farmers has earned returns from khandsari sugar for planted sugarcane greater than that of others, the Post hoc test has been applied. The results of the post hoc test are shown in Table 3.28.

Table 3.28: Returns from Khandsari Sugar Planted Sugarcane for Different Size of Farms -
Multiple Comparisons

Land holding (I)	Land holding(J)	Mean difference(I-J)	Std.Error
Small	Medium	9236.24	1.37
	Large	21830.09	1.35
Medium	Small	-9236.24	1.37
	Large	12593.85*	1.35
Large	Small	-21830.09	1.37
	Medium	-12593.85*	1.37

*Significant at 5% level

Table 3.28 depicts that the returns from khandsari sugar in planted sugarcane differ significantly among the three sizes of farms. For small farms returns from khandsari sugar in planted sugarcane per acre is more than that of the medium and large farms. Further, it is concluded that the returns from khandsari sugar in planted sugarcane varies with the size of land holdings.

3.12.2. *Size of Farms and Returns from Khandsari Sugar for Ratoon Sugarcane*

In order to test whether there exists any significant difference in returns from the khandsari sugar for ratoon sugarcane per acre by the three sizes of farms, viz., Small, Medium and Large farms, ANOVA has been applied. Then to find out which group of farms has earned higher return among the three groups, Post hoc test has been applied. The mean scores of the three sizes of farms viz., Small, Medium and Large farms regarding returns from khandsari sugar for ratoon sugarcane per acre are presented in Table 3.29.

Table 3.29: Returns from Khandsari Sugar in Ratoon Sugarcane for Different Size of Farms

Size of farms	No. of farmers	Mean	Std. Deviation
Small	9	65347.50	5162.587
Medium	89	52529.10	14055.073
Large	117	45930.71	7467.522
Total	215	49409.14	11431.922

Table 3.29 reveals that the mean score of the small farms (65347.50) is more than the other two sizes of farms. Hence, to test the significance of the difference in mean scores of the different size of the farms for the returns from khandsari sugar for ratoon sugarcane, the analysis of variance has been applied. The results of ANOVA are presented in Table 3.30.

Table 3.30: Returns from Khandsari Sugar in Ratoon Sugarcane for Different Size of Farms -
ANOVA

Variation	Sum of Squares	Degrees of freedom	Mean Square	F- Value	Result
Between Groups	1051263646.015	2	5.256	4.601	Significant @ 5 per cent level
Within Groups	5483178634.024	213	1.142		
Total	6534442280.039	215			

Table 3.30 clearly states that the calculated value of 'F' (4.601) is greater than the table value (2.99). Hence, the hypothesis is not accepted. It indicates that there is a significant difference in the returns from the production of khandsari sugar for ratoon sugarcane among the Small, Medium and Large farms.

To find out which category of farms has earned returns from khandsari sugar for ratoon sugarcane greater than that of others, the Post hoc test has been applied. The results of the post hoc test are shown in Table 3.31.

Table 3.31: Returns from Khandsari Sugar in Ratoon Sugarcane for Different Size of Farms-Multiple Comparisons

Land holding (I)	Land holding(J)	Mean difference(I-J)	Std.Error
Small	Medium	12818.41	7909.24
	Large	19416.79*	7822.79
Medium	Small	-12818.41	7909.24
	Large	6598.38*	3085.35
Large	Small	-19416.79*	7822.79
	Medium	-6598.38*	3085.35

*Significant at 5 % level

Table 3.31 depicts that the returns from khandsari sugar for ratoon sugarcane differ significantly among the three sizes of farms. For small farms, return from khandsari sugar for ratoon sugarcane per acre is more than that of the medium and large farms. Further, it is concluded that the returns from khandsari sugar for ratoon sugarcane varies with the size of land holdings.

3.13. Production Function Analysis

The challenges of every farmer in agriculture faces are to increase output and minimize the cost. In this, farmer must know how the efficiently are using the inputs, identify the inputs that are inefficiently used and then measures can be suggested that to increase production and also to minimize cost. In order to identify the efficient use of inputs for increase the production, production function analysis is the relevant technique. The production function analysis gives an explicit idea regarding the use of inputs and their influence on output. The production function analysis determines the productivity levels of different inputs and asses the contribution at margin to the output. To know the input-output relationship in sugarcane cultivation, Cobb-Douglas production function technique is applied.

In this section, Cobb-Douglas type of production function could effectively be used to ascertain the possibility or otherwise to increase the production through increase in doses of important inputs. Two equations of Cobb-Douglas function (non–linear) have been estimated on the basis of goodness of fit (r^2). The farmers are cultivating both planted sugarcane and ratoon sugarcane. In view of this, two equations are estimated. One equation for planted sugarcane farming and the other for ratoon sugarcane farming. This is because ratoon sugarcane does not involve setts cost. The specification of function is given below. The estimation is made separately for sugarcane farmers those who are marketing sugarcane and those who are producing own khandsari sugar. The data are therefore, subjected to functional analysis by using following form of equation.

$$Y = ax_1^{b1}. x_2^{b2}. \ldots\ldots x_n^{bn}. ei$$

Where,

Y = dependent variable

X_l = independent variable

a = Constant representing intercept of production function

bi = Regression co-efficient of respective resource variable

The regression co-efficient obtained from this function directly represents the elastic ties of production, which remain constant throughout the relevant ranges of inputs. The sum of co-efficient i.e. bi indicates the nature of returns to scale. This function can be presented into linear form making logarithmic transformation.

$$Log\ y = log\ a + b_1 logx_1 + b_2 logx_2 + \ldots\ldots + b_n log\ x_n + loge$$

For fitting production function in sugarcane cultivation nine inputs (variables) have been considered as important factors by considering the problem of multi-colinearity in estimating production function and the equation fitted is of the following formula.

$$Y = ax_1^{b1}. x_2^{b2}. x_3^{b3}. x_4^{b4}. x_5^{b5}. x_6^{b6}.x_7^{b7}. x_8^{b8}. x_9^{b9}$$

Where,

Y = yield (tonne per acre)

a = intercept of production function

b1 = Regression co-efficient of the respective resource

Variable (i = 1, 2, 3 ....9)

$$Log\ y = log\ a + b_1 logx_1 + b_2 logx_2 + b_3 logx_3 + b_4 logx_4 + b_5 logx_5 + b_6 logx_6 + b_7 logx_7 + b_8 logx_8 + b_9 log\ x_9$$

Where,

y = Value of **output** per acre

X_1 = Land Preparation

X_2 = Sowing

X_3 = Manure & Fertilizer Application

X_4 = Irrigation Operation

X_5 = Intercultural Operation

X_6 = Plant Protection Measures

X_7 = Setts

X_8= Manure and fertilizer

X_9 =Labour for crushing

Sugarcane Farmers (Planted Sugarcane)

It includes all the above stated variables except X_9 i.e., Labour for crushing.

Sugarcane Farmers (Ratoon Sugarcane)

It includes the above stated variables except X_2 i.e., Sowing, X_7 i.e., Setts and X_9 i.e., Labour for crushing.

Khandsari Sugar Farmers (Plant Sugarcane)

For own producer of khandsari sugar for plant farming, all the above these variables are included.

Khandsari Sugar Farmers (Ratoon Sugarcane)

For own producer of khandsari sugar for ratoon farming, it includes the above stated variables except X_2 i.e., Sowing and X_7 i.e., Setts.

Output

The gross value of output valued at prices received by the farmers. Gross value of output is the dependent variable.

Land Preparation

In all the villages, tractors are used for ploughing. Thus, the actual cost incurred by farmer for ploughing is considered for those who do not own a tractor.

Sowing

In sugarcane crop, sowing is the operational cost. The cost incurred for planting the seed. It is lease basis on number of setts or daily wages basis.

Manure and Fertilizers Application

The actual cost incurred by farmer for application of manure and fertilizers is considered in sugarcane crop.

Irrigation Charges

This cost is measured as the actual cost incurred by farmers for application of irrigation in sugarcane cultivation to the particular crop.

Intercultural Operation

Human labour is specified in terms of eight hours per day. The assumed differences in the efficiency of labour between male and females are standardized. In the area, the wage rates of female labourer ₹150 per day and male labourer ₹ 300 per day.

Plant Protection

Plant protection cost incurred by the farmers for the purchased cost and applied cost in sugarcane crop.

Setts

Setts are one of important items of production function. In sugarcane cultivation home grown setts generally do not exists. Thus, the cost incurred in the purchase of setts is considered for plant sugarcane while for ratoon farming setts cost does not exist.

Manure & Fertilizers

The expenditure on manure and fertilizer is aggregated into a single variable. The cost of manure is measured in terms cost per cart-load, while fertilizer is valued at purchased cost.

Labour for Crushing

In own producer of khandsari sugar farmers incurred the labour cost for crushing of the sugarcane converted into khandsari sugar. The regression co-efficient of cultivation of sugarcane for different size of farms has been worked out in Table 3.32.

Table 3.32: Production Function Analysis for Sugarcane Farmers (N=385)

Independent Variables	PLANTEDSUGARCANE		RATOON SUGARCANE	
	Regression co-efficient	t-ratio	Regression co-efficient	t-ratio
Land Preparation (X_1)	0.536	2.91***	0.1782	4.01***
Sowing (X_2)	0.661	2.31**	-	-
Manure & Fertilizer Application (X_3)	-0.262	-1.67*	-0.013	-1.75*
Irrigation Operation (X_4)	-0.390	-6.70***	-0.005	-1.62
Intercultural Operation (X_5)	0.266	3.02***	-0.011	-1.92*
Plant Protection Measures (X_6)	0.043	0.46	-0.017	-2.02**
Setts(X_7)	-0.168	-1.78*	-	-
Manure and fertilizers (X_8)	0.140	3.36***	-0.072	-0.03
R^2	0.8391		0.2553	

Note: *** 1% level of significance, **5% level of significance, *10% level of significance

Table 3.32 clearly indicates that the regression co-efficient for manure & fertilizers (-2.62), irrigation operation (-3.90) and setts (-0.168) are negative and regression co-efficient of manure & fertilizers and setts are showing significant at 10 per cent level of significance but the contribution of irrigation operation is significant at 1 per cent level of significance. The manure and fertilizers (3.36) is highly significant at 1 per cent level of significance followed by intercultural operation (3.02) land preparation (2.91) and sowing (2.31) also significant at 1 and 5 per cent level of significance. This means increase in yield level of sugarcane is directly proportional to increase in use of these inputs. The elasticity of production variable manure & fertilizer is 0.140 which means one per cent increase in manure & fertilizer increase the yield of sugarcane by 0.140 per cent. Similarly 1 per cent increase in intercultural operation, land preparation and sowing increase the sugarcane yield by 0.266, 0.536 and 0.661 per cent respectively.

In ratoon sugarcane, there is no cost for setts and sowing. The land preparation (4.01) is highly significant at 1 per cent level of significance. The plant protection measures (-0.017), manure and fertilizers (-0.013) and intercultural operation (-0.011) are negative and regression co-efficient are showing significant at 5 and 10 per cent level of significance.

The co-efficient of multiple determination (R^2) is 0.8391 which indicates that 83.91 per cent variance in sugarcane production has been explained by the all independent variables. In the case, of ratoon sugarcane the R^2 value 0.2553 which indicates 25.53 percent variance in sugarcane production has been explained by all independent variables.

The regression co-efficient of cultivation of sugarcane and production of khandsari sugar for different size of farms has been worked out in Table 3.33.

Table 3.33: Production Function Analysis for Farmers Producing Khandsari Sugar (N=215)

Independent Variables	PLANTEDSUAGRCANE		RATOON SUGARCANE	
	Regression co-efficient	t-ratio	Regression co-efficient	t-ratio
Land Preparation(X_1)	0.174	2.53**	0.017	3.10***
Sowing(X_2)	-0.034	-0.90	-	-
Manure & Fertilizer Application (X_3)	-0.017	-0.37	-0.014	-1.20
Irrigation Operation(X_4)	-0.020	-1.81*	-0.024	-0.87
Intercultural Operation(X_5)	-0.270	-1.72*	-0.051	-1.05
Plant Protection Measures(X_6)	-0.003	-0.29	0.016	0.15
Setts(X_7)	0.017	1.78*	-	-
Manure and fertilizers (X_8)	-0.348	-4.07***	-0.098	-2.13**
Labour for crushing(X_9)	-0.025	-2.42**	-0.033	-0.52
R^2	0.313		0.129	

Note: *** 1% level of significance, **5% level of significance, *10% level of significance

Table 3.33 clearly indicates that the regression co-efficient for manure & fertilizer (-0.348), labour for crushing (-0.025), irrigation operation (-0.020) and intercultural operation (-0.270) are negative and statistically significant at 1, 5 and 10 per cent level of significance. The land preparation (2.53) is highly significant at 5 per cent level of probability followed by setts

(1.78) also significant at 1 per cent level of significance. This means increases in yield level of sugarcane and return of khandsari sugar are directly proportional to increase in use of these inputs.

In ratoon sugarcane, land preparation (3.10) is highly significant at 1 per cent level of significance. The manure & fertilizers (-0.098) is negative and regression co-efficient are showing significant at 5 per cent level of significance. The other input whose elasticity co-efficient are not statistically significant.

The co-efficient of multiple determination (R^2) 0.313 which indicates 31.3 per cent variance in sugarcane production has been explained by the all independent variables. In the case of ratoon sugarcane the (R^2) value 0.129 which indicates 12.9 percent variance in sugarcane production has been explained by independent variables.

3.14. Summary

In this chapter, cultivation practices in sugarcane in the area have been highlighted. Further, factors influencing the farmers to cultivate sugarcane, cost & returns from sugarcane cultivation and production of khandsari sugar have been examined. The following are the major findings of this chapter:

- For analysing the factors influencing the farmers to cultivate sugarcane, factor analysis has been applied. From the analysis, it is found that crop orientation factor and economic factor are identified as the most significant factors influencing the farmers to cultivate sugarcane.
- For analysing the reasons for not following intercropping in sugarcane cultivation, Garrett Ranking technique has been applied. From the analysis, it is found that the 'High input price' is identified as the most important reason for not following intercropping in sugarcane cultivation.
- It is also found that majority of the farmers (50.67 per cent) used borrowed fund for cultivation of sugarcane, majority of farmers (57.33 per cent) are purchasing setts from factory and majority of the farmers (54.17 per cent) use upto 20000 setts per acre in sugarcane cultivation.
- It is found that majority of farmers (93.67 per cent) cultivating Co 86032 variety in sugarcane cultivation and it is also found that as per the Garrett ranking technique 'High yielding' variety has been identified as the most significant reason for using a particular variety.

- In cost of cultivation analysis, it is found that the cost of cultivation per acre incurred for small, medium and large farms are ₹ 59,314.20, ₹ 65,442.90 and ₹ 70,560.58 respectively for plant sugarcane crop. For ratoon sugarcane, the cost of cultivation is ₹ 51,659.26, ₹ 57,507.50 and ₹ 60,392.54 respectively.

- By applying 'F' test, it is found that there is a significant difference in the average total cost incurred per acre for cultivation of sugarcane plant and ratoon sugarcane among the three sizes of farms. It is also found that there is a significant difference in average return per acre from sugarcane cultivation and production of khandsari sugar.

- By applying Post-hoctest, it is found that large farms spent more cost for sugarcane cultivation than small and medium farms. It is also found that small farms get more returns from sugarcane cultivation than small and medium farms.

- By applying Cobb-Douglas production function analysis for sugarcane cultivation, it is found that the regression co-efficient for manure & fertilizers, irrigation operation and setts are negative and it shows that the farmers that they have not utilised these resources to the fullest capacity.

- By applying Cobb-Douglas production function analysis for production of khandsari sugar farmers, it is found that the regression co-efficient for manure & fertilizer, labour for crushing, irrigation operation and intercultural operation are negative. This indicates that the sugarcane farmers who produce khandsari sugar have not fully utilised these resources in proper and an efficient way.

CHAPTER IV

ADOPTION OF DRIP IRRIGATION SYSTEM IN SUGARCANE CULTIVATION

Keywords

Factors influencing the farmers to cultivate sugarcane under Drip Irrigation System - Satisfaction of farmers in adoption of Drip Irrigation System - Problems faced by the farmers in adoption of Drip Irrigation System in Sugarcane Cultivation - Reasons for Non-Adoption of Drip Irrigation System in sugarcane cultivation.

4.1. Introduction

Irrigation is the major input for agriculture. The development of agriculture is mainly depending on proper utilization of various sources of irrigation. The development of agriculture or mechanization and modernization of agriculture depends on the availability of irrigation facilities. The level of ground water depends on rainfall and tank irrigation. Due to the uneven rainfall in the country, it is necessary to improve the canal source of irrigation through proper utilisation of rainfall.

Sugarcane is a crop of about one year duration and it has to pass through all the seasons of the year irrespective of the time of planting. Some months are moisture deficit, some are with adequate moisture supply and in some there is moisture surplus. Water requirement of the crop is high during the deficit period compared to the surplus period. Providing optimum soil moisture conditions throughout its growing period is of paramount importance to realise high yields. Water is a prime resource and at the same time, it is over exploited resource due to rapid commercialization of agriculture and urbanisation. The ground water in Tamil Nadu has been exploited to the tune of 80-85 per cent of its potential. Many areas have slipped into 'Black Zone' from 'White' and 'Grey'.

Drip irrigation also known as trickle irrigation or micro irrigation, is an irrigation method which saves water by allowing water to drip slowly to the roots of plants, either onto the soil surface or directly onto the root zone of plants, through network of valves, pipes, tubing and emitters. It is a positive approach for farmers to avoid huge wastage and improve the farmers' income. Drip irrigation for sugarcane cultivation is available technology and an essential foundation for the development of sustainable sugarcane cultivation with the shrinking water resources. Drip irrigation is a recent technology in sugarcane which is being practiced since 2006 in Tamil Nadu State. During the year 2012-2013, drip irrigation has been adopted in

7807 hectares under various crops such as sugarcane, cotton, maize and coconut. Drip irrigation was popularized as a technology highlighting the concepts of water saving and yield increase. On the whole, water saving (40-50 per cent), labour saving, easy application of fertilizers, increasing yield (35-45 per cent), reduction in weeds, increase in cultivable area, provides uniform irrigation to entire crop and easy to maintain large farms were the main reasons for adoption of drip irrigation system in sugarcane cultivation.

There are two systems of drip irrigation method for sugarcane crop. They are surface and subsurface irrigation. In surface drip irrigation system, water moves over and across the land by simple gravity flow in order to wet it and to infiltrate into the soil. It can be subdivided into furrow, border-strip or basin irrigation. Subsurface drip irrigation system uses permanently or temporarily buried dripper line or drip tape located at or below the plants root zone.

This chapter is analysed by using the data collected from the 123 sugarcane farmers who follow drip irrigation system in sugarcane cultivation. The factors influencing the farmers to adopt the drip irrigation system in sugarcane cultivation has been analysed with help of factor analysis. Satisfaction of the farmers about the adoption of drip irrigation system in sugarcane cultivation has been analysed with help of chi-square test, F-test, Z-test and multiple regression analysis. The problems faced by the farmers in adoption of drip irrigation system and reasons for non-adoption of drip irrigation system in sugarcane cultivation have been analysed with help of Garrett Ranking Technique.

4.2. Factors Influencing the Farmers to Cultivate Sugarcane under Drip Irrigation System

The farmers are influenced by number of factors to cultivate sugarcane under drip irrigation. In the area, on the basis of outcome of the study, farmers are interviewed to disclose the factors which influence them to adopt the drip irrigation in sugarcane cultivation. To examine the influencing factors, seventeen factors such as water saving, high yield, less labour requirements, long term usages, to get subsidy from Government, minimum work, flexibility, no drainage requirement, easy fertilizer application, reduction in weeds, increase in cultivable area, efficient & uniform irrigation, suitable to large farmers, convenience in irrigation, can have good yield even in drought, useful if frequent power failure, possibility of multiratooning have been considered. The sample farmers have been required to assess each factor on its own significance. The factors to influence in cultivation of sugarcane under drip irrigation are narrated with the help of factor analysis and results of analysis are shown in Table 4.1.

Table 4.1: KMO and Bartlett's Test

Kaiser-Meyer-Olkin Measure of Sampling Adequacy		0.681
Bartlett's Test of Sphericity	Approx. Chi-Square	1972.26
	Sig.	0.000

Table 4.1 reveals that the measured value of Kaiser-Meyer-Olkin measure of sampling adequacy is 0.681 which is greater than 0.50. So, that ensures the appropriateness of sampling. Hence, it is decided to apply the Factor Analysis.

Rotated Component Matrix

The score of the variable leading to factors influencing the farmers to cultivate sugarcane under drip irrigation system have been included for the factor analysis. The rotated component matrixes for the influencing variables are given in Table 4.2.

Table 4.2: Factors Influencing the Farmers to Cultivate Sugarcane under Drip Irrigation System-Rotated Component Matrix

	Component		
VARIABLES	**1**	**2**	**3**
Efficient and uniform irrigation	**0.944**	0.056	0.213
Water saving	**0.884**	0.451	0.352
Useful if frequent power failure	**0.839**	0.396	0.334
Convenience in irrigation	**0.788**	0.255	0.073
No drainage requirement	**0.791**	0.235	0.070
Reduction in weeds	-0.178	**0.842**	0.334
Less labour requirements	0.419	**0.835**	0.326
Increase in cultivable area	0.412	**0.828**	0.284
Easy fertilizer application	0.258	**0.773**	0.417
Flexibility	0.382	**0.715**	0.157
Minimum work	0.089	**0.690**	0.466
Suitable to large farmers	-0.053	**0.647**	0.588
High yielding	0.056	0.213	**0.942**
Can have good yield in even drought	-0.049	0.087	**0.934**
Possibility of multiratooning	0.067	0.328	**0.886**
Long term usages	0.588	-0.053	**0.647**
To get subsidy from the Government	0.263	0.292	**0.512**

Extraction Method : Principal Component Analysis

Rotation Method: Varimax with Kaiser Normalization

The factor analysis narrated the seventeen variables into three factors namely Irrigation, maintenance and yield. The highly correlated variable of the Irrigation factor is 'Efficient and uniform irrigation'. It has the factor loading of 0.944. The variable 'Reduction in weeds' is the highly correlated variable of the Maintenance factor since it has the highest factor loading of 0.842. 'High yielding' variable of the Yield factor has the highest factor loading of 0.942.

The number of variables in each factor, Eigen value and the per cent of variation explained by each factor are presented in Table 4.3.

Table 4.3: Factors Influencing the Farmers to Cultivate Sugarcane under Drip Irrigation System - Principal Component Analysis

S. No.	Factors	Number of variables	Eigen value	Per cent of Variation explained	Cumulative per cent of Variation explained
1	Irrigation	5	7.944	37.827	37.827
2	Maintenance	7	5.629	26.805	64.632
3	Yield	5	3.744	17.827	82.460

The most important factors influencing the farmers to cultivate sugarcane under drip irrigation system are 'Irrigation factors' and 'Maintenance factors' since their Eigen values are 7.944 and 5.629 respectively. The Irrigation factors consists of five variables with the variation explained by 37.827 per cent. The Maintenance factor consists of seven variables with the variation explained by 26.805 per cent. The third factor is 'Yield factor' since its respective Eigen value is 3.744 and it also consists of five variables with the percent of variation explained by this factor is 17.827.

It is concluded that irrigation factors are influencing the farmers to adopt the drip irrigation system in sugarcane cultivation.

4.3. Satisfaction of Farmers in Adoption of Drip Irrigation System

In the present study, by considering the importance and benefits on drip irrigation in sugarcane cultivation, an attempt is made to analyse the farmers' satisfaction about the adoption of drip irrigation system in sugarcane cultivation. The level of satisfaction of farmers about the adoption of drip irrigation system in sugarcane cultivation has been analysed with the help of χ^2 test, F- test, Z-test and multiple regression analysis.

4.3.1. Quantification and Scoring Procedure

To measure the level of satisfaction of the farmers about the adoption of drip irrigation system in sugarcane cultivation, Rensis Likert's summated five point scaling technique has been adopted. Fifteen statements relating to the adoption of drip irrigation system in sugarcane cultivation have been constructed and included in interview schedule. All these statements are generated on the basis of the experience gained during the pilot study and also based on review of relevant literature.

The farmers have been asked to indicate their satisfaction regarding each statement in the likert's 5 point scale. The scale values 5, 4, 3, 2 and 1 have been used to measure the satisfaction level of the sample farmers. The scale value 5 indicates 'Highly Satisfied', 4 indicates 'Satisfied', 3 indicates 'Neutral', 2 indicates Dissatisfied and the scale value 1 indicates that the farmers are 'Highly Dissatisfied' about the statements. The scores of 123 farmers have been calculated. An individual's score is the mere summation of the scores secured from the 15 statements. The expected score of the farmers ranged from 15 to 75. The average score is 45.

Further, for the purpose of analysis based on the satisfaction average score, the farmers have been grouped into two viz., low satisfaction and high satisfaction. The farmers who have scored between 15 and 45 are classified as 'Low satisfaction'. The farmers who have scored between 46 and 75 are classified as 'High satisfaction'. Table 4.4 represents the distribution of farmers based on their level of satisfaction.

Table 4.4: Distribution of Farmers based on their Satisfaction Level

Satisfaction level	Number of farmers	Average satisfaction Score	S.D
Low (15-45)	44(35.77)	53.45	16.703
High (46-75)	79(64.23)	79.69	3.081
Total	**123 (100.00)**	**70.31**	**16.245**

(Figures in parentheses represent percentages)

Table 4.4 shows that the average satisfaction scores of 123 farmers are 70.31. Among 123 farmers, 79(64.23%) farmers have high level of satisfaction and 44 (35.77%) farmers have low level of satisfaction about the adoption of drip irrigation system in sugarcane cultivation. Therefore, it is concluded that majority (64.23%) of the farmers are highly satisfied with the adoption of drip irrigation system in sugarcane cultivation.

4.3.2. *Relationship between Independent Variables of the Farmers and their Satisfaction Level about the Adoption of Drip Irrigation System in Sugarcane Cultivation*

An attempt has been made in this chapter to examine the relationship between the personal & socio-economic characteristics of the farmers and their level of satisfaction about the adoption of drip irrigation system in sugarcane cultivation for which the following null hypothesis has been framed.

H_0: There is no significant relationship between the personal and socio-economic characteristics (Age, Educational level, Occupation, Nature of family, Size of the family, Number of family members involved in Agriculture, Annual Income, Annual Expenditure, Experience in Agriculture, Experience in Sugarcane Cultivation, Sources of water for drip irrigation, Methods of drip irrigation) of the farmers and their level of satisfaction about the adoption of drip irrigation system in sugarcane cultivation. This hypothesis has been tested by using χ^2- test, F-test, Z-test and multiple regression analysis.

4.3.3. *Age and Satisfaction Level*

Age is an important factor which may influence the farmers to adopt the drip irrigation system in sugarcane cultivation. The young and middle aged farmers may be more aware than the old aged farmers as they like to reap more benefits within the available resources by way of using modern technology, new varieties and drip irrigation etc., On the other hand, old aged farmers may be well experienced in agriculture and it may influence to adopt of drip irrigation. For the purpose of analysis, the farmers have been classified into three categories according to their age viz., Young (upto 30 years), Middle (31 and 50 years) and Old (above 50 years). Table 4.5 exhibits the distribution of the farmers on the basis of age and their satisfaction level.

Table 4.5: Age and Satisfaction Level: χ^2- TEST

Age	Satisfaction Level		Total
	Low	High	
Young	9(60.00)	6(40.00)	15(100.00)
Middle	19(29.20)	46(70.80)	65(100.00)
Old	16(37.20)	27(62.80)	43(100.00)
Total	**44 (35.80)**	**79 (64.20)**	**123 (100.00)**

χ^2= 5.081 DF -2 Table Value- 2.706 @10% (Figures in Parentheses represent Percentage)

Table 4.5 reveals that among the three age groups of farmers, a high percentage (70.8%) of middle aged group farmers have high level of satisfaction about the adoption of drip irrigation system in sugarcane cultivation as compared to old and young aged group.

The calculated value of chi square (5.081) is more than the table value (2.706) for degrees of freedom 2 at 10 per cent level of significance. Hence, the hypothesis is not accepted. Therefore, it can be concluded that there is a significant relationship between age group of farmers and their satisfaction level. Table 4.6 gives results of 'F' test for Age and average satisfaction score.

Table 4.6: Age and Satisfaction: F-test

Age	Number of farmers	Per cent	Average Score	F-Value
Young	15	12.20	63.60	6.126*
Middle	65	52.85	73.40	
Old	43	34.95	67.98	
Total	**123**	**100.00**	**70.31**	

* Significant at 5% level, Table Value - 2.99

Table 4.6 displays that the average score of middle aged group farmers (73.40) is higher than the other two groups. The calculated value of 'F' (6.126) is more than the table value (2.99) for 2 & 120 degrees of freedom at 5 per cent level of significance. Hence, the hypothesis is not accepted. Therefore, it can be concluded that the relationship between the average satisfaction score of different groups of farmers according to their age and their satisfaction level is significant.

4.3.4. *Educational Level and Satisfaction Level*

Education is a vital factor for the socio economic development. An education not only widens knowledge but also helps a person to make use of rational and scientific approach to solve problems. In rural areas, most of the farmers do not have the record up-to-date information on how to produce efficiently and economically. Therefore, it is expected that there may be a relationship between Educational level of the farmers and their level of satisfaction about the adoption of drip irrigation system in sugarcane cultivation. Hence, an attempt is made to examine the relationship between the Educational level and level of satisfaction. For the purpose of analysis, the farmers have been classified into three groups' according to their educational level viz., No formal education, School level education and College level education. Table 4.7 exhibits the distribution of the farmers on the basis of Educational level and their satisfaction level.

Table 4.7: Educational Level and Satisfaction Level: χ2- Test

Educational level	Satisfaction Level		Total
	Low	High	
No formal education	14(58.30)	10(41.70)	24(100.00)
School level	10(18.50)	44(81.50)	54(100.00)
College level	20(44.40)	25(55.60)	45(100.00)
Total	**44 (35.80)**	**79 (64.20)**	**123 (100.00)**

χ2 - 13.787   DF-2 Table Value - 5.991 @5% (Figures in Parentheses represent Percentage)

Table 4.7 clearly indicates that among the three Educational level groups of farmers, a high percentage (81.50%) of school level educated farmers have high level of satisfaction as compared to groups.

It is found that the calculated value of chi-square (13.787) is more than the table value (5.991) for degrees of freedom 2 at 5 per cent level of significance. Hence, the hypothesis is not accepted. Therefore, it is evident that there exists a significant relationship between the Educational level of farmer and their level of satisfaction about the adoption of drip irrigation system in sugarcane cultivation. Table 4.8 gives results of 'F' test for Educational level and average satisfaction score.

Table 4.8: Educational Level and Satisfaction: F-Test

Educational level	Number of Farmers	Per cent	Average Score	F-Value
No formal education	24	19.51	60.75	9.390*
School level	54	43.90	76.33	
College level	45	36.59	68.18	
Total	**123**	**100.00**	**70.31**	

* Significant at 5% level, Table Value - 2.99

Table 4.8 indicates that the average score of school level education farmers (76.33) is higher than the other level of education. It is found that the calculated value of 'F' (9.390) is more than the table value (2.99) for 2 & 120 degrees of freedom at 5 per cent level of significance. Hence, the hypothesis is not accepted. Therefore, it is concluded that there is a significant relationship between the average satisfaction score of different groups of farmers according to their Educational level and their satisfaction.

4.3.5. Occupation and Satisfaction Level

The occupation of the farmers may influence the level of satisfaction about the adoption of drip irrigation system. Most of the people are engaged in agriculture with other occupation such as business, employment and profession. Hence, it is decided to analyse the relationship between the occupation of the farmers and their satisfaction level. Table 4.9 exhibits the distribution of the farmers on the basis of occupation and their satisfaction level.

Table 4.9: Occupation and Satisfaction Level: χ2- Test

Occupation	Satisfaction Level		Total
	Low	High	
Agriculture only	25 (39.70)	38 (60.30)	63 (100.00)
Agriculture &others	19 (31.70)	41 (68.30)	60 (100.00)
Total	**44 (35.80)**	**79 (64.20)**	**123 (100.00)**

χ2– 0.859 DF- 1 Table Value - 3.841 @ 5%, (Figures in Parentheses represent Percentage)

Table 4.9 indicates that among the occupation groups of farmers, a high percentage (68.30%) of the farmers belonging to Agriculture & others group has high level of satisfaction as compared to those farmers who engaged in Agriculture only.

It is found that the calculated value of Chi-square (0.859) is less than the table value (3.841) for 1 degree of freedom at 5 per cent level of significance. Hence, the hypothesis is accepted. Therefore, it is concluded that there is no significant association between the occupation of the farmers and their satisfaction level about the adoption of drip irrigation system in sugarcane cultivation. Table 4.10 gives the results of 'Z' test for occupation and average satisfaction score.

Table 4.10: Occupation and Satisfaction : Z-Test

Occupation	Number of Farmers	Per cent	Average Score	Z-Value
Agriculture only	63	51.22	70.71	0.534
Agriculture &others	60	48.78	69.88	
Total	**123**	**100.00**	**70.31**	

Table Value - 2.99

Table 4.10 indicates that the average score of farmers belonging to Agriculture only (70.71) is higher than the farmers belonging to Agriculture & others. It is found that the calculated value of 'Z' (0.534) is less than the table value (2.99) for 2 & 121 degrees of freedom at 5 per cent level of significance. Hence, the hypothesis is accepted. Therefore, it is concluded that there is no significant relationship between the average satisfaction score of different groups of farmers according to their occupation and their satisfaction level.

4.3.6. Nature of the Family and Satisfaction Level

Generally, family environment decides various aspects of agriculture activities. It is common view that nature of the family (either joint family or nuclear family) affects the farmers' satisfaction about the adoption of drip irrigation system in sugarcane cultivation. An attempt has been made to examine the association between the nature of the family and satisfaction about the adoption of the drip irrigation system. Table 4.11 exhibits the distribution of the farmers on the basis of nature of the family and their satisfaction level.

Table 4.11: Nature of the Family and Satisfaction Level : χ2- Test

Nature of the Family	Satisfaction Level		Total
	Low	High	
Joint	31 (47.00)	35(53.00)	66(100.00)
Nuclear	13(22.80)	44(77.20)	57(100.00)
Total	**44(35.80)**	**79(64.20)**	**123(100.00)**

χ2– 7.772 DF- 1 Table Value - 3.841 @ 5%, (Figures in Parentheses represent Percentage)

Table 4.11 shows that among the family groups, a high percentage (77.20%) of the farmers belonging to nuclear family group has high level of satisfaction on adoption of drip irrigation system in sugarcane cultivation as compared to joint family group.

It is found that the calculated value of chi-square (7.772) exceeds the table value (3.841) for 1 degree of freedom at 5 per cent level of significance. Hence, the hypothesis is not accepted. Therefore, it is concluded that there is a significant association between the nature of the family of the farmers and their satisfaction level. Table 4.12 gives the results of 'Z' test for nature of the family and average satisfaction score.

Table 4.12: Nature of the Family and Satisfaction : Z-Test

Nature of the Family	Number of Farmers	Per cent	Average Scores	Z-Value
Joint	66	53.66	69.15	
Nuclear	57	46.34	71.65	4.017*
Total	**123**	**100.00**	**70.31**	

* Significant at 5% level, Table Value - 2.99

Table 4.12 indicates that the average score of the farmers belonging to nuclear family (71.65) is higher than the farmers belonging to joint family. It is found that the calculated value of 'Z' (4.017) is more than the table value (2.99) for 2 & 121 degrees of freedom at 5 per cent level of significance. Hence, the hypothesis is not accepted. Therefore, it is concluded that there is a significant relationship between the average satisfaction score of different groups of farmers according to their nature of the family and their satisfaction level.

4.3.7. Size of the Family and Satisfaction Level

A family is defined as a group of persons, all related to each other. The number of members in it constitutes a family's size. If there is more number of members in the family, it is possible to do some activities which concerns about the adoption of drip irrigation in sugarcane cultivation. The size of the family reflects on the economic status of the farmers and this plays an important role in determining the viability of agricultural economy. Number of members in the farmers' family ranged from 2 to 8. The role played by size of the family in satisfaction of the farmers about the adoption of drip irrigation is considered as relevant. It is felt that there would be an association between the size of family and satisfaction. In this regard, farmers are divided into three groups' according to their size of the family viz., Small (family with 3 members), Medium (family with 4 to 6 members) and Large (family with above 6 members). Table 4.13 exhibits the distribution of the farmers on the basis of size of the family and their satisfaction level.

Table 4.13: Size of the Family and Satisfaction Level: χ2- TEST

Size of the family	Satisfaction Level		Total
	Low	High	
Small	7(15.20)	39(84.80)	46(100.00)
Medium	24(40.00)	36(60.00)	60(100.00)
Large	13(76.50)	4(23.50)	17(100.00)
Total	**44(35.80)**	**79(64.20)**	**123(100.00)**

χ2 – 21.181 DF- 2 Table Value - 5.991 @ 5% (Figures in Parentheses represent Percentage)

Table 4.13 indicates that among the three groups, a high percentage (84.80%) of the farmers who belongs to small family have high level of satisfaction about the adoption of drip irrigation system in sugarcane cultivation as compared to other two groups.

It is found that the calculated value of chi-square (21.181) exceeds the table value (5.991) for 2 degrees of freedom at 5 per cent level of significance. Hence, the hypothesis is not accepted. Therefore, it is concluded that there is a significant association between the size of the family of the farmers and their satisfaction level. Table 4.14 gives the results of 'F' test for the size of the family and average satisfaction score.

Table 4.14: Size of the Family and Satisfaction: F-Test

Size of the family	Number of Farmers	Per cent	Average Score	F-Value
Small	46	37.40	73.80	4.147*
Medium	60	48.78	69.83	
Large	17	13.82	62.53	
Total	**123**	**100.00**	**70.31**	

* Significant at 5% level, Table Value - 2.99

Table 4.14 depicts that the average score (73.80) of the farmers belonging to small family is higher than the other two groups. It is found that the calculated value of 'F' (4.147) is more than the table value (2.99) for 2 & 120 degrees of freedom at 5 per cent level of significance. Hence, the hypothesis is not accepted. Therefore, it is concluded that there is a significant relationship between the average satisfaction score of different groups of farmers according to their size of the family of farmers and their satisfaction level.

4.3.8. Number of Members Involved in Agriculture and Satisfaction Level

Number of family members involved in agriculture may influence the level of satisfaction of farmers towards the adoption of drip irrigation system. When there are more family members involved in sugarcane cultivation, there is a scope for adoption of drip irrigation by having discussions with each other as every one of them is well experienced. Table 4.15 exhibits the distribution of the farmers on the basis of number of members involved in agriculture and their satisfaction level.

Table 4.15: Number of Members Involved in Agriculture and Satisfaction Level: χ2- TEST

Number of members	Satisfaction Level		Total
	Low	High	
Upto 3 members	31(51.70)	29(48.30)	60(100.00)
Above 3members	13(20.60)	50(79.40)	63(100.00)
Total	44(35.80)	79(64.20)	123(100.00)

χ2 – 12.880 DF- 1   Table Value - 3.841 @ 5% (Figures in Parentheses represent Percentage)

Table 4.15 shows that among the above two groups of farmers, a high percentage (79.40%) of the farmers belonging to above 3 members involved in agriculture group has high level of satisfaction on adoption of drip irrigation system in sugarcane cultivation as compared to upto 3 members group.

It is found that the calculated value of Chi-square (12.880) is more than the table value (3.841) for degree of freedom 1at 5 per cent level of significance. Hence, the hypothesis is not accepted. Therefore, it is concluded that there is a significant association between number of members involved in agriculture of farmers' family and their satisfaction level. Table 4.16 gives the results of 'Z' test for number of members involved in agriculture and average satisfaction score.

Table 4.16: Number of Members Involved in Agriculture and Satisfaction: Z-Test

Number of members	Number of Farmers	Per cent	Average Score	Z-Value
Upto 3 members	60	48.78	66.18	-3.18*
Above 3 members	63	51.22	74.24	
Total	123	100.00	70.31	

* Significant at 5% level, Table Value - 2.99

Table 4.16 indicates that the average score (74.24) of the farmers with above 4members involved in agriculture is higher than the other group of farmers. It is found that the calculated value of 'Z' (-3.18) is more than the table value (2.99) for 2 & 121 degrees of freedom at 5 per cent level of significance. Hence, the hypothesis is not accepted. Therefore, it is concluded that there is a significant relationship between number of members involved in agriculture in farmers' family and their satisfaction level.

4.3.9. *Annual Income and Satisfaction Level*

Income plays a vital role in the growth of the family. Every family depends on its income for its survival and growth. Annual income of the farmers is one of the important criteria which may influence the level of satisfaction. On the basis of annual income the farmers have been classified into three groups' viz., Low income group (below ₹ 100000), Medium income group (₹ 100000 to ₹ 300000) and High income group (above ₹ 300000). Table 4.17 exhibits the distribution of the farmers on the basis of annual income and their satisfaction level.

Table 4.17: Annual Income and Satisfaction Level: χ2- Test

Annual income	Satisfaction Level		Total
	Low	High	
Low income	20(38.50)	32(61.50)	52(100.00)
Medium income	4(12.90)	27(87.10)	31(100.00)
High income	20(50.00)	20(50.00)	40(100.00)
Total	**44(35.80)**	**79(64.20)**	**123(100.00)**

χ2 –10.744 DF- 2 Table Value - 5.991 @ 5%, (Figures in Parentheses represent Percentage)

Table 4.17 reveals that among the three income groups of farmers, a high percentage (87.10%) of the farmers belonging to medium income group have high level of satisfaction on adoption of drip irrigation system in sugarcane cultivation as compared to other two income groups.

It is found that the calculated value of chi-square (10.744) is more than the table value (5.991) for degrees of freedom 2at 5 per cent level of significance. Hence, the hypothesis is not accepted. Therefore, it is concluded that there is a significant association between the annual income of the family of the farmers and their satisfaction level. Table 4.18 gives the results of 'F' test for annual income and average satisfaction score.

Table 4.18: Annual Income and Satisfaction: F-Test

Annual Income	Number of Farmers	Per cent	Average Score	F-Value
Low income	52	42.28	69.62	4.32*
Medium income	31	25.20	76.29	
High income	40	32.52	66.58	
Total	**123**	**100.00**	**70.31**	

* Significant at 5% level, Table Value - 2.99

Table 4.18 indicates that the average score (76.29) of medium income group farmers is higher than the other two groups of farmers. It is found that the calculated value of 'F' (4.32) is more than the table value (2.99) for 2 & 120 degrees of freedom at 5 per cent level of significance. Hence, the hypothesis is not accepted. Therefore, it is concluded that there is a significant relationship between annual income of farmers and their satisfaction level.

4.3.10. Annual Expenditure and Satisfaction Level

It is perceived that the annual expenditure of the farmers would likely influence the farmer's adoption of drip irrigation in sugarcane cultivation. In the present study, the annual expenditure refers to farmers expenses in all activities both agricultural and non-agricultural. On the basis of annual expenditure, the farmers have been classified into three groups' viz., Low expenditure (below ₹ 100000), Medium expenditure (₹100000 to ₹ 300000) and High expenditure (above ₹ 300000). Table 4.19 exhibits the distribution of the farmers on the basis of annual expenditure and their satisfaction level.

Table 4.19: Annual Expenditure and Satisfaction Level: χ2- Test

Annual Expenditure	Satisfaction Level		Total
	Low	High	
Low expenditure	20(38.50)	32(61.50)	52(100.00)
Medium expenditure	11(21.60)	40(78.40)	51(100.00)
High expenditure	13(65.00)	7(35.00)	20(100.00)
Total	**44(35.80)**	**79(64.20)**	**123(100.00)**

χ2 – 12.078 DF- 2 Table Value - 5.991 @ 5%, (Figures in Parentheses represent Percentage)

Table 4.19 reveals that among three expenditure groups of the farmers, a high percentage (78.40%) of the farmers belonging to medium expenditure group have high level of satisfaction on adoption of drip irrigation system in sugarcane cultivation as compared to other two expenditure groups.

It is found that the calculated value of chi-square (12.078) is greater than the table value (5.991) for degrees of freedom 2 at 5 per cent level of significance. Hence, the hypothesis is not accepted. Therefore, it is concluded that there is a significant association between the annual expenditure of the family of the farmers and their satisfaction level. Table 4.20 gives the results of 'F' test for annual expenditure and average satisfaction score.

Table 4.20: Annual Expenditure and Satisfaction: F-Test

Annual Expenditure	Number of Farmers	Per cent	Average Score	F-Value
Low expenditure	52	42.28	69.62	4.426*
Medium expenditure	51	41.46	75.43	
High expenditure	20	16.26	59.05	
Total	**123**	**100.00**	**70.31**	

* Significant at 5% level, Table Value - 2.99

Table 4.20 indicates that the average score (75.43) of medium expenditure group of farmers is higher than the other two expenditure groups of farmers. It is found that the calculated value of 'F' (4.426) is more than the table value (2.99) for 2 & 120 degrees of freedom at 5 per cent level of significance. Hence, the hypothesis is not accepted. Therefore, it is concluded that there is a significant relationship between annual expenditure of farmers and their satisfaction level.

4.3.11. Experience in Agriculture and Satisfaction Level

The farm experience of the farmers would play a significant role to induce the farmers to adopt the drip irrigation in sugarcane cultivation. Due to experience, farmers can assess the natures, quality, availability, cost and the benefits in adoption of drip irrigation. Hence, an attempt has been made to examine the relationship between their experience in agriculture and their level of satisfaction towards the adoption of drip irrigation in sugarcane cultivation. For the purpose of analysis, the farmers have been grouped into three categories based on their experience in agriculture viz., Low experience (upto 10 years), Medium experience (10-20 years) and High experience (above 20 years). Table 4.21 exhibits the distribution of the farmers on the basis of experience in agriculture and their satisfaction level.

Table 4.21: Experience in Agriculture and Satisfaction Level: χ^2- Test

Experience in Agriculture	Satisfaction Level		Total
	Low	High	
Low experience	11(35.50)	20(64.50)	31(100.00)
Medium experience	11(34.40)	21(65.60)	32(100.00)
High experience	22(36.70)	38(63.30)	60(100.00)
Total	**44(35.80)**	**79(64.20)**	**123(100.00)**

χ^2 - 0.049 DF- 2 Table Value - 5.991 @ 5% (Figures in Parentheses represent Percentage)

Table 4.21 states that among three experience groups of the farmers, a high percentage (65.60%) of the farmers who belong to medium experience group have high level of satisfaction about the adoption of drip irrigation system in sugarcane cultivation as compared to other two experience groups of farmers. It is found that the calculated value of chi-square (0.049) is less than the table value (5.991) for degrees of freedom 2 at 5 per cent level of significance. Hence, the hypothesis is accepted. Therefore, it is concluded that there is no significant association between the experience in agriculture of the farmers and their satisfaction level. Table 4.22 gives the results of 'F' test for experience in agriculture and average satisfaction score.

Table 4.22: Experience in Agriculture and Satisfaction: F-Test

Experience in Agriculture	Number of Farmers	Per cent	Average Score	F-Value
Low experience	31	25.20	67.90	0.457
Medium experience	32	26.02	70.84	
High experience	60	48.78	71.27	
Total	**123**	**100.00**	**70.31**	

Table Value - 2.99

Table 4.22 indicates that the average score (71.27) of high experience group of farmers is higher than the other two experience groups of farmers. It is found that the calculated value of 'F' (0.457) is less than the table value (2.99) for 2 & 120 degrees of freedom at 5 per cent level of significance. Hence, the hypothesis is accepted. Therefore, it is concluded that there is no significant relationship between experience in agriculture of farmers and their satisfaction level.

4.3.12. Experience in Sugarcane Cultivation and Satisfaction Level

The experience of the farmers in sugarcane cultivation plays a significant role in adoption of drip irrigation in sugarcane cultivation. They assess the crop difficulties, need to adopt the drip irrigation, benefits of drip irrigation in sugarcane cultivation. Hence, an attempt has been made to examine the relationship between the experience of the farmers in cultivation of sugarcane and their level of satisfaction towards the adoption of drip irrigation system in sugarcane cultivation. For the purpose of analysis, the farmers have been divided into three groups' on the basis of their experience in sugarcane cultivation viz., Low experience (upto 10 years), Medium experience (10-20 years) and High experience (above 20 years). Table 4.23 exhibits the distribution of the farmers on the basis of Experience in sugarcane cultivation and their satisfaction level.

Table 4.23: Experience in Sugarcane Cultivation and Satisfaction Level: χ2- TEST

Experience in Sugarcane Cultivation	Satisfaction Level		Total
	Low	**High**	
Low experience	15(44.10)	19(55.90)	34(100.00)
Medium experience	5(16.10)	26(83.90)	31(100.00)
High experience	24(41.40)	34(58.60)	58(100.00)
Total	44(35.80)	79(64.20)	123(100.00)

χ2 – 7.030 DF- 2 Table Value - 5.991 @ 5% (Figures in Parentheses represent Percentage)

Table 4.23 states among three experience groups of farmers, a high percentage (83.90 per cent) of famers belong to medium experience in sugarcane cultivation have high level of satisfaction about the adoption of drip irrigation system in sugarcane cultivation as compared to other two experience groups of farmers.

It is found that the calculated value of Chi-square (7.030) is more than the table value (5.991) for degrees of freedom 2 at 5 per cent level of significance. Hence, the hypothesis is not accepted. Therefore, it is concluded that there is a significant association between the experience in sugarcane cultivation of the farmers and their level of satisfaction. Table 4.24 gives the results of 'F' test for experience in sugarcane cultivation and average satisfaction score.

Table 4.24: Experience in Sugarcane Cultivation and Satisfaction: F-Test

Experience in Sugarcane Cultivation	Number of Farmers	Per cent	Average Score	F-Value
Low experience	34	27.64	64.41	5.856*
Medium experience	31	25.20	77.65	
High experience	58	47.15	69.84	
Total	**123**	**100.00**	**70.31**	

* Significant at 5% level, Table Value - 2.99

Table 4.24 indicates that the average score (77.65) of medium experience group of farmers is higher than the other two experience groups of farmers. It is found that the calculated value of 'F' (5.856) is more than the table value (2.99) for 2 & 120 degrees of freedom at 5 per cent level of significance. Hence, the hypothesis is not accepted. Therefore, it is concluded that there is a significant relationship between experience in sugarcane cultivation of farmers and their satisfaction level.

4.3.13. Sources of Water for Drip Irrigation and Satisfaction Level

Sources of irrigation is one of the most important factors which have direct impact on farmers to adopt drip irrigation system. Based on availability of water, one goes to decide whether to adopt drip irrigation or not. By considering this, an attempt has been made to examine the association between the sources of irrigation and level of farmers' satisfaction towards the adoption of drip irrigation system in sugarcane cultivation. In the area, open well source and bore well source are commonly used for adopt the drip irrigation system. Table 4.25 exhibits the distribution of the farmers on the basis of sources of water for drip irrigation and their satisfaction level.

Table 4.25: Sources of Water for Drip Irrigation and Satisfaction Level: χ2- TEST

Sources of water for drip irrigation	Satisfaction Level		Total
	Low	High	
Open well	11(39.30)	17(60.70)	28(100.00)
Bore well	33(34.70)	62(65.30)	95(100.00)
Total	44(35.80)	79(64.20)	123(100.00)

χ2 – 0.195 DF- 1   Table Value - 3.841 @ 5% (Figures in Parentheses represent Percentage)

Table 4.25 reveals that among two sources of water for drip irrigation groups, high percentage (65.30%) of the farmers who use bore well as source of drip irrigation have high level of satisfaction about the adoption of drip irrigation system in sugarcane cultivation as compared to other two groups of farmers.

It is found that the calculated value of chi-square (0.195) is less the table value (3.841) for degree of freedom 1 at 5 per cent level of significance. Hence, the hypothesis is accepted. Therefore, it is concluded that there is no significant association between the sources of water for drip irrigation of the farmers and their satisfaction level. Table 4.26 gives the results of 'Z' test for sources of water for drip irrigation system and average satisfaction score.

Table 4.26: Sources of Water for Drip Irrigation and Satisfaction: Z-Test

Sources of water for drip irrigation	Number of Farmers	Per cent	Average Score	Z-Value
Open well	28	22.76	69.00	0.484
Bore well	95	77.24	70.70	
Total	123	100.00	70.31	

Table Value - 2.99

Table 4.26 indicates that the average score (70.70) of the farmers who belong to bore well as sources of water for drip irrigation of farmers is higher than the other group open well sources of water for drip irrigation of farmers. It is found that the calculated value of 'Z' (0.484) is less than the table value (2.99) for 2 & 121 degrees of freedom at 5 per cent level of significance. Hence, the hypothesis is accepted. Therefore, it is concluded that there is no significant relationship between sources of water for drip irrigation of farmers and their satisfaction level.

4.3.14. Methods of Drip Irrigation and Satisfaction Level

There are two methods of drip irrigation system for sugarcane cultivation. They are: surface drip irrigation and subsurface drip irrigation. In the study area, both methods of drip irrigation system are followed by the sugarcane farmers. Hence, it is decided to analyse the relationship between the farmers' satisfaction towards drip irrigation system in sugarcane cultivation and methods of drip irrigation system they follow for sugarcane cultivation. Table 4.27 exhibits the distribution of the farmers on the basis of methods of drip irrigation and their satisfaction level.

Table 4.27: Methods of Drip Irrigation and Satisfaction Level: $\chi2$- Test

Methods of Drip Irrigation	Satisfaction Level		Total
	Low	High	
Sub-surface	19(47.50)	21(52.50)	40(100.00)
Surface	25(30.10)	58(69.90)	83(100.00)
Total	44 (35.80)	79 (64.20)	123 (100.00)

$\chi2$– 3.548 DF- 1 Table Value - 2.706 @ 10%, (Figures in Parentheses represent Percentage)

Table 4.27 indicates that method of drip irrigation, a high percentage (69.90%) of the farmers' surface drip irrigation methods has high level of satisfaction about the adoption of drip irrigation system in sugarcane cultivation as compared to other sub-surface method of drip irrigation. It is found that the calculated value of Chi-square (3.548) is more than table value (2.706) for degree of freedom 1 at 10 per cent level of significance. Hence, the hypothesis is not accepted. Therefore, it is concluded that there is a significant association between the methods of drip irrigation of the farmers and their satisfaction level. Table 4.28 gives the results of 'Z' test for methods of drip irrigation and average satisfaction score.

Table 4.28: Methods of Drip Irrigation and Satisfaction: Z - Test

Methods of drip irrigation	Number of Farmers	Per cent	Average Score	Z-Value
Sub-surface	40	32.52	69.90	5.136*
Surface	83	67.48	70.51	
Total	123	100.00	70.31	

* Significant at 5% level, Table Value - 2.99

Table 4.28 indicates that the average score (70.51) of the farmers who follow surface methods of drip irrigation is higher than the farmers who follow sub-surface methods of drip irrigation. It is found that the calculated value of 'Z' (5.136) is more than the table value (2.99) for 2 & 121 degrees of freedom at 5 per cent level of significance. Hence, the hypothesis is not accepted. Therefore, it is concluded that there is a significant relationship between methods of drip irrigation of farmers and their satisfaction level.

4.3.15. Satisfaction of Farmers in Adoption of Drip Irrigation System-Multiple Regression Analysis (Step-wise Model)

This section is devoted to a discussion on the variables influencing the satisfaction of the farmers. In this connection, the hypothesis that the satisfaction of the farmers is influenced by Age, Educational level, Nature of the Family, Size of the Family, Number of Members Involved in Agriculture, Experience in Sugarcane Cultivation, earning members in the Family, Annual Income, Annual Expenditure which are tested with the help of Regression Analysis. The test aims at finding out whether the independent variables $(X1, X_2, X_3.....X_9)$ do actually have any significant influence on the dependent variable (Y).

Regression analysis is used to make prediction about the level and type of association exists between two variables. Simple or Bivariate regression analysis is a statistical technique that uses information about the relationship between one independent variables and dependent variables. Regression analysis involves estimating an equation, which is usually a linear one and independent variables are considered to be statistically independent. It is well known that multi-collinearity does not exist in case of large samples[75].

The Multiple Linear Equation is:

$$Y = b_0 + b_1X_1 + b_2X_2 + b_3X_3 + b_4X_4 + b_5X_5 + b_6X_6 + b_7X_7 + b_8X_8 + b_9X_9$$

Where

  Y   = Total Satisfaction score on adoption of drip irrigation system

  X_1 = Number of Members involved in Agriculture

  X_2 = Size of the Family

  X_3 = Experience in Sugarcane Cultivation

  X_4 = Age

---

[75] Srivastava, V. K., Shenoy, G. V. and Sharma, S. C., (1997), Quantitative Techniques for Managerial Decisions, New Delhi: New Age International, p. 345.

X_5 = Educational level

X_6 = Annual Income

X_7 = Nature of the Family

X_8 = Earning members in the family

X_9 = Annual Expenditure

b_0 = Regression constant and

$b_1, b_2, b_3....b_9$ = Regression co-efficient of independent variables

The easiest way to analyse the relationships is to examine the regression co-efficient for each independent variable. These co-efficient describe the average amount of change to be expected in Y given a unit change in the value of the particular independent variable. Moreover, each particular regression co-efficient describes the strength of the relationship between an individual independent variables and the dependent variable.

With the addition of more than one independent variable, a couple of new issues have to be considered. One concern is the possibility that each independent variable may be measured using a different scale. When multiple independent variables are measured with different scales, it is not possible to make relative comparisons between regression co-efficient to see which independent variable has the most influence on the dependent variable.

The results of a regression model are tested to examine the significance that include the R^2, the model F statistic, the individual regression co-efficient for each independent variable, their associate 't' statistics and the individual beta co-efficient. The appropriate procedure to follow in evaluating the results of a regression analysis is as follows: a) assess the statistical significance of the overall regression model by using the F statistic and its associated probability b) evaluate the obtained R^2 to see how large it is andc) examine the individual regression co-efficient to assess relative influence.

In this study, nine independent variables are worked out to ascertain the influence of different sets of independent variables on satisfaction. The regressions are estimated using cross-section data of 123 farmers. In the present study, satisfaction score has been taken as a dependent variable and personal and socio-economic characteristics are taken as independent variables. The results of nine regression equations are summarised in Table 4.29.

Table 4.29: Satisfaction Level: Multiple Regression Analysis (Step Wise Model)

DEPENDENT VARIABLE: TOTAL SATISFACTION ON ADOPTION OF DRIP IRRIGATION SYSTEM IN SUGARCANE CULTIVATION										
		REGRESSION MODEL								
Regressor		I	II	III	IV	V	VI	VII	VIII	IX
Number of members involved in Agriculture	β	2.138	2.285	1.900	2.255	2.960	3.157	2.689	2.908	1.985
	t	3.32	3.69	3.13	3.86	4.91	5.54	4.66	5.06	3.22
Size of the Family	β		-1.828	-2.134	-1.667	-2.310	-2.675	-2.558	-2.430	-2.897
	t		-3.42	-4.08	-3.26	-4.37	-5.26	-5.16	-4.96	-5.91
Experience in Sugarcane Cultivation	β			-1.199	-2.683	-2.385	-2.465	-2.693	-2.547	-2.827
	t			-3.31	-5.10	-4.64	-5.08	-5.64	-5.38	-6.13
Age	β				0.176	0.2170	0.241	0.247	0.221	0.159
	t				3.74	4.61	5.38	5.66	4.98	3.43
Educational level	β					2.830	7.742	7.890	7.522	8.162
	t					3.23	5.21	5.47	5.28	5.92
Annual Income	β						-2.855	-3.097	-3.010	-7.293
	t						-3.98	-4.41	-4.37	-5.06
Nature of the Family (Nuclear)	β							-1.730	-1.709	-2.929
	t							-2.89	-2.87	-4.32
Earnings Members in the family	β								-1.127	-2.033
	t								-2.29	-3.74
Annual Expenditure	β									4.640
	t									3.34
Summary Statistics and Join Tests										
SER		4.098	3.928	3.775	3.585	3.45	3.25	3.155	3.099	2.969
R		0.289	0.406	0.485	0.562	0.610	0.669	0.695	0.712	0.742
R^2		**0.083**	**0.165**	**0.235**	**0.316**	**0.372**	**0.447**	**0.484**	**0.506**	**0.551**
Adjusted R^2		0.076	0.151	0.216	0.293	0.345	0.419	0.452	0.472	0.515
N		123	123	123	123	123	123	123	123	123

From the Table 4.29 the various multiple regression analysis for farmers satisfaction reveals that the model fit increases from 0.289 to 0.742 by adding more variables such as Number of members involved in Agriculture, Size of the Family, Experience in Sugarcane Cultivation, Age, Educational level, Annual Income, Nature of the Family, Earning members in the family, Annual Expenditure to the independent variable in a step-by-step process. The adjusted R square also shows an increase from 0.076 to 0.515. This indicates that the increasing trend of nine independent variables is significant in affecting satisfaction level of drip irrigation system in sugarcane cultivation.

4.4. Problems Faced by the Farmers in Adoption of Drip Irrigation System in Sugarcane Cultivation

Most of the farmers faced the problems in adoption of drip irrigation system in sugarcane cultivation. Against this background, an attempt has been made to identify and evaluate the problems in adoption of drip irrigation system in sugarcane cultivation by the farmers. Based on the pilot study, it is understood that there are ten problems in adoption of drip irrigation system in sugarcane cultivation in the area. These problems such as improper after sales service, risk in application of fertilizer, used only for one crop, not suitable for small land holding, problems in getting subsidies, rat, rodent, insect & human damage to drip lines, problems in drip equipment, high maintenance charges, risk during the period of harvest, need of acid treatment. These problems are included in the interview schedule, farmers are asked to rank these problems on the basis of significance.

Scale values as per Garrett ranking technique for first to ten ranks are: 81.86, 70.37, 63.30, 57.61, 52.49, 47.52, 42.39, 36.70, 29.63 and 18.14 respectively. The percentage position of each rank is made into score by referring problems and summed up for assigning ranks. Table 4.30 shows the problems faced by the farmers in adoption of drip irrigation system in sugarcane cultivation as per Garrett Ranking Technique.

Table 4.30: Problems Faced by Farmers in Adoption of Drip Irrigation System in Sugarcane Cultivation - Garrett Ranking Technique

S.No	PROBLEMS	Ranks	SCALE AND SCORE VALUES OF RANKS										Total score	Mean score	Rank

S.No	PROBLEMS	Ranks	I	II	III	IV	V	VI	VII	VIII	IX	X	Total score	Mean score	Rank
		Scale Value (x)	81.86	70.37	63.30	57.61	52.49	47.52	42.39	36.70	29.63	18.14			
1	Improper after sales service	F	2	4	9	7	6	11	2	42	23	17	123	39.61	IX
		FX	163.72	281.48	569.70	403.27	314.94	522.72	84.78	1541.40	681.49	308.38	4871.88		
2	Risk in application of fertilizer	F	4	5	10	18	20	28	18	11	6	3	123	49.83	V
		FX	327.44	351.85	633.00	1036.98	1049.80	1330.56	763.02	403.70	177.78	54.42	6128.55		
3	Used only for one crop	F	3	6	8	4	2	14	42	23	13	8	123	43.33	VII
		FX	245.58	422.22	506.40	230.44	104.98	665.28	1780.38	844.10	385.19	145.12	5329.69		
4	Not suitable for small land holding	F	2	8	9	3	14	10	4	11	20	42	123	37.46	X
		FX	163.72	562.96	569.70	172.83	734.86	475.20	169.56	403.70	592.60	761.88	4607.01		
5	Problems in getting subsidies	F	5	6	4	12	12	16	4	5	37	22	123	40.77	VIII
		FX	409.30	422.22	253.20	691.32	629.88	760.32	169.56	183.50	1096.31	399.08	5014.69		
6	Rat, rodent, insect & human damage to drip lines	f	2	6	47	30	13	8	7	2	4	4	123	56.20	IV
		FX	163.72	422.22	2975.10	1728.30	682.37	380.16	296.73	73.40	118.52	72.56	6913.08		
7	Problems in drip equipment	F	4	2	5	12	35	20	19	5	5	16	123	46.27	VI
		FX	327.44	140.74	316.50	691.32	1837.15	950.40	805.41	183.50	148.15	290.24	5690.85		
8	High maintenance charges	F	38	25	4	12	8	5	11	9	4	7	123	61.09	II
		FX	3110.68	1759.25	253.20	691.32	419.92	237.60	466.29	330.30	118.52	126.98	7514.06		
9	Risk during the period of harvest	F	46	29	14	5	7	4	7	4	5	2	123	66.39	I
		FX	3765.56	2040.73	886.20	288.05	367.43	190.08	296.73	146.80	148.15	36.28	8166.01		
10	Need of acid treatment	F	17	32	13	20	6	7	9	11	6	2	123	59.07	III
		FX	1391.62	2251.84	822.90	1152.20	314.94	332.64	381.51	403.70	177.78	36.28	7265.41		

Source: Primary Data

Table 4.30 clearly indicates that the 'Risk during the period of harvest' is the most important problem with the highest mean score value of 66.39 under Garrett ranking technique. 'High maintenance charges' (61.09) has been identified as the second most important problem. The third rank has been given to the problem of Need of acid treatment (59.07). 'Not suitable for small land holding' has got the least mean score (37.46) among the ten problems listed. Thus, it may be concluded that as per the Garrett Ranking technique, Risk during the period of harvest is identified as the most significant problem in adoption of drip irrigation system in sugarcane cultivation.

4.5. Reasons for Non-adoption of Drip Irrigation System in Sugarcane Cultivation

In the present study, out of total farmers, majority (79.50 per cent) of the farmers have not adopted the drip irrigation system in sugarcane cultivation. For non-adoption of drip irrigation system in sugarcane cultivation, the reasons are: availability of adequate water, high risk in sugarcane crop, inadequate finance, high maintenance and investment cost, reduce soil fertility and imbalanced land. In order to identify the significant reason for non-adoption of drip irrigation system in sugarcane cultivation, Garrett ranking technique has been applied. Scale values as per Garrett ranking technique for first to six ranks are: 77.00, 63.30, 54.15, 46.85, 36.70 and 23.00 respectively. The percentage position of each rank is made into score by referring reasons and summed up for assigning rank. The results of the analysis are presented in Table 4.31.

Table 4.31: Reasons for Non-adoption of Drip Irrigation System in Sugarcane Cultivation - Garrett Ranking Technique

			SCALE AND SCORE VALUES OF RANKS								
S. No	Reasons	Ranks	I	II	III	IV	V	VI	Total Score	Mean score	Rank
		Score value (x)	77.00	63.30	54.15	46.85	36.70	23.00			
1	Availability of adequate water	F	16	102	75	168	90	26	477	49.31	IV
		FX	1232.00	6456.60	4061.25	7870.80	3303.00	598.00	23521.65		
2	High risk in sugarcane crop	F	120	47	128	22	76	84	477	52.20	II
		FX	9240.00	2975.10	6931.20	1030.70	2789.20	1932.00	24898.20		
3	High initial investment	F	151	49	145	102	18	12	477	59.32	I
		FX	11627.00	3101.70	7851.75	4778.70	660.60	276.00	28295.75		
4	High maintenance cost	F	73	127	12	75	135	55	477	50.40	III
		FX	5621.00	8039.10	649.80	3513.75	4954.50	1265.00	24043.15		
5	Reduce soil fertility	F	75	53	17	13	137	182	477	41.66	VI
		FX	5775.00	3354.90	920.55	609.05	5027.90	4186.00	19873.40		
6	Imbalanced land	F	42	99	100	97	21	118	477	48.10	V
		FX	3234.00	6266.70	5415.00	4544.45	770.70	2714.00	22944.85		

Source: Primary Data

From the Table 4.31, it is found that high initial investment is identified as the most significant reason for non-adoption of drip irrigation system in sugarcane cultivation with the highest mean score of 59.32 followed by high risk in sugarcane crop, high cost of maintenance, availability of adequate water, imbalanced land and reduces soil fertility.

Hence, it is concluded that high initial investment is identified as the most significant reason for non-adoption of drip irrigation system in sugarcane cultivation.

4.6. Summary

In this chapter, the factors to influence the farmers to adopt the drip irrigation system in sugarcane cultivation has been analysed with help of factor analysis. Satisfaction of the farmers about the adoption of drip irrigation system in sugarcane cultivation has been analysed with help of chi-square test, F-test, Z-test and multiple regression analysis. The problems faced by the farmers in adoption of drip irrigation system and reasons for non-adoption of drip irrigation system in sugarcane cultivation have been analysed with help of Garrett Ranking Technique.

The following are the major findings of this chapter: For analysing the factors influencing the farmers to cultivate sugarcane factor analysis has been applied.

- From the analysis, it is found that Irrigation factor and Maintenance factors are identified as the most significant factors influencing the farmers to adopt the drip irrigation system in sugarcane cultivation.

- By applying Chi-square analysis, it is found that there is a significant relationship between independent variables (Age, Educational level, Nature of the family, Size of the family, Number of Members involved in Agriculture, Annual income, Annual Expenditure, Experience in Sugarcane cultivation, Methods of drip irrigation) and their level of satisfaction about the adoption of drip irrigation system in sugarcane cultivation. Further, it is found that there is insignificant relationship between independent variables like Occupation, Experience in Agriculture and Sources of water for drip irrigation and their level of satisfaction about the adoption of drip irrigation system in sugarcane cultivation.

- By applying Multiple Regression Analysis, it is found that the model fit increases from 0.289 to 0.742 by adding more variables such as Number of members involved in Agriculture, Size of the Family, Experience in Sugarcane Cultivation, Age, Educational level, Annual Income, Nature of the Family, Earning members in the family, Annual Expenditure to the independent variable in a step-by-step process. The adjusted R square also shows an increase from 0.076 to 0.515. This indicates that the increasing trend of nine independent variables is significant in affecting satisfaction level of drip irrigation system in sugarcane cultivation.

- By applying Garrett Ranking Technique, it is found that 'high initial investment' is identified as the most important reason for non-adoption of drip irrigation system in sugarcane cultivation. It is also found that 'risk during the period of harvest' is identified as the most significant problem in adoption of drip irrigation system in sugarcane cultivation.

CHAPTER V

MARKETING PRACTICES OF SUGARCANE FARMERS

Keywords

Factors Motivating the farmers to market their sugarcane - Sugarcane Marketing Channels - Factors Motivating the farmers to market their sugarcane through Channel-I - Farmers Satisfaction about the functioning of sugarcane marketing channel-I (Sugarcane Farmers - Sugar Factory) - Factors Motivating the farmers to market their sugarcane through channel - II - Farmers Satisfaction about the functioning of sugarcane marketing channel-II (Sugarcane Farmers-Jaggery Producers) - Marketing Cost incurred by the farmers to market their Sugarcane through different marketing channels - Price Spread of sugarcane marketing - Production of Khandsari Sugar - Marketing of Khandsari Sugar - Khandsari Sugar marketing channels - Factors motivating the farmers to market their Khandsari Sugar through channel-I - Factors Motivating the farmers to market their Khandsari Sugar through channel-II - Farmers Satisfaction about the functioning of Khandsari Sugar marketing channels - Marketing Cost incurred by farmers to market their Khandsari Sugar - Marketing Cost incurred by market functionaries - Price Spread of Khandsari Sugar.

5.1.   Introduction

Agricultural marketing is the study of all activities, agencies and policies involved in the procurement of farm inputs by the farmers and the movement of agricultural products from the farms to consumers. The agricultural marketing system is a link between the farm and non-farm sectors[76]. The agricultural marketing systems play a dual role in economic development in countries whose resources are primarily agricultural. An efficient agricultural marketing system leads to the optimisation of resource use and output management. It ensures higher levels of income for the farmers, reducing the number of middlemen or by restricting the cost of marketing services and the malpractices. It helps in growth of agro based industries in the adoption of new technology and the overall development process of the economy.

Agricultural sector needs well-functioning markets to drive growth, employment and economic prosperity in rural areas. Due to an increased accent on liberalization, privatisation and globalization of the economy, agricultural marketing has become the key driver of the agricultural sector. Though our farmers have succeeded in the production front, they have not achieved appreciably in terms of price realization for their produce owing to their

---

[76]Acharya S. S and Agarwal N. L., (2004), "Agricultural Marketing in India", Oxford and IBH publishing Company Pvt. Ltd., New Delhi.

inaccessibility of efficient and scientific marketing system. An efficient and organised marketing system would ensure maximum price realization to the farmers which will induce them to produce more and market their produce in an increasing proportion.

Sugarcane is an important cash crop grown in India. The farmers have the option to sell the sugarcane or own crushing for produce of khandsari sugar. In case of supply of sugarcane as raw material to sugar factory or jaggery producers. Generally, based on the price of sugarcane, the farmers are supplying to sugar factory before the beginning seasons enter into an agreement with sugar factory. If price of khandsari sugar is high, the farmer makes own crushing to produce khandsari sugar.

An attempt has been made in this chapter to identify the factors which motivate the farmers to market their sugarcane and khandsari sugar, to study the marketing cost, price spread and level of satisfaction of farmers about the functioning of sugarcane and khandsari sugar marketing channels.

5.2. Factors Motivating the Farmers to Market their Sugarcane

Sugarcane is less perishable nature. In the present study, it is decided to analyse the factors motivating the farmers to market their sugarcane. Out of 600 farmers, 385 farmers market their sugarcane to factory and jaggery producers. For analysing this, eight factors are considered on the basis of the results of pilot study and review of previous studies. They are: remunerative price for sugarcane, fixed price, convenience in during rainy seasons, labour shortage, non-availability of trained labourer for crushing, less work, attention to ratoon crop and non-availability of crushing machines. In order to identify the most significant factor motivating the farmers to market their sugarcane, simple ranking technique has been employed. The results of the simple ranking technique are shown in Table 5.1.

Table 5.1: Factors Motivating the Farmers to Market their Sugarcane

No	Factors	HM	M	N	LM	NM	Total score	Mean score	Rank
1	Remunerative price for Sugarcane	175(45.45)	120(31.17)	42(10.91)	30(7.79)	18(4.68)	1559	4.05	VII
2	Fixed price	245(63.64)	98 (25.45)	18 (4.68)	13(3.38)	11(2.86)	1708	4.44	I
3	Convenience in during rainy seasons	215(55.84)	73 (18.96)	45(11.69)	31(8.05)	21(5.45)	1585	4.12	VI
4	Labour shortage	241(62.60)	90 (23.38)	28 (7.27)	12(3.12)	14(3.64)	1687	4.38	II
5	Non availability of trained labourer for crushing	180(46.75)	145(37.66)	14 (3.64)	26(6.75)	20(5.19)	1594	4.14	V
6	Less work	219(56.88)	114(29.61)	17 (4.42)	20(5.19)	15(3.90)	1657	4.30	IV
7	Attention to ratoon crop	241(62.60)	95 (24.68)	14 (3.64)	20(5.19)	15(3.90)	1682	4.37	III
8	Non-availability of crushing machines	200(51.95)	82 (21.30)	45(11.69)	28(7.27)	30(7.79)	1549	4.02	VIII

Source: Primary Data, (HM- Highly motivated, M- Motivated, N- Neutral, LM- Less motivated, NM- Not motivated)

(Figures in parentheses represent percentages)

Table 5.1 exhibits that the fixed price is the vital factor which motivates the farmers to market their sugarcane with the highest mean score value of 4.44. Labour shortage is the second important factor (4.38) followed by the attention to ratoon crop (4.37), less work (4.30), non-availability of trained labourer for crushing (4.14), convenience during rainy seasons (4.12), remunerative price for sugarcane (4.05) and non-availability of crushing machines (4.02). Hence, it is concluded that the fixed price is the vital factor which motivates the farmers to market their sugarcane.

5.3.   Sugarcane Marketing Channels

Marketing channels are routes through which agricultural products move from producers to consumers. The length of the marketing channels for agricultural products varies from commodity to commodity, country to country, time to time, depending on the quantity to be moved, the form of consumer demand and degree of regional specialization in production.[77] Marketing channels for sugarcane is different from other crops. Sugarcane is generally marketed by either to sugar factories or jaggery producers. Based on the pilot study, it is found that there are two important marketing channels functioning for sugarcane market for selling their sugarcane in this area. They are:

Channel-I: Sugarcane Farmer-Sugar Factory

Channel-II: Sugarcane Farmer-Jaggery Producers

The details about selection of channel by the farmers are presented in Table 5.2.

Table 5.2: Marketing Channels Preference of Sugarcane Farmers

Marketing Channels	Number of Farmers	Per Cent
Channel-I	313	81.30
Channels-II	72	18.70
Total	385	100.00

Table 5.2 depicts that the 313 (81.30 per cent) farmers prefer to market their sugarcane through channel-I. In this channel, the farmers sell their sugarcane to factory. Channel-II has been chosen by 72 (18.70 per cent) farmers. In this channel, the farmers sell their sugarcane to jaggery producers.

Thus, it may be concluded that majority of the farmers preferred channel-I for marketing their sugarcane.

---

[77] Acharya and S.S Agarwal N. L., (2004), "Agricultural Marketing in India", Oxford and IBH publishing Company Pvt Ltd, New Delhi, p. 191.

5.4. Factors Motivating the Farmers to Market their Sugarcane through Channel-I

In this area, there are two sugar factories. Supply of sugarcane to sugar factory does not involve any responsibility of farmers as it is the responsibility of sugar factory to harvest and transport the sugarcane from farmers' field to sugar factory. On the basis of this information obtained from the farmers through the pilot study, it is understand that there are fourteen reasons for preferring marketing channel-I to market their sugarcane. Out of 385 farmers who market sugarcane, 313 farmers prefer channel-I to market their sugarcane. Table 5.3 explains the factors motivating the farmers to market their sugarcane through channel-I according to simple ranking technique.

Table 5.3: Factors Motivating the Farmers to Market their Sugarcane through Channel–I

S. No	Factors	HM	M	N	LM	NM	Total score	Mean score	Rank
1	Fixed price	235(75.08)	25(7.99)	17(5.43)	21(6.71)	15(4.79)	1383	4.42	I
2	Loan facilities	202(64.54)	58(18.53)	24(7.67)	11(3.51)	18(5.75)	1354	4.33	II
3	Arrangement of setts	161(51.44)	94(30.03)	21(6.71)	25(7.99)	12(3.83)	1306	4.17	IV
4	Provision of machinery for cultivation work	72(23.00)	178(56.87)	57(18.21)	4(1.28)	2(0.64)	1253	4.00	VIII
5	Labour facilities	218(69.66)	32(10.22)	30(9.58)	12(3.83)	21(6.71)	1353	4.32	III
6	Provision of fertilizer by factory	157(50.17)	51(16.29)	70(22.36)	1(0.32)	34(10.86)	1235	3.95	IX
7	Timely harvesting	166(53.03)	68(21.73)	30(9.58)	21(6.71)	28(8.95)	1262	4.03	VII
8	Proper payment	40 (12.78)	25(7.99)	120(38.34)	73(23.32)	55(17.57)	861	2.75	XIV
9	Crop insurance facility	148(47.29)	70(22.36)	21(6.71)	44(14.06)	30(9.58)	1201	3.84	XI
10	Getting assistance and advice from factory for cultivation activities	35(11.18)	40(12.78)	145(46.33)	55(17.57)	38(12.14)	918	2.93	XIII
11	Long term practice	81(25.89)	178(56.87)	12(3.83)	30(9.58)	12(3.83)	1225	3.91	X
12	No transportation cost	137(43.77)	63(20.13)	59(18.85)	24(7.67)	30(9.58)	1192	3.81	XII
13	Quick harvesting	182(58.15)	51(16.29)	34(10.86)	25(7.99)	21(6.71)	1287	4.11	V
14	No fear of loss of cash	168(53.68)	80(25.56)	12(3.83)	32(10.22)	21(6.71)	1281	4.09	VI

Source: Primary Data, (HM- Highly motivated, M- Motivated, N- Neutral, LM- Less motivated, NM- not Motivated) (Figures in parentheses represent percentages)

Table 5.3 reveals that fixed price is the important factor which motivates the farmers to market their sugarcane through factory with the highest mean score value of 4.42, followed by the loan facilities (4.33), labour facilities (4.32), arrangement of setts (4.17), quick harvesting (4.11), no fear of loss of cash (4.09), timely harvesting (4.03), provision of machinery for cultivation work (4.00), provision of fertilizer by factory (3.95), long term practice (3.91), crop insurance facility (3.84), no transportation cost (3.81), getting assistance and advice from factory for cultivation activities (2.93) and proper payment (2.75). Thus, it is concluded that fixed price is the significant factor which motivates the farmers to market their sugarcane to factory (channel-I).

5.5. Farmers Satisfaction about the Functioning of Sugarcane Marketing Channel-I (Sugarcane Farmers - Sugar Factory)

In this chapter, an attempt has been made to study the level of farmers' satisfaction about the functioning of sugarcane marketing channel-I (Sugarcane farmers-Factory). For the purpose of analysing the relationship between personal and socio economic characteristics of farmers and their level of satisfaction, Logistic Regression model has been applied. Table 5.4 gives the results of simple ranking technique on farmers satisfaction about the functioning of sugarcane marketing channel-I.

Table 5.4: Farmers Satisfaction about the Functioning of Sugarcane Marketing Channel - I

S. No.	Factors	HS	S	N	DS	HDS	Total Score	Mean Score	Rank
1	Arrangement of finance	241(77.00)	25(7.99)	15(4.79)	11(3.51)	21(6.71)	1393	4.45	I
2	Sugarcane registration formalities	128(40.89)	109(34.82)	38(12.14)	14(4.47)	24(7.68)	1242	3.97	IV
3	Reasonable price	66 (21.09)	87(27.8)	115(36.74)	34(10.86)	11(3.51)	1102	3.52	VIII
4	Arrangement of setts	178(56.87)	72(23.00)	18(5.75)	21(6.71)	24(7.67)	1298	4.15	II
5	Arrangement of machineries for cultivation work	160(51.12)	51(16.29)	38(12.14)	46(14.70)	18(5.75)	1228	3.92	V
6	Correct weighing	22(7.03)	118(37.7)	99(31.63)	55(17.57)	19(6.07)	1008	3.22	XII
7	Immediate payment	31(9.90)	20(6.39)	142(45.37)	62(19.81)	58(18.53)	843	2.69	XV
8	Crop insurance facility	96(30.67)	63(20.13)	78(24.92)	55(17.57)	21(6.71)	1097	3.50	IX
9	Timely harvesting	102(32.59)	126(40.26)	45(14.38)	25(7.99)	15(4.78)	1214	3.88	VI
10	Good quality of setts and new varieties	170(54.31)	67(21.41)	28(8.95)	30(9.58)	18(5.75)	1280	4.09	III
11	Price of fertilizers	13(4.15)	138(44.09)	97(30.99)	45(14.38)	20(6.39)	1018	3.25	XI
12	Provision of training programme	19(6.07)	139(44.41)	100(31.95)	38(12.14)	17(5.43)	1044	3.34	X
13	Cutting &loading charges	15(4.79)	124(39.62)	84(26.84)	69(22.04)	21(6.71)	982	3.14	XIII
14	Assistance &advice from officials	28(8.95)	178(56.87)	64(20.44)	29(9.26)	14(4.47)	1116	3.57	VII
15	Supply of sugar in minimum price	13(4.15)	130(41.53)	85(27.16)	47(15.02)	38(12.14)	972	3.11	XIV

Source: Primary Data, HS-Highly Satisfied, S-Satisfied, N-Neutral, Ds-Dissatisfied, HDS-Highly Dissatisfied (Figures in parentheses represent percentages)

Table 5.4 depicts that farmers have high level of satisfaction on arrangement of finance with the highest mean score value of 4.45 and farmers have low level of satisfaction on immediate payment with the lowest mean score value of 2.69 about the functioning of sugarcane marketing channel-I. Thus, it is concluded that farmers have high level of satisfaction on arrangement of finance with the highest mean score value of 4.45 about the functioning of sugarcane marketing channel-I.

5.5.1. Quantification and Scoring Procedure

To measure the level of satisfaction of the farmers about functioning of sugarcane marketing channel-I, Rensis Likerts five points scaling technique has been adopted. In interview schedule, fifteen statements relating to the functioning of sugarcane marketing channel-I have been included. All these statements are generated on the basis of the experience gained during the pilot study and also based on review of relevant literature. The farmers have been asked to indicate their level of satisfaction regarding each statement by using the likert's 5 point scale. The scale values 5, 4, 3, 2 and 1 have been used to measure the satisfaction level of the farmers. The scale 5 indicates that the farmers are Highly Satisfied, the scale value 4 indicates that the farmers are 'Satisfied', the scale value 3 indicates that the farmers are 'Neutral', the scale value 2 indicates that the farmers are Dissatisfied and the scale value 1 indicates that the farmers are Highly Dissatisfied about the functioning of sugarcane marketing channel-I. The total score of each statement has been calculated for all the fifteen statements using the above scoring procedure.

The scores of 313 farmers have been calculated. An individual's score is the mere summation of the scores secured from the 15 statements. The expected score of the farmers ranging from 15 to 75. Further, for the purpose of analysis based on the satisfaction score, the farmers have been grouped into two viz., low satisfaction and high satisfaction. The farmers who have scored 45 or less are classified as 'Low Satisfaction'; the farmers who have scored above 46 are classified as 'High Satisfaction'. Table 5.5 shows the distribution of farmers on the basis of their level of satisfaction about the functioning of sugarcane marketing channel-I.

Table 5.5: Distribution of Farmers on the Basis of their Satisfaction level

Level of Satisfaction	Number of farmers	Per cent	Mean score
Low (15 to 45)	38	12.16	29.33
High (46 to 75)	275	87.84	50.29
Total	**313**	**100.00**	**47.74**

Table 5.5 shows that the mean score of all the farmers is 47.74. Among 313 farmers, 275 (87.84 per cent) farmers have high level of satisfaction about the functioning of marketing channel- I where as 38 (12.16 per cent) farmers have low level of satisfaction about the functioning of marketing channel-I. Hence, it is concluded that majority (275) of the farmers have high level of satisfaction about the functioning of sugarcane marketing channel-I.

5.5.2. *Regression Analysis: Logistic Model*

To estimate the qualitative response regression model, there is a need to consider about binary response regression. There are three approaches to develop a probability model for a binary response variable and one such model is logistic. The present study uses log it model (also known as logistic model) and pointed out its usefulness when the dependent variable is nominal (values are high and low) and it takes the values either 1 or 0. Logistic regression equation also allows using nominal independent variable.

The level of satisfaction of farmers about the functioning of marketing channel-I is hypothesized to be a function of the 15 statements (measured on a 5- point likert type scale). The statements include Arrangement of finance, Sugarcane registration formalities, Reasonable price, Arrangement of setts, Arrangement of machineries for cultivation work, Correct weighing, Immediate payment, Crop insurance facility, Timely Harvesting, Good quality of setts and new varieties, Price of fertilizers, Provision of Training Programme, Cutting & Loading Charges, Assistance & Advice from officials and Supply of sugar in minimum price. Level of satisfaction = 1 if the respondent is highly satisfied (above 45) with the functioning of marketing channel-I; 0 otherwise (45 or less). The statistical relationship between the level of satisfaction of farmers and their personal and socio-economic characteristics such as Age, Educational level, Occupation, Size of the family, Earnings members in the family, Annual expenditure, Experience in agriculture, Experience in sugarcane cultivation, Years of Supplying to the Factory is determined with the help of logistic model.

Logistic regression model

$$\text{In}(y) = \beta_0 + \beta_1 \chi_1 + \beta_2 \chi_2 + \dots\dots\dots + \beta_k \chi_k + \varepsilon$$

Where y = odds ratio

In (y) = natural logarithm of the odds ratio

$\chi_1, \chi_2, \chi_3, \dots\dots \chi_K$:Independent variables

χ_1 = Age (in years)

χ_2 = Educational level (in years)

χ_3 = Occupation (Agriculture)

χ_4 = Size of the family (Number of Members)

χ_5 = Earnings members in the family (Number of Members)

χ_6 = Annual expenditure (₹)

χ_7 = Experience in agriculture (years)

χ_8 = Experience in sugarcane cultivation (years)

χ_9 = Year of supplying to the factory (years)

$\beta_0, \beta_1 \dots\dots\dots, \beta_k$: co-efficient of the independent variables

ε = error variable

The logistic regression model is similar to linear regression except for the dependent variable. Logistic regression equation:

$$\text{In}(\hat{y}) = b_0 + b_1 \chi_1 + b_2 \chi_2 + \dots\dots\dots + b_k \chi_k$$

In this logistic regression equation, the dependent variable (Y) is nominal, the least squares technique is not appropriate. Logistic is used to estimate the probability that a particular outcome will occur. The dependent variable in logistic regression is the odds ratio, which is another way to express probability[78].

The values of $\hat{y}$ is the estimated odds ratio, that is:

$$\hat{Y} = e^{\ln(\hat{y})} \text{ (Y-hat means fitted or calculated value of y)}$$

$$\text{Estimated probability of the event} = \frac{\hat{y}}{\hat{y}+1}$$

(Satisfaction of farmers)

Statistical software package performs the above required calculations. The co-efficient is estimated using a statistical technique called maximum likelihood estimation. The results of logistic regression are presented in Table 5.6.

Table 5.6: Satisfaction of Farmers-Logistic Regression Analysis

	Co-efficient	S. E	Z	p-value
Constant	0.556	0.386	1.44	0.151
Age (χ_1)	0.744	0.147	5.07	0.000 ***
Educational level (χ_2)	0.062	0.245	0.25	0.801
Occupation (χ_3)	0.091	0.159	0.57	0.568
Size of the family (χ_4)	-0.586	0.168	-3.49	0.000 ***
Earning members in the family (χ_5)	-0.099	0.349	-0.28	0.777
Annual expenditure (χ_6)	-0.480	0.308	-1.56	0.119
Experience in agriculture (χ_7)	-0.639	0.295	-2.17	0.030 **
Experience in sugarcane cultivation (χ_8)	-0.552	0.300	-1.84	0.065 *
Years of supplying to the Factory(χ_9)	0.136	0.144	0.95	0.344

*** 1 Per cent level of Significance, **5 Per cent level of Significance,*10 Per cent level of Significance

The logistic regression is In $(\hat{y})$ = 0.556 $_+$ 0.744χ_1 + 0.062χ_2 + 0.091χ_3 - 0.586χ_4 - 0.099χ_5 - 0.480χ_6 - 0.639χ_7 - 0.552χ_8 + 0.136χ_9

Interpreting the co-efficient of the logistic regression is somewhat more complex. If a co-efficient is positive, an increase in that independent variable will result in an increase in the probability of the event. The co-efficient of χ_4, χ_5, χ_6, χ_7 and χ_8, are negative. This tells us an increase in the independent variable will result in a decrease in the probability of the event. If the size of the family of farmers increases, it has a higher probability of getting low satisfaction or dissatisfaction about the functioning of marketing channel-I. Among the nine independent variables Age (χ_1), Size of the family (χ_4), Experience in agriculture (χ_7) and Experience in sugarcane cultivation (χ_8) is significantly related to level of satisfaction of farmers about the functioning of sugarcane marketing channel-I. The variable χ_1 is the positive change in the

---

[78]Gerald Keller., (2008), "Statistics for Management and Economics", Seventh edition, Cengage learning, New Delhi.

value of y. Because, this model has been developed with the use of observational data from the farmers.

Model Fit

In logistic regression (binary logistic), commonly used measures of model fit are based on the level of satisfaction of farmers and are Cox & Snell R square and Nagel kerke R Square. Both these measures are similar to R^2 in multiple regressions. The Cox and Snell are constrained in such a way that it cannot be equal 1.0, even if the model perfectly fits the data. The model fit is assessed by determining the proportion of correct prediction. If the estimated probability is greater than 0.5, then the predicted value of Y is set to 1. On the other hand, if the estimated probability is less than 0.5, then the predicted value of Y is set to 0. The predicted values of Y can then be compared to the corresponding actual values to determine the percentage of correct predictions.

Table 5.7: Model Summary on R Square

Model Summary on R Square			
Step	-2Log likelihood	Cox & Snell R Square	Nagelkerke R Square
1	32.774[a]	0.257	0.492

Table 5.7 shows that the Cox & Snell R square and Nagel kerke R square tells that all explanatory variables in the significantly fitted model could explain 25.7 per cent and 49.2 per cent of variance in satisfaction of farmers about the functioning of sugarcane marketing channel-I.

Table 5.8: Classification by Model

Observed	Predicted		
	Low (0)	High (1)	Percentage Correct
Low	8	30	22.2
High	4	271	98.5
Overall Percentage			89.2

Table 5.8 reveals that the 22.2 per cent of low satisfaction farmers are correctly classified by the model and 98.5 per cent of the high satisfaction farmers are correctly classified by the model. Overall 89.2 per cent of cases could be accurately classified by the model. False prediction either negative or positive is below 20 per cent. Hence, the above logistic model can be used for predicting the satisfaction of farmers regarding functioning of sugarcane marketing channel-I with 89.2 per cent accuracy.

5.6. Factors Motivating the Farmers to Market their Sugarcane Through Channel - II

Jaggery processing is an important cottage industry in sugarcane growing regions of Tamil Nadu. The development of this industry is contributing to the industrial growth and to the general well-being of the rural people. The per capita consumption of jaggery during the year 2012-2013 is estimated at 18.2 as compared to 12.5 of sugar. The jaggery price is more fluctuating than the white sugar price. Because the price of jaggery is determined by the forces of supply and demand in the free market. On the other hand, the price of white sugar is administered and price fluctuation in sugar market is not high. However, sugar and jaggery are close substitutes and the changes in the price of one commodity affect the price of the other. It is generally observed that the high price of jaggery in one year induces the farmers to market their sugarcane to jaggery producers in the following year rather than supply of sugarcane to the factory. Therefore, marketing of sugarcane depends upon the price of jaggery in the market.

In this area, unorganised jaggery producing units are also available. The farmers prefer to market their sugarcane to jaggery producers depends upon the price of sugarcane and return of sugarcane. If the farmers market their sugarcane to jaggery producers they need not wait for a particular time to harvest and there is no marketing cost involved in this channel. Out of 385 farmers who market sugarcane, 72 farmers prefer channel-II to market their sugarcane. For the analysing purpose, seven motivating factors are considered on the basis of outcome of pilot study. In order to identify the most important factor motivating the farmers to market their sugarcane. Table 5.9 describes the factors motivating the farmers to prefer channel-II according to simple ranking technique.

Table 5.9: Factors Motivating the Farmers to Market their Sugarcane through Channel-II

S. No	Factors	HM	M	N	LM	NM	Total score	Mean score	Rank
1	Higher return	38(52.78)	15(20.83)	8(11.11)	6(8.33)	5(6.94)	291	4.04	V
2	Flexibility in harvesting	57(79.17)	9(12.5)	3(4.17)	1(1.39)	2(2.78)	334	4.64	I
3	Easy to market	5(6.94)	4(5.56)	42(58.33)	13(18.06)	8(11.11)	201	2.79	VII
4	Immediate payment	51(70.83)	15(20.83)	1(1.39)	3(4.17)	2(2.78)	326	4.53	II
5	Quick harvesting	48(66.67)	13(18.06)	2(2.78)	4(5.56)	5(6.94)	311	4.32	IV
6	No transport &cutting charges	52(72.22)	7(9.72)	4(5.56)	5(6.94)	4(5.56)	314	4.36	III
7	Correct weighing can be ensured	11(15.28)	10(13.89)	35(48.61)	8(11.11)	8(11.11)	224	3.11	VI

Source: Primary Data, (HM-Highly motivated, M-motivated, N-neutral, LM-less motivated, NM-not motivated), (Figures in parentheses represent percentages)

Table 5.9 indicates that flexibility in harvesting is the significant factor which motivates the farmers to market their sugarcane to jaggery producers with the highest mean score value of

4.64, followed by the immediate payment (4.53), no transport & cutting charges (4.36), quick harvesting (4.32), higher return (4.04), correct weighing can be ensured (3.11) and easy to market (2.79).

Thus, it is concluded that 'flexibility in harvesting' is the significant factor which motivates the farmers to market their sugarcane to Jaggery producers.

5.7. Farmers Satisfaction about the Functioning of Sugarcane Marketing Channel-II (Sugarcane Farmers-Jaggery Producers)

In this chapter, an attempt has been made to analyse the level of farmers' satisfaction about the functioning of marketing channel-II (Sugarcane farmers- Jaggery producers). For the purpose of analysing the relationship between personal and socio- economic characteristics of farmers and their level of satisfaction, Logistic Regression model has been applied. Table 5.10 gives the results of simple ranking technique on farmers' satisfaction about the functioning of sugarcane marketing channel-II.

Table 5.10: Farmers Satisfaction about the Functioning of Sugarcane Marketing Channel – II

S. No.	Factors	HS	S	N	DS	HDS	Total score	Mean Score	Rank
1	Reasonable Price	46(63.89)	14(19.44)	4(5.56)	1(1.39)	7(9.72)	307	4.26	I
2	Timely and quick harvesting	5(6.94)	13(18.06)	41(56.94)	10(13.89)	3(4.17)	223	3.10	IV
3	Correct weighing	6(8.33)	39(54.17)	20(27.78)	2 (2.78)	5(6.94)	255	3.54	III
4	Immediate payment	47(65.28)	11(15.28)	1(1.39)	5(6.94)	8(11.11)	300	4.17	II
5	Sugarcane cutting method	8(11.11)	5(6.94)	38(52.78)	17(23.61)	4(5.56)	212	2.94	V
6	Provision of setts	2(2.78)	4(5.56)	40(55.56)	18(25.00)	8(11.11)	190	2.64	VI

Source: Primary Data, (Figures in parentheses represent percentages) HS-Highly Satisfied, S-Satisfied, N-Neutral, Ds-Dissatisfied, HDS-Highly Dissatisfied

Table 5.10 reveals that farmers have high level of satisfaction on reasonable price with the highest mean score value of 4.26 and farmers have low level of satisfaction on provision of setts with the lowest mean score value of 2.64 about the functioning of sugarcane marketing channel-II.

Thus, it is concluded that farmers have high level of satisfaction on reasonable price with the highest mean score value of 4.26 about the functioning of sugarcane marketing channel-II.

5.7.1. Quantification and Scoring Procedure

To measure the level of satisfaction of the farmers about functioning of marketing channel-II, Rinsis likerts five point scaling technique has been adopted. In interview schedule, six statements relating to the functioning of marketing channel-II have been included. All these statements are generated on the basis of the experience gained during the pilot study and also based on review of relevant literature. The farmers have been asked to indicate their level of satisfaction regarding each statement by using likert's 5 point scale. The scale values 5, 4, 3, 2 and 1 have been used to measure the satisfaction level of the farmers. The scale 5 indicates that the farmers are Highly Satisfied, the scale value 4 indicates that the farmers are 'Satisfied', the scale value 3 indicates that the farmers are 'Neutral', the scale value 2 indicates that the farmers are Dissatisfied and the scale value 1 indicates that the farmers are Highly Dissatisfied about the functioning of sugarcane marketing channel-II. The total score of each statement has been calculated for all the six statements using the above scoring procedure.

The score of 72 farmers have been calculated. An individual's score is the mere summation of the scores secured from the 6 statements. The score of the farmers ranging from 6 to 30. Further, the purpose of analysis based on the satisfaction score, the farmers have been grouped into two viz., low satisfaction and high satisfaction. The farmers who have scored 18 or less are classified as 'Low Satisfaction' the farmers who have scored above 18 are classified as 'High Satisfaction'. Table 5.11 shows the distribution of farmers on the basis of their level of satisfaction about the functioning of sugarcane marketing channel-II.

Table 5.11: Distribution of Farmers on the Basis of their Satisfaction Level

Satisfaction	Number of farmers	Per cent	Mean score
Low (6 to 18)	47	64.71	21.82
High (19 to 30)	25	35.29	20.67
Total	**72**	**100.00**	**21.41**

Table 5.11 displays that the mean score of all the farmersis21.41. Among 72 farmers, 47 (64.71 per cent) farmers have low level of satisfaction about the functioning of sugarcane marketing channel-II whereas 25 (35.29 per cent) farmers have high level of satisfaction about the functioning of sugarcane marketing channel-II. Thus, it is concluded that majority 47 (64.71 per cent) farmers have low level of satisfaction about the functioning of sugarcane marketing channel-II.

5.7.2. *Regression Analysis: Logistic Model*

The same logistic model is applied for analysing the relationship between personal and socio-economic characteristics of the farmers and their level of satisfaction about the functioning of sugarcane marketing channel-II. The level of satisfaction of farmers about the functioning of sugarcane marketing channel-II is hypothesized to be a function of the 6 statements (measured on a 5-point likert type scale). The statements include Reasonable Price, Timely and quick harvesting, correct weighing, immediate payment, Sugarcane cutting method,

Provision of setts. Level of satisfaction=1 if the respondent is highly satisfied (above 18) with functioning of sugarcane marketing channel II; 0 otherwise (18 or less). The statistical relationship between the level of satisfaction and their personal and socio-economic characteristics of farmers are determined with the help of logistic model. The results of logistic regression are presented in Table 5.12.

Table 5.12: Satisfaction of Farmers - Logistic Regression Analysis

Constant	Co-efficient	S. E	Z	p-value
	1.936	0.535	3.62	0.000***
Age(χ_1)	0.304	0.195	1.56	0.119
Educational level (χ_2)	0.175	0.328	0.53	0.593
Occupation (χ_3)	0.393	0.219	1.79	0.074*
Size of the family (χ_4)	-0.025	0.223	-0.11	0.911
Earning members in the family (χ_5)	-1.758	0.447	-3.93	0.000***
Annual expenditure (χ_6)	-0.600	0.439	-1.37	0.171
Experience in agriculture (χ_7)	-0.437	0.427	-1.02	0.306
Experience in sugarcane cultivation (χ_8)	0.083	0.446	0.19	0.853
Years of supplying to the jaggery producers (χ_9)	-0.231	0.190	-1.21	0.226

*** 1 Per cent level of Significance, *10 Per cent level of Significance

The logistic regression is In ($\hat{y}$) = +1.936 $_+$ 0.304χ_1 $_+$ 0.175χ_2 $_+$ 0.393χ_3 -0.025χ_4 -1.758χ_5 $_-$ 0.600χ_6 -0.437χ_7 $_+$0.083χ_8 -0.231χ_9

Interpreting the co-efficient of the logistic regression is somewhat more complex. If a co-efficient is positive, an increase in that independent variable will result in an increase in the probability of the event. The co-efficient of χ_4, χ_5, χ_6, χ_7 and χ_9, are negative. This tells us an increase in the independent variable will result in a decrease in the probability of the event. If the earning members in the family increases has a higher probability of getting low satisfaction or dissatisfaction about the functioning of sugarcane marketing channel-II.

Among the nine independent variables Occupation (χ_3) and Earnings members in the family (χ_5) is significantly related to level of satisfaction of farmers about the functioning of marketing channel-II. The variable χ_3 is the positive change in the value of y. Because, this model has been developed with the use of observational data from the farmer.

Model Fit

In logistic regression (binary logistic), commonly used measures of model fit is based on the level of satisfaction of farmers and are Cox & Snell R square and Nagelkerke R Square. Model summary on R square is presented in Table 5.13.

Table 5.13: Model Summary on R Square

Model Summary on R Square			
Step	**-2Log likelihood**	**Cox & Snell R Square**	**Nagelkerke R Square**
1	16.252[a]	0.329	0.443

Table 5.13 shows that the Cox & Snell R square and Nagelkerke R square tell that all explanatory variables in the significantly fitted model could explain 32.9 per cent and 44.3 per cent of variance in satisfaction of farmers about the functioning of sugarcane marketing channel-II.

Table 5.14: Classification by Model

Observed	**Predicted**		
	Low (0)	**High (1)**	**Percentage Correct**
Low	37	10	78.72
High	2	23	92.00
Overall Percentage			83.33

Table 5.14 reveals that the 92.00 per cent of high satisfaction farmers are correctly classified by the model and 78.72 per cent of low satisfaction farmers are correctly classified by the model. Overall, 83.33 per cent of cases could be accurately classified by the model. False prediction either negative or positive is below 20 per cent. Hence, above logistic model can be used for predicting the satisfaction of farmers regarding the functioning of marketing channel II with 83.33 per cent accuracy.

5.8. Marketing Cost Incurred by the Farmers to Market their Sugarcane through Different Marketing Channels

The marketing cost incurred by the farmers which differ significantly in different identified channels. Marketing cost for sugarcane farmers constitutes the expenses like cutting charges, loading and unloading charges and transport cost. In this area, out of 600 farmers, 385 farmers market their sugarcane to the factory and jaggery producers. While marketing the sugarcane to factory only cutting charges incurred as marketing cost to the farmers and transport cost is bear by the sugar factory. But the marketing of sugarcane to jaggery producers, there is no marketing cost. Table 5.15 shows the details of marketing cost incurred by the farmers in different marketing channels.

Table 5.15: Marketing Cost Incurred by the Farmers to Market their Sugarcane in Different Marketing Channels

Expenses	**Channel-I (₹)**	**Channel-II (₹)**
Cutting Charge	535.95 (100.00)	0.00
Total	**535.95 (100.00)**	**0.00**

Source: Primary Data (Figures in parentheses represent percentages)

Table 5.15 reveals that cutting charge ₹ 535.95 is marketing cost incurred by the farmers to market their sugarcane through channel-I. There is no marketing cost in channel-II for their marketing of sugarcane. Hence, it is concluded that cutting charge ₹ 535.95 is marketing cost incurred by the farmers to market their sugarcane to sugar factory.

5.9.   Price Spread of Sugarcane Marketing

In the marketing of agricultural commodities, the difference between the price paid by consumer and price received by the producer for an equivalent quantity of farm produce is often known as price spread. Sugarcane is a raw material to produce other products such as white sugar, jaggery and khandsari sugar. In this book, an attempt has been made to know the net price received by the farmer in marketing of sugarcane. Table 5.16 exhibits the price spread of sugarcane in different marketing channels.

Table 5.16: Price Spread of Sugarcane in Different Marketing Channels

Price Spread	Channel-I		Channel-II	
	Amount(₹/ tonne)	Per cent	Amount (₹/tonne)	Per cent
Net price received by farmer	1849.05	77.53	1912.94	100.00
Marketing Cost	535.95	22.47	0.00	0.00
Selling Price	**2385.00**	**100.00**	**1912.94**	**100.00**

Source: Primary Data

From the Table 5.16, it is observed that the farmers received the maximum price (net) of ₹ 1912.94 in channel-II and ₹ 1849.05 in channel-I. Hence, it is concluded that the farmers received the maximum price (net) of ₹ 1912.94 in channel-II.

5.10. Production of Khandsari Sugar

In this area, out of 600 farmers, 215 farmers produced khandsari sugar. Hence, an attempt has been made to know the factors motivating the farmers to produce khandsari sugar. For examining this, eleven factors are considered on the basis of the outcome of pilot study. In order to know the most significant factor motivating the sugarcane farmers to go for production of khandsari sugar, simple ranking technique has been applied. The results of simple ranking technique on factors motivating the farmers to produce of khandsari sugar are presented in Table 5.17.

Table 5.17: Factors Motivating the Farmers to Produce Khandsari SUGAR

S. No	Factors	HM	M	N	LM	NM	Total score	Mean score	Rank
1	Remunerative price for sugar	125(58.14)	30(13.95)	34(15.81)	13(6.05)	13 (6.05)	886	4.12	I
2	Flexibility in harvesting	123(57.21)	25(11.63)	42(19.53)	8(3.72)	17 (7.91)	874	4.07	II
3	Availability of machinery for crushing	113(52.56)	17(7.91)	21(9.77)	13(6.05)	51 (23.72)	773	3.60	VIII
4	Availability of labour	34(15.81)	93(43.26)	59(27.44)	8(3.72)	21 (9.77)	756	3.52	IX
5	Availability of storage facilities	13(6.05)	8(3.72)	59(27.44)	89(41.4)	46 (21.4)	498	2.32	XI
6	Domestic consumption	38(17.67)	84(39.07)	51(23.72)	8(3.72)	34 (15.81)	729	3.39	X
7	Improper road facility	122(56.74)	30(13.95)	21(9.77)	4(1.86)	38 (17.67)	839	3.90	V
8	Long term practice	55(25.58)	118(54.88)	17(7.91)	8(3.72)	17 (7.91)	831	3.87	VI
9	Increase in return	118(54.88)	34(15.81)	25(11.63)	21(9.77)	17 (7.91)	860	4.00	III
10	Can cultivate any variety	55(25.58)	97(45.12)	21(9.77)	8(3.72)	34 (15.81)	776	3.61	VII
11	Easy to market	55(25.58)	126(58.6)	17(7.91)	4(1.86)	13 (6.05)	851	3.96	IV

Source: Primary Data, (HM-highly motivated, M-motivated, N-neutral, LM-less motivated, NM-not motivated), (Figures in parentheses represent percentages)

Table 5.17 displays that remunerative price for sugar is the primary factor which motivates the farmers to produce the khandsari sugar by themselves (4.12), flexibility in harvesting is the second factor for motivating the own production of khandsari sugar (4.07), is followed by the increase in return (4.00), easy to market (3.96), improper road facility (3.90), long term practice (3.87), can cultivate any variety (3.61), availability of machinery for crushing (3.60), availability of labour (3.52), domestic consumption (3.39) and availability of storage facilities (2.32). Hence, it is concluded that remunerative price for sugar is the prime factor which motivates the farmers to produce the khandsari sugar in their own.

5.11. Marketing of Khandsari Sugar

In the area, khandsari sugar market is located at Kavindapadi and Chittode as regulated market and private market. After production of khandsari sugar, immediately the farmers bring it to the market for the need of money or lack of storage facilities. Out of 600 farmers, 215 farmers market their khandsari sugar through commission agent or through regulated market.

5.12. Khandsari Sugar Marketing Channels

Marketing of sugarcane does not involve any complicated process of marketing and it is transferred directly from the farmer to the sugar factory or jaggery producer for processing of jaggery. But khandsari sugar is complicated one for producing and involving a long marketing channel and number of middlemen to market their khandsari sugar. Out of 600 farmers, 215 farmers are producing of khandsari sugar in their own. Based on pilot study, it has been identified that the two important marketing channels of khandsari sugar in the area. These are:

Channel-I: Farmers-Wholesaler-Retailer-Consumer (through commission agent)

Channel-II: Farmers–Consumer (Wholesaler) (through regulated market)

The study of channel preference provides an insight into how the farmers arrive at the disposal decision and the variables which influence their decision. Once the influencing variables have been identified, the traders can manipulate them so as to induce the farmer in a positive sales decision. The farmers produce khandsari sugar either through commission agent or direct market through regulated market. It is a known fact that the farmers producing khandsari sugar prefer any of the identified two channels for their own convenience. The details about selection of channel by the farmers are presented in Table 5.18.

Table 5.18: Marketing Channels Preference of Khandsari Sugar Farmers

Marketing Channels	Number of Farmers	Per cent
Channel-I	130	60.47
Channel-II	85	39.53
Total	**215**	**100.00**

Table 5.18 reveals that the 130 (60.47 per cent) farmers prefer to market their khandsari sugar through Channel-I. In this channel, the farmers sell the khandsari sugar through commission agent. Channel-II has been chosen by 85 (39.53 per cent) farmers. In this channel, the farmers sell the khandsari sugar through regulated market. Thus, it is concluded that majority of the farmers (60.47 per cent) prefer Channel-I for marketing their khandsari sugar.

5.13. Factors Motivating the Farmers to Market their Khandsari Sugar through Channel-I

In the area, out of 215 farmers who producing khandsari sugar, 130 farmers are marketing their khandsari sugar through commission agent to wholesaler. On the basis of the information obtained from the farmers through the pilot study, it is understood that there are nine reasons for preferring a particular marketing channel-I for marketing their khandsari sugar such as no rental charges, less risk in arrangement of workers, less risk in packing, remunerative price for sugar, arrangement of transport facility by agent, proper maintenance (less wastage), good amenities, availability of agent and to get advance money. Table 5.19 describes the factors motivating the farmers to prefer channel-I according to simple ranking technique.

Table 5.19: Factors Motivating the Farmers to Market their Khandsari Sugar through

Commission Agent

S. No	Factors	HM	M	N	LM	NM	Total score	Mean score	Rank
1	No rental charges	33(25.38)	55(42.31)	25(19.23)	4(3.08)	13 (10.00)	481	3.70	VI
2	Less risk in arrangement of workers	58(44.62)	34(26.15)	4(3.08)	13(10.00)	21 (16.15)	485	3.73	V
3	Less risk in packing	59(45.38)	29(22.31)	21(16.15)	13(10.00)	8 (6.15)	508	3.91	II
4	Remunerative price for sugar	8(6.15)	59(45.38)	42(32.31)	13(10.00)	8 (6.15)	436	3.35	VIII
5	Arrangement of transport facility by agent	37(28.46)	55(42.31)	21(16.15)	13(10.00)	4 (3.08)	498	3.83	III
6	Proper maintenance	29(22.31)	42(32.31)	34(26.15)	17(13.08)	8 (6.15)	457	3.52	VII
7	Good amenities	21(16.15)	29(22.31)	50(38.46)	13(10.00)	17 (13.08)	414	3.18	IX
8	Availability of agent	54(41.54)	13(10.00)	42(32.31)	17(13.08)	4 (3.08)	486	3.74	IV
9	To get advance money	63(48.46)	38(29.23)	4(3.08)	17(13.08)	8 (6.15)	521	4.01	I

Source: Primary Data, (HM-highly motivated, M-motivated, N-neutral, LM-less motivated, NM-not motivated), (Figures in parentheses represent percentages)

Table 5.19 reveals that to get advance money is the most significant factor which motivates the farmers to market their khandsari sugar through commission agent with the highest mean score value of 4.01, followed by the less risk in packing (3.91), arrangement of transport facility by agent (3.83), availability of agent (3.74), less risk in arrangement of workers (3.73), no rental charges (3.70), proper maintenance (less wastage) (3.52), remunerative price for sugar (3.35) and good amenities (3.18).

Hence, it is concluded that 'to get advance money' is the most significant factor which motivates the farmers to market their khandsari sugar through commission agent with the highest mean score value of 4.01.

5.14. Factors Motivating the Farmers to Market their Khandsari Sugar through Channel-II

In the present study, out of 215 farmers who produced khandsari sugar, 85 farmers are marketing their khandsari sugar through regulated market. On the basis of the information obtained from the farmers through the pilot study, it is understood that there are nine reasons for preferring a particular marketing channel-II for marketing their khandsari sugar such as higher sugar price, correct weighing, proper maintenance, good amenities, availability of pledge loan, availability of insurance facilities, no commission charge, availability of storage facility for low rental charges, availability of packing materials, direct marketing, immediate cash payment and market news service. Table 5.20 describes about the factors motivating the farmers to prefer channel-II according to simple ranking technique.

Table 5.20: Factors Motivating the Farmers to Market their Khandsari Sugar through Regulated Market

S. No	Factors	HM	M	N	LM	NM	Total score	Mean score	Rank
1	Higher sugar price	52 (61.18)	17(20.00)	9 (10.59)	3(3.53)	4(4.71)	365	4.29	IV
2	Correct weighing	25 (29.41)	21(24.71)	17 (20.00)	13(15.29)	9(10.59)	295	3.47	XI
3	Proper maintenance	49 (57.65)	18(21.18)	10 (11.76)	5(5.88)	3(3.53)	360	4.24	VI
4	Good amenities	50 (58.82)	10(11.76)	6 (7.06)	11(12.94)	8(9.41)	338	3.98	VIII
5	Availability of pledge loan	55 (64.71)	12(14.12)	9 (10.59)	4(4.71)	5(5.88)	363	4.27	V
6	Availability of insurance facilities	40 (47.06)	20(23.53)	4 (4.71)	11(12.94)	10(11.76)	324	3.81	IX
7	No commission charge	56 (65.88)	21(24.71)	1(1.18)	5(5.88)	2(2.35)	379	4.46	II
8	Availability of storage facility for low rental charges	25 (29.41)	10(11.76)	36(42.35)	6(7.06)	8(9.41)	293	3.45	XII
9	Availability of packing materials	35 (41.18)	20(23.53)	18(21.18)	2(2.35)	10(11.76)	323	3.80	X
10	Direct marketing	59 (69.41)	15(17.65)	3(3.53)	1(1.18)	7(8.24)	373	4.39	III
11	Immediate cash payment	61 (71.76)	11(12.94)	9(10.59)	3(3.53)	1(1.18)	383	4.51	I
12	Market news services	52 (61.18)	15(17.65)	4(4.71)	10(11.76)	4(4.71)	356	4.19	VII

Source: Primary Data,(HM- highly motivated, M- motivated, N- neutral, LM- less motivated, NM- not motivated), (Figures in parentheses represent percentages)

Table 5.20 indicates that immediate cash payment is the prime factor which motivates the farmers to market their khandsari sugar through regulated market with the highest mean score value of 4.51, followed by no commission charge (4.46), direct marketing (4.39), higher sugar price (4.29), availability of pledge loan (4.27), proper maintenance (4.24), market news services (4.19), good amenities (3.98), availability of insurance facilities (3.81),availability of packing materials (3.80), correct weighing (3.47) and availability of storage facility for low rental charges (3.45). Thus, it is concluded that 'immediate cash payment' is the prime factor which motivates the farmers to market their khandsari sugar through regulated market.

5.15. Farmers Satisfaction about the Functioning of Khandsari Sugar Marketing Channels

In this chapter, an attempt has been made to study the level of farmers' satisfaction about the functioning of khandsari sugar marketing channels. For the purpose of analysing the relationship between personal and socio-economic characteristics of farmers and their level of satisfaction, Logistic Regression model has been applied. Table 5.21 gives the results of simple ranking technique on farmers' satisfaction about the functioning of khandsari sugar marketing channels.

Table 5.21: Farmers Satisfaction about the Functioning of Khandsari Sugar Marketing Channels

S. No.	Factors	HS	S	N	DS	HDS	Total Score	Mean Score	Rank
1	Reasonable Price	8 (3.72)	59 (27.44)	105 (48.84)	13 (6.05)	30 (13.95)	647	3.01	XII
2	Rental charges for storage	84 (39.07)	59 (27.44)	55 (25.58)	10 (4.65)	7 (3.26)	848	3.94	VI
3	Weighing process	102 (47.44)	60 (27.91)	18 (8.37)	20 (9.30)	15 (6.98)	859	4.00	IV
4	Immediate cash payment	105 (48.84)	46 (21.40)	43 (20.00)	11 (5.12)	10 (4.65)	870	4.05	II
5	Commission charges/ market fees	84 (39.07)	62 (28.84)	45 (20.93)	10 (4.65)	14 (6.51)	837	3.89	VII
6	To get advance money/ pledge loan	97 (45.12)	75 (34.88)	32 (14.88)	4 (1.86)	7 (3.26)	896	4.17	I
7	Transport cost	21 (9.77)	31 (14.42)	130 (60.47)	21 (9.77)	12 (5.58)	673	3.13	XI
8	Storage facility	42 (19.53)	93 (43.26)	45 (20.93)	21 (9.77)	14 (6.51)	773	3.60	IX
9	Behaviour of agent/ officials of regulated market	101 (46.98)	40 (18.60)	37 (17.21)	12 (5.58)	25 (11.63)	825	3.84	VIII
10	Grading and analysis	89 (41.4)	55 (25.58)	61 (28.37)	4 (1.86)	6 (2.79)	862	4.01	III
11	Packing of sugar	68 (31.63)	90 (41.86)	40 (18.6)	12 (5.58)	5 (2.33)	849	3.95	V
12	Insurance facility for sugar	72 (33.49)	21 (9.77)	51 (23.72)	25 (11.63)	46 (21.40)	693	3.22	X

Source: Primary Data, (Figures in parentheses represent percentages) HS-Highly Satisfied, S-Satisfied, N-Neutral, DS-Dissatisfied, HDS-Highly Dissatisfied

Table 5.21 displays that farmers have high level of satisfaction on 'to get advance money/ pledge loan' with the highest mean score value of 4.17 and farmers have low level of satisfaction on reasonable price with the lowest mean score value of 3.01 about the functioning of khandsari sugar marketing channels. Thus, it is concluded that farmers have high level of satisfaction on 'to get advance money/pledge loan' with the highest mean score value of 4.17 about the functioning of khandsari sugar marketing channels.

5.15.1. Quantification and Scoring Procedure

To measure the level of satisfaction of the farmers about the functioning of khandsari sugar marketing channels, Rensis likert five point scaling technique has been adopted. In interview schedule, twelve statements relating to the functioning of khandsari sugar marketing channels have been constructed. All these statements are generated on the basis of the experience gained during the pilot study and also based on review of relevant literature. The farmers have been asked to indicate their satisfaction regarding each statement in the likert's 5 point scale. The total score of each statement has been calculated for all the twelve statements using the scoring procedure.

The score of 215 farmers have been calculated. An individual's score is the mere summation of the scores secured from the 12 statements. The score of the farmers ranges from 12 to 60. Further, for the purpose of analysis based on the satisfaction score, the farmers have been grouped into two viz., low satisfaction and high satisfaction. The farmers who have scored 36 or less are classified as 'Low Satisfaction', the farmers who have scored above 36 are classified as 'High Satisfaction'. Table 5.22 shows the distribution of farmers on the basis of their level of satisfaction about the functioning of khandsari sugar marketing channels.

Table 5.22: Distribution of Farmers on the Basis of their Satisfaction Level

Satisfaction	No. of farmers	Per cent	Mean score
Low (12 to36)	118	54.90	42.11
High (37 to 60)	97	45.10	53.30
Total	**215**	**100.00**	**47.16**

Table 5.22 shows that the mean score of all the farmers is 47.16. Among 215 farmers, 97 (45.10 per cent) farmers have high level of satisfaction about the functioning of khandsari sugar marketing channels whereas 118 (54.90 per cent) farmers have low level of satisfaction about the functioning of khandsari sugar marketing channels.

Thus, it is concluded that 118 (54.90 per cent) farmers have low level of satisfaction about the functioning of khandsari sugar marketing channels.

5.15.2. Regression Analysis: Logistic Model

The same logistic model is applied for analysing the relationship between personal and socio-economic characteristics of the farmers and their level of satisfaction about the functioning of khandsari sugar marketing channels.

The level of satisfaction of farmers about the functioning of khandsari sugar marketing channels is hypothesized to be a function of the 12 statements (measured on a 5- point likert type scale). The statements include reasonable price, rental charges for storage, weighing process, immediate cash payment, commission charge/market charge, to get advance money/pledge loan, transport cost, storage facility, behaviour of agent/officials of regulated market, grading and analysis, packing of sugar and insurance facility for sugar. Level of satisfaction = 1 if the respondent is highly satisfied (above 36) with functioning of khandsari sugar marketing channels 0 otherwise (18 or less). The statistical relationship between the level of satisfaction and their personal and socio economic characteristics of farmers are determined with the help of logistic model. The results of logistic regression are presented in Table 5.23.

Table 5.23: Satisfaction of Farmers - Logistic Regression Analysis

	Co-efficient	S .E	Z	p-value
Constant	-1.639	1.099	-1.49	0.136
Age (χ_1)	-0.029	0.136	-0.21	0.837
Educational level (χ_2)	-0.039	0.136	-0.28	0.777
Occupation (χ_3)	-0.344	0.172	-1.99	0.046
Size of the family (χ_4)	0.158	0.155	1.02	0.308
Earning members in the family (χ_5)	1.524	1.092	1.40	0.163
Annual expenditure (χ_6)	1.308	1.091	1.19	0.231
Experience in agriculture (χ_7)	0.976	1.091	0.89	0.371
Experience in Sugarcane cultivation (χ_8)	0.863	1.097	0.79	0.432
Years of producing khandsari sugar(χ_9)	-0.028	0.141	-0.19	0.843

The logistic regression is In $(\hat{y})$ = -1.639 -0.029χ_1 -0.039χ_2 -0.344χ_3+0.158χ_4 +1.524χ_5 +1.308χ_6 +0.976χ_7 +0.863χ_8 -0.028χ_9

Interpreting the co-efficient of the logistic regression is somewhat more complex. If a co-efficient is positive, an increase in that independent variable will result in an increase in the probability of the event. The co-efficient of χ_1, χ_2, χ_3 and χ_9, are negative. This tells us an increase in the independent variable will result in a decrease in the probability of the event. If the age of respondent increases, has a higher probability of getting low satisfaction or dissatisfaction about the functioning of khandsari sugar marketing channels. Among the nine independent variables insignificantly related to level of satisfaction of farmers about the functioning of khandsari sugar marketing channels.

Model Fit

The same model is applied to the functioning of khandsari sugar marketing channels. The Model summary on r square is presented in Table 5.24.

Table 5.24: Model Summary on R Square

Model Summary on R Square			
Step	**-2Log likelihood**	**Cox & Snell R Square**	**Nagelkerke R Square**
1	37.407[a]	0.174	0.335

Table 5.24 indicates that the Cox & Snell R square and Nagelkerke R Square tells that all explanatory variables in the significantly fitted model could explain 17.4 per cent and 33.5 per cent of variance in satisfaction of about the functioning of khandsari sugar marketing channels.

Table 5.25: Classification by Model

Observed	Predicted		
	Low (0)	**High (1)**	**Percentage Correct**
Low	105	13	89.3
High	21	76	78.3
Overall Percentage			84.3

Table 5.25 it is noticeable to that 89.3 per cent of low satisfaction farmers are correctly classified by the model and 78.3 per cent of the high satisfaction farmers are correctly classified by the model. Overall 84.3 per cent of cases could be accurately classified by the model. False prediction either negative or positive is below 20 per cent. Hence, logistic model

can be used for predicting the satisfaction of farmers regarding the functioning of khandsari sugar marketing channels with 84.3 per cent accuracy.

5.16. Marketing Cost Incurred by Farmers to Market their Khandsari Sugar

Marketing costs refer to the cost incurred for various marketing functionaries who performed various marketing functions[79]. It includes all the marketing charges from local assembling to retail in the marketing process i.e. the cost of performing the various marketing functions and of operating various agencies.[80] Generally, high marketing costs and margins are considered to be indicators of inefficiency in the marketing process. But this is not always true. It is known fact that a major part of the consumer's rupee is spent on marketing cost. A number of factors may operate to cause a high proportion of marketing cost, without any reflection on the efficiency of the marketing system.[81]

Marketing cost is the cost incurred to move the product from the producer to the consumer is known as marketing cost. In other words, the cost of performing the various marketing functions is known as marketing cost.[82] The study of marketing of any commodity is incomplete if it does not cover the cost involved in the marketing of the commodity. The marketing cost assumes a focal point of interest in the marketing of most commodities, since marketing cost directly affect the net returns to producers' as well as consumers' satisfaction. Therefore, cost of marketing is frequently considered s an index to measure the marketing efficiency. In this regard, it is decided to analyse the price spread, marketing cost and marketing margin.

In this area, the marketing costs incurred by farmers differ significantly in the identified two channels. Marketing cost for khandsari sugar farmers constitutes the expenses like loading and unloading cost, packing cost, transport cost, storage cost, commission paid to commission agent and miscellaneous expenses etc., In marketing of khandsari sugar, one bag of khandsari sugar is 60 kg. The marketing cost incurred by farmers in marketing one bag of khandsari sugar has been worked out and are presented in Table 5.26.

---

[79]Deokate T.D. and Tilekar H.R., (2011), "Marketing of jaggery in western Maharashtra", Indian Journal of Agricultural Marketing, Vol.25, No.1.

[80]Jitender Singh and Subhash Chandra (2007), "Economic aspects of Sugarcane Marketing in Faizabad district of eastern Uttar Pradesh", Agricultural Marketing, Vol. L, No. 1, April-June.

[81]Acharya S.S and Agarwal N.L., (1994), Agricultural Marketing in India, Oxford & IBH Publishing Company Private Limited, New Delhi.

[82]Kohi (1964), "Marketing of Agricultural Product", Third Edition, The Macmillan Company, New Delhi.

Table 5.26: Marketing Cost Incurred by Farmers to Market their Khandsari Sugar

Marketing Cost	Channels-I		Channels-II	
	Amount (₹/bag)	Per cent	Amount (₹/bag)	Per cent
Loading and unloading cost	12.36	27.12	13.48	29.15
Packing cost	14.26	31.29	15.35	33.19
Transport cost	16.12	35.37	16.42	35.50
Storage cost	0.00	0.00	1.00	2.16
Commission paid to commission agent	1.58	3.47	0.00	0.00
Miscellaneous expenses	1.25	2.74	0.00	0.00
Total Cost	45.57	100.00	46.25	100.00

Source: Primary Data

Table 5.26 depicts that the total expense incurred by farmers in marketing of khandsari sugar is ₹ 45.57 per bag through channel I and channel II ₹ 46.25 per bag. Transport cost is the major cost which constituted to the cost of khandsari sugar marketing followed by packing cost, loading and unloading, commission paid to commission agent, miscellaneous expenses and storage cost.

Hence, it is concluded that transport cost and packing cost are the major costs incurred by farmers to market their khandsari sugar.

5.17. Marketing Cost Incurred by Market Functionaries

In this area, farmers to market their khandsari sugar either through commission agent or through regulated market. In khandsari sugar market, wholesaler and retailer act as marketing functionaries in the khandsari sugar market. In this market, the farmers market their khandsari sugar through commission agent. The marketing cost incurred by the wholesalers and retailers have been worked out and are presented in Table 5.27.

Table 5.27: Marketing Cost Incurred by Market Functionaries

Marketing Cost	Wholesaler		Retailer	
	Amount (₹/bag)	Per cent	Amount (₹/bag)	Per cent
Loading and unloading	14.78	14.36	13.20	9.47
Rent	1.36	1.32	0.00	0.00
Transport cost	22.47	21.82	18.26	13.10
Market fees	4.72	4.58	0.00	0.00
Labour &packing cost	1.70	1.65	26.72	19.17
Miscellaneous expenditure	1.04	1.01	1.38	0.99
Commission paid to commission agent	56.89	55.25	0.00	0.00
Weight loss	0.00	0.00	79.84	57.27
Total	102.96	100.00	139.40	100.00

Table 5.27 exhibits that the total expenses incurred by wholesaler for marketing of khandsari sugar are ₹ 102.96 per bag. Commission paid to commission agent (55.25 per cent) is the major cost which constituted to the total cost of marketing of khandsari sugar for wholesaler followed by transport cost, loading & unloading, market fees, labour & packing cost, rent and miscellaneous expenditure.

The total expenses incurred by retailer for marketing of khandsari sugar are ₹ 139.40 per bag. Weight loss (57.27 per cent) is the major cost which constituted to the total cost of marketing of khandsari sugar for retailer followed by labour & packing cost, transport cost, loading & unloading and miscellaneous expenditure. Hence, it is concluded that 'Commission paid to commission agent' and 'Weight loss' are major costs incurred by the wholesaler and retailer for marketing of khandsari sugar.

5.18. Price Spread of Khandsari Sugar

The price of khandsari sugar is fluctuating on the basis of season and demand. Further, the price available to farmers producing khandsari sugar is purely based on demand and supply. To analyse the marketing efficiency in various identified channels, the farmers have been asked to reveal the price realised by them for one bag of khandsari sugar from the intermediaries. Such collected data have been averaged and the same is used for analysis purpose. On this basis, price received by the farmers producing khandsari sugar in the first channel is worked out as ₹ 1893.55 per bag. In the second channel, it is ₹ 1957.28 per bag.

Price spread is one of the important measures of marketing efficiency. It indicates the difference between the price paid for by the consumer and price received by producer for the same quantity of produce. This spread consists of marketing cost and margins of the intermediaries which ultimately determine the overall effectiveness of the marketing system. The market is said to be efficient if the price spread is minimum. The price spread varies, depending on the number of intermediaries involved in the marketing channel. Hence, more the number of intermediaries, higher are the price spread and vice versa. Generally, the channel having the lowest price spread is preferred. The price is one of the important factors which will have a decisive impact on the profit margin of the producers. Table 5.28 shows the price spread of khandsari sugar in channel-I.

Table 5.28: Price Spread for Khandsari Sugar in Channel-I

S. No.	Price Spread	Amount (₹/bag)	Per cent
1	Farmer Net Price received	1847.98	81.17
	Marketing cost	45.57	2.00
	Gross Price Received	**1893.55**	**83.17**
2	Wholesaler price paid	1893.55	83.17
	Marketing cost	102.96	4.52
	Marketing margin	48.20	2.12
	Price Received	**2044.71**	**89.81**
3	Retailer price paid	2044.71	89.81
	Marketing cost	139.40	6.12
	Marketing margin	92.67	4.07
4	**Price Received or Price Paid by consumer**	**2276.78**	**100.00**
5	Producer's share in consumer's price	81.17	
6	**Price Spread**	**428.80**	

It is observed from the Table 5.28 that the farmer received the maximum price of ₹ 1847.98 through channel-I (sold through commission agent). The marketing cost incurred by the farmers for marketing their khandsari sugar through channel-I ₹ 45.57.

The marketing cost incurred by wholesaler is ₹ 102.96 and retailer is ₹ 139.40 for marketing of khandsari sugar. The marketing margin charged by wholesaler is ₹ 48.20 and retailer is ₹ 92.67 when khandsari sugar is sold through channel-I. Price paid by consumer ₹ 2276.78 in channel-I and the producers' share in consumer rupee is 81.17.

Hence, it is concluded that price spread is ₹ 428.80 for marketing of khandsari sugar. Table 5.29 shows the price spread of khandsari sugar in channel-II.

Table 5.29: Price Spread for Khandsari Sugar in Channel-II

S. No.	Price Spread	Amount (₹/bag)	Per cent
1	Farmer Net Price received	1911.03	97.64
	Marketing cost	46.25	2.36
	Gross Price received	**1957.28**	**100.00**
2	Wholesaler price paid	1957.28	100.00
3	**Price Received or Price Paid by consumer**	**1957.28**	
4	Producer's share in consumer's price	97.64	
5	Price spread	46.25	

It is observed from the Table 5.29 that the farmer received the maximum price of ₹ 1911.03 through channel-II (sold through regulated market). The marketing cost incurred by the farmers for marketing their khandsari sugar through channel-II ₹ 46.25. Price paid by consumer ₹ 1957.28 in channel-II and the producers' share in consumer rupee is 97.64. Hence, it is concluded that price spread is ₹ 46.25 for marketing of khandsari sugar through channel-II.

5.19. Summary

In this chapter, an attempt has been made to identify the factors which motivate the farmers to market their sugarcane and khandsari sugar. To study the marketing cost, price spread and level of satisfaction of farmers about the functioning of sugarcane and khandsari sugar marketing channels. The major findings of this chapter are:

- It is found that the majority (81.30 per cent) of farmers prefer channel-I (Farmer- Factory) to market their sugarcane. It is also found that fixed price is the significant factor which motivates the farmers to market their sugarcane to factory.
- It is found that flexibility in harvesting is the significant factor which motivates the farmers to market their sugarcane to jaggery producers.
- It is found that remunerative price for sugar is the main factor which motivates the farmers to produce of khandsari sugar. It is found that getting advance money is the

most significant factor which motivates the farmers to market their khandsari sugar through channel-I (through commission agent) and it is also found that the immediate cash payment is the important factor which motivates the farmers to market their khandsari sugar through channel-II (through regulated market).

- By applying Logistic Regression Model, it is found that Age, Size of the family, Experience in agriculture and Experience in sugarcane cultivation are significantly related to the level of satisfaction of farmers about the functioning sugarcane marketing channel-I (Farmers-Factory). It is also found that Occupation and Earnings members in the family are significantly related to the level of satisfaction of farmers about the functioning sugarcane marketing channel-II (Farmers-Jaggery producers). Further, it is found that all nine independent variables (Age, Educational level, Occupation, Size of the family, Earning members in the family, Annual Expenditure, Experience in agriculture, Experience in sugarcane cultivation, Years of producing khandsari sugar) are insignificantly related to the level of satisfaction of farmers who produce of khandsari sugar.

- In price spread analysis, it is found that transport cost and packing cost are the major costs incurred by farmers to market their khandsari sugar through channel-I. Price paid by consumer ₹ 2276.78 in channel-I and the producers' share in consumer rupee is 81.17. Hence, it is concluded that price spread is ₹ 428.80 for marketing of khandsari sugar through channel-I.

- Further, it is found that price paid by consumer ₹ 1957.28 in channel-II and the producers' share in consumer rupee are 97.64. Hence, it is concluded that price spread is ₹ 46.25 for marketing of khandsari sugar through channel-II.

CHAPTER VI

CULTIVATION AND MARKETING PROBLEMS OF SUGARCANE FARMERS

Keywords

Problems in Cultivation of Sugarcane - Problems faced by farmers in production of Khandsari Sugar - Problems in marketing of sugarcane and Khandsari Sugar.

6.1. Introduction

Agriculture is the backbone of the Indian economy and it continues to be the most predominant sector of Indian economy.

In future as majority of the population depends directly or indirectly on it. Agricultural has been considered as the primary occupation in the developing countries.

Now-a-days in the agricultural sector in India, cultivable land has been declined due to rapid urbanisation and industrialisation. It has been subjected to countless problems such as untapped groundwater level, non-availability of agricultural labourers, loss of soil fertility, inadequate credit support, high cost of fertilizers, not tapping the potential yields, imbalanced fertilizer use, low price for agricultural products, poor economic policies, non-availability of machineries, diversion of cultivable land for non-agricultural purposes, improper cultivation practices and lack of government support for farmers, poorly maintained irrigation systems. Farmers' access to market is hampered by poor roads, rudimentary market infrastructure and excessive regulations and almost universal lack of good extension services are responsible factors. It leads the farming community a hand to mouth existence.

Agricultural sector is not well developed and faces lots of problems resulting in low productivity of crops. As 43 per cent of land in India is used for farming but contributes only 18 per cent of the nation's GDP. The poor condition of agriculture is the main concern for Indians. The rural farmers in India suffer from poverty and most of them are illiterate, so there is a lack of good extension services. Agricultural sector growth was lower at 1.9 per cent in 2012-2013 as compared to 3.6 per cent in 2011-2012[83]. Agriculture Growth Rate in India's GDP has slowed down because the production in this sector has reduced over the years.

---

[83] Government of India (2013), op.cit., p.5.

The agricultural sector has had low production due to a number of factors such as illiteracy, insufficient finance and inadequate marketing of agricultural product. Further, the reason for the decline in Agriculture Growth Rate in India's GDP are that in the sector the average size of the farms are very small which in turn has resulted in low productivity. This sector has not adopted modern technology in agricultural practices and has insufficient irrigation facilities. As a result of this, the farmers are dependent on rainfall, which is however very unpredictable[84].

This chapter focused to identify the problems faced by farmers in cultivation and marketing of sugarcane. For identifying the problems faced by the farmers in sugarcane cultivation, Simple Ranking Technique, Reliability Analysis, Factor Analysis and Discriminant Function Analysis have been employed. The problems faced by the farmers in the production of khandsari sugar has been analysed with the help of Ranking Analysis. The problems in marketing of sugarcane and khandsari sugar have been analysed with the help of Rank Based Quotient Technique (RBQ).

6.2.   Problems in Cultivation of Sugarcane

Sugarcane is a long duration crop as compared to other cash crops grown in the country. It requires great skill and huge investment in the form of inputs on the part of the farmers to grow this labour-intensive and cost-oriented crop. On the basis of results of the pilot study, the problems like shortage and high wages of labourers, water scarcity, severity of diseases and new diseases, increased rats, weeds etc., Shortage and high cost of fertilizer and pesticides, poor quality of setts, poor quality of fertilizer & pesticides, non-availability of high yield and new varieties, low yield in ratoon crop, inadequate loan facilities, non-availability of sugarcane cultivation machinery, decrease & difference in yield, difficulties in unfavourable conditions, frequent power failure, repeated sugarcane cultivation reduces yield, poor knowledge in irrigation practices, risk in crop maintenance and low awareness to use improved cultivation practices. For identifying the most important problems faced by the farmers in cultivation of sugarcane with the help of Ranking Analysis, Reliability Analysis, Factor Analysis and Discriminant Function Analysis have been employed and the results are displayed in Table 6.1.

---

[84]Ramesh Kumar P., (2013), "Globalisation and Indian Agricultural Performance", Kisan World, Vol. 40, No. 8, August, pp. 35-39.

Table 6.1: Problems in Cultivation of Sugarcane-Simple Ranking Technique

S. NO	Cultivation Problems	Most Important	Important	Medium	Less Important	Not Important	Total Score	Mean Score	Rank
1	Shortage and high wages of labourers	435 (72.50)	76 (12.67)	34 (5.67)	25 (4.17)	30 (5.00)	2661	4.44	I
2	Water scarcity	97 (16.17)	80(13.33)	250(41.67)	97(16.17)	76(12.67)	1825	3.04	XVI
3	Severity of diseases and new diseases	203(33.83)	177(29.50)	127(21.17)	51(8.50)	42(7.00)	2248	3.75	IV
4	Increased rats, weeds etc.	173 (28.83)	46(7.67)	178(29.67)	118(19.67)	85(14.17)	1904	3.17	XV
5	Shortage and high cost of fertilizer and pesticides	110 (18.33)	299(49.83)	106(17.67)	34(5.67)	51(8.50)	2183	3.64	VII
6	Poor quality of setts	25 (4.17)	46(7.67)	369(61.50)	118(19.67)	42(7.00)	2017	3.36	XI
7	Poor quality of fertilizer & pesticides	139 (23.17)	203(33.83)	165(27.50)	48(7.00)	45(8.50)	2143	3.57	VIII
8	Non availability of high yield and new varieties	156(26.00)	229(38.17)	118(19.67)	55(9.17)	42(7.00)	2202	3.67	VI
9	Low yield in ratoon crop	245 (40.83)	153(25.50)	101(16.83)	63(10.50)	38(6.33)	2304	3.84	III
10	Inadequate loan facilities	68(11.33)	59(9.83)	228(38.00)	169(28.17)	76(12.67)	1674	2.79	XVIII
11	Non availability of sugarcane cultivation machinery	55(9.17)	194(32.33)	190(31.67)	123(20.50)	38(6.33)	1905	3.18	XIV
12	Decrease & difference in yield	220(36.67)	181(30.17)	55(9.17)	76(12.67)	68(11.33)	2209	3.68	V
13	Difficulties in unfavourable conditions	42(7.00)	245(40.83)	80(13.33)	123(20.50)	110(18.33)	1786	2.98	XVII
14	Frequent power failure	110(18.33)	248(41.33)	85(14.17)	85(14.17)	72(12.00)	2039	3.40	X
15	Repeated sugarcane cultivation reduces yield	38(6.33)	177(29.50)	304(50.67)	30(5.00)	51(8.50)	1921	3.20	XIII
16	Poor knowledge in irrigation practices	203 (33.83)	186(31.00)	63(10.50)	42(7.00)	106(17.67)	2138	3.56	IX
17	Risk in crop maintenance	423(70.50)	46(7.67)	55(9.17)	42(7.00)	34(5.67)	2582	4.30	II
18	Low awareness to use improved cultivation practices	173(28.83)	127(21.17)	118(19.67)	93(15.50)	89(14.83)	2002	3.34	XII

Source: Primary Data; (Figures in parentheses represents percentages)

Table 6.1 depicts that shortage and high wages of labourers (4.44) is identified as the most important problem in cultivation of sugarcane followed by the risk in crop maintenance (4.30), low yield in ratoon crop (3.84), severity of diseases and new diseases (3.75), decrease & difference in yield (3.68), non-availability of high yield varieties and new varieties (3.67), shortage and high cost of fertilizer and pesticides (3.64), poor quality of fertilizer & pesticides (3.57), poor knowledge in irrigation practices (3.56), frequent power failure (3.40), poor quality of setts (3.36), low awareness to use improved cultivation practices (3.34), repeated sugarcane cultivation reduces yield (3.20), non-availability of sugarcane cultivation machinery

(3.18), increased rats, weeds etc., (3.17), water scarcity (3.04), difficulties in unfavourable climate conditions (2.98) and inadequate loan facilities (2.79).

Hence, it is concluded that shortage and high wages of labourers (4.44) is identified as the most important problem in cultivation of sugarcane.

6.2.1. *Reliability Analysis for Problems in Cultivation of Sugarcane*

To carry out factor analysis, initially the reliability test has been applied. The reliability of scales used in this study is based on cronbach's co-efficient alpha. cronbach's alpha reliability co-efficient normally ranges between 0 and 1. However, there is no lower limit to the co-efficient. The closer cronbach's alpha reliability co-efficient is to 1.0 greater the internal consistency of the items in the scale. If the co-efficient alpha values exceed the minimum standard error of 0.50 then it gives good estimates of internal consistency reliability. Table 6.2 depicts the reliability test for problems in cultivation of sugarcane.

Table 6.2: Problems in Cultivation of Sugarcane- Reliability Analysis

Source		Sum of Squares	Mean Square	F- Value	Significant	Cronbach's
Between People		236.461	1.677	94.122	0.000*	0.651
Within People	Between Items	1195.925	54.36			
	Residual	1791.554	0.578			
	Total	2987.78	0.956			
Total		3223.939	0.987			

*Significance at 5 per cent level

Table 6.2 reveals that all the eighteen measurement scale items are reliable as the Cronbach alpha efficient is 0.651. It is greater than the threshold level of 0.50. It has provided acceptable estimates of internal consultancy reliability and also co-efficient alpha values for all constructs. It indicates that the scales used in this study are reliable. It clearly indicates that the above scale items are consistent with each other and they are reliable measure to find out the problems in cultivation of sugarcane. Hence, it has been applied for factor analysis.

6.2.2. *Problems in Cultivation of Sugarcane - Factor Analysis*

The problems in cultivation of sugarcane are narrated with the help of factor analysis. The results of the findings are shown in Table 6.3.

Table 6.3: KMO and Bartlett's Test

Kaiser-Meyer-Olkin Measure of Sampling Adequacy		0.647
Bartlett's Test of Sphericity	Approx. Chi-Square	2119.00
	Sig.	0.000

Table 6.3 reveals that the measured value of Kaiser-Meyer-Olk in measure of sampling adequacy is 0.647 which is greater than 0.50. So, that ensures the appropriateness of sampling. Hence, it is decided to apply the Factor Analysis.

Rotated Component Matrix

The scores of the variable leading to problems in cultivation of sugarcane have been included in the factor analysis. The rotated component matrixes for the influencing variables are given in Table 6.4.

Table 6.4: Problems in Cultivation of Sugarcane-Rotated Component Matrix

VARIABLES	COMPONENT					
	1	**2**	**3**	**4**	**5**	**6**
Shortage and high cost of fertilizer and pesticides	**0.877**	-0.07	0.197	0.089	-0.031	0.096
Shortage and high wages of labourers	**-0.518**	-0.056	0.035	0.052	-0.42	-0.051
Low yield in ratoon crop	0.169	**0.804**	0.08	0.047	0.024	0.030
Decrease & difference in yield	0.181	**0.658**	0.111	0.022	0.302	0.129
Risk in crop maintenance	-0.305	**0.617**	0.288	0.147	-0.487	-0.200
Non-availability of sugarcane cultivation machinery	0.370	**-0.546**	0.312	0.046	0.051	-0.470
Severity of diseases and new diseases	0.241	-0.191	**0.788**	0.154	0.092	0.137
Poor quality of setts	-0.098	0.258	**0.768**	0.122	-0.245	0.142
Non-availability of high yield varieties and new varieties	-0.052	-0.002	**-0.605**	-0.167	0.183	-0.183
Low awareness to use improved cultivation practices	0.226	-0.066	0.032	**0.796**	-0.102	-0.061
Poor knowledge in irrigation practices	-0.339	0.064	0.361	**0.748**	0.116	0.023
Increased rats, weeds etc.	0.438	-0.072	0.259	**0.547**	-0.253	0.044
Poor quality of fertilizer & pesticides	-0.015	-0.611	0.016	-0.122	**0.625**	-0.182
Inadequate loan facilities	0.177	0.567	-0.019	-0.325	**0.568**	0.13
Frequent power failure	-0.046	-0.312	-0.008	-0.008	-0.140	**0.888**
Repeated sugarcane cultivation reduces yield	-0.067	0.053	0.025	0.250	0.011	**-0.816**
Difficulties in unfavourable climate conditions	0.164	0.115	0.388	0.071	-0.031	**-0.735**
Water scarcity	-0.244	0.018	-0.124	-0.055	0.363	**0.628**

Extraction Method: Principal Component Analysis. Rotation Method: Varimax with Kaiser Normalization.

The factor analysis narrated the eighteen variables into six factors Cost orientation, Crop orientation, Seed orientation, Maintenance orientation, Input orientation and General problem. The highly correlated variable of the Cost orientation is 'Shortage and high cost of fertilizer and pesticides'. It has the factor loading of 0.877. The variable 'Low yield in ratoon crop' is the highly correlated variable of the Crop orientation since it has the highest factor loading of 0.804. Severity of diseases and new diseases variable of the Seed orientation has the highest factor loading of 0.788. In case of Maintenance orientation, the variable 'Low awareness to use improved cultivation practices' has the highest factor loading of 0.796. The highly correlated variable of the Input orientation is Poor quality of fertilizer & pesticides which has the factor loading of 0.625. Regarding the General problem, higher correlation is noticed in the case of variable 'Frequent power failure', since it has the highest factor loading of 0.888.

The number of variables in each factor, Eigen value and the per cent of variation explained by each factor are presented in Table 6.5.

Table 6.5: Problems in Cultivation of Sugarcane-Principal Component Analysis

S.No.	Problems	No. of variables	Eigen Value	Per cent of Variation Explained	Cumulative per cent of Variation Explained
1	CostOrientation	2	3.289	14.301	14.301
2	Crop Orientation	4	3.212	13.964	28.265
3	SeedOrientation	3	3.117	13.552	41.817
4	MaintenanceOrientation	3	2.713	11.794	53.611
5	Input Orientation	2	2.680	11.651	65.261
6	General problem	4	1.329	5.778	71.039

Table 6.5 shows that the most important problems in sugar cane cultivation are 'Cost orientation' and 'Crop Orientation' since their Eigen values are 3.289 and 3.212 respectively. The Cost orientation consists of two variables with the variation explained by 14.301 per cent. The Crop orientation consists of four variables with the variation explained by 13.964 per cent. The third and fourth factors are 'Seed orientation' and 'Maintenance orientation' since their respective Eigen values are 3.117 and 2.713 with consists of three variables and the percent of variation explained by these two factors are 13.552 and 11.794 respectively. The fifth and sixth factors are 'Input orientation' and 'General problem' since their respective Eigen values are2.680 and 1.329 respectively. The Input orientation consists of two variables with the variation explained by 11.651 per cent and General problem consists of four variables with the variation explained by 5.778 per cent. Hence, it is concluded that cost orientation problem is the major problem in cultivation of sugarcane.

6.2.3. *Construction of Discriminant Function*

The Discriminant Function Analysis is a multivariate analysis which provides more complete explanation for complex phenomena. A discriminant function is a regression equation with a dependent variable that represents group membership[85]. It is used to classify objects into two groups or more. In the present study, the farmers are classified into two groups' viz., low problem and high problem. An attempt has been made to determine how the low problem differs from high problem with respect to problems in cultivation of sugarcane.

Discriminant Function Analysis is used to construct a function with the variables in order to differentiate the farmers belonging to either of the two groups at the maximum. The discriminant function model includes in sugarcane cultivation problems and personal factors. All these variables are selected based on Mahalanobis Minimum D squared method. The Mahalanobis procedure is based on the Generalized Squared Euclidean Distance that adjusts for unequal variances in the variables. It is the preferred procedure to get the available information to the maximum extent. In computing discriminant function, step-wise method is

---

[85]Krishnaswami O.R and Ranganatham M., (2011), "Methodology of Research in Social Science", Himalaya publishing house, Mumbai.

used where the independent variables in the discriminant function are entered one at a time on the basis of their discriminating power.

The stepwise approach begins by choosing the single best discriminating variable. It is then paired with each of the other independent variables one at a time and a second variable is chosen. The second variable is one of the best to improve the discriminating power of the function in combination with the first variable. The subsequent variables are selected in a similar manner. Addition variables are included, some of the already selected variables may be removed if the information they contain about group differences is available in some combination of the other already included variables (multicollinearity). Eventually, either all independent variables have been included in the function or the excluded variables have been judged as not contributing significantly to further discrimination. By sequentially selecting the next best discriminating variable at each step, variables that are not useful in discriminating between the groups are eliminated and reduced set of variables is identified. The results of the discriminant function analysis with the values of canonical discriminant function co-efficient for each of the discriminating variables are shown in Table 6.6.

Table 6.6: Problems in Cultivation of Sugarcane - Canonical Discriminant Function Co-Efficient

S. No.	Variables	Function Co-efficient
1	Size of the family	-0.111
2	Earnings members in the family	0.403
3	Nature of the family	-0.456
4	Age	-0.887
5	Annual expenditure	0.050
6	Sugarcane cultivation knowledge	0.438
7	Experience in sugarcane cultivation	0.595
8	Agricultural information	-0.028
9	Source of irrigation	-0.126
10	Source of finance	0.580

Table 6.6 shows that out of eighteen variables selected for analysis, step-wise approach included only ten variables in the model. The discriminant function (Z) for study can be written as,

$$Z = \alpha - 0.111X_1 + 0.403X_2 - 0.456X_3 - 0.887X_4 + 0.050X_5 + 0.438X_6 + 0.595X_7 - 0.028X_8 - 0.126X_9 + 0.580X_{10}$$

Where,

X_1 = Size of the family

X_2 = Earnings members in the family

X_3 = Nature of the family

X_4 = Age

X_5= Annual expenditure

X_6= Sugarcane cultivation knowledge

X_7= Experience in sugarcane cultivation

X_8= Agricultural information

X_9= Source of irrigation

X_{10}=Source of finance

The canonical discriminant function is shown in Table 6.7.

Table 6.7: Problems in Cultivation of Sugarcane - Canonical Discriminant Function

Canonical Correlation	Wilk's Lambda	Chi-square	Result
0.396	0.844	22.965	Significant

It is clear from the Table 6.7 that discriminant function is significant at 1 per cent level as chi-square test (22.965) value and wilk's lambda value (0.844) are significant at 1 per cent level. It further reveals that the correlation is 0.396. This shows that there is a moderate level of canonical correlation between the grouping variable and the independent variables.

The discriminant score for each farmer is calculated by substituting the values for discriminating variables from the analysis data with the help of discriminant function. Then the mean scores for low problem group (Z_0) and high problem group (Z_1) are calculated. It is known as group centroids. The results are shown in Table 6.8.

Table 6.8: Problems in Cultivation of Sugarcane- Canonical Discriminant Function at Group

Function at Group Centrodis	
Farmers groups	Function
Low problem	0.282
High problem	-0.649

Table 6.8 reveals that the group means for the discriminant functions are 0.282 for low problem group farmers and -0.649 for high problem group farmers. Prior probabilities are then calculated for each group based on the proportionate size of the sample in the respective groups. The prior probabilities for groups are shown in Table 6.9.

Table 6.9: Problems in Cultivation of Sugarcane - Prior Probabilities for Groups

Farmers groups	Prior probabilities	No. of farmers
Low problem farmers	0.697	418 (69.70)
High problem farmers	0.303	182 (30.30)
Total	**1.000**	**600 (100.00)**

Table 6.9 shows that the prior probabilities low problem group farmers are 0.697 and high problem group farmers are 0.303. It is identified that 69.70 per cent of the farmers are categorised as low problem group farmers and 30.30 per cent of the farmers are high problem

group farmers. The structure matrix which measures the simple linear correlations between each independent variable and the discriminant function is shown in Table 6.10.

Table 6.10: Problems in Cultivation of Sugarcane - Structure Matrix

Variables	Function (R)	R²
Age	-0.535	28.62
Sugarcane cultivation knowledge	0.465	21.62
Source of finance	0.391	15.29
Earnings members in the family	0.388	15.05
Experience in sugarcane cultivation	-0.258	6.66
Annual expenditure	0.216	4.67
Nature of the family	-0.200	4.00
Sources of irrigation	0.079	0.62
Agricultural information	-0.036	0.13
Size of the family	0.009	0.01

It is clear from the Table 6.10 that R^2 gives the percent contribution of each variable to discriminant function. It is found that the variable 'Age' is the maximum discriminating variable i.e. 28.62 per cent between low and high problem group farmers followed by Sugarcane cultivation knowledge (21.62 per cent), Source of finance (15.29 per cent), Earnings members in the family (15.05 per cent), Experience in sugarcane cultivation (6.66 per cent), Annual expenditure (4.67 per cent), Nature of the family (4.00 per cent), Source of irrigation (0.62 per cent), Agricultural information (0.13 per cent), Size of the family (0.01 per cent). The variables namely Nature of the family, Source of irrigation, Agricultural information and Size of the family less than 5 per cent discrimination between the low and high problem group farmers in cultivation of sugarcane. Thus, it is concluded that the variable 'Age' is the maximum discriminating variable is 28.62 per cent between low and high problem group farmers in cultivation of sugarcane.

6.3.   Problems Faced by Farmers in Production of Khandsari Sugar

In the present study, out of 600 farmers only 215 farmers are producing khandsari sugar. It is interesting to note that the processors are capable of engaging family members as workers for processing work of khandsari sugar production. On the basis of outcome of the pilot study, the problems like financial problem, high wage rate, non-availability of trained abourers, high rental charge of machinery, high fluctuation of sugar prices, problem in ratoon crops growth, high cost of chemicals and problems due to rainy seasons. For identifying the most important problem faced by the farmers in production of khandsari sugar, Simple ranking technique has been applied. The results of simple ranking technique are displayed in Table 6.11.

Table 6.11: Problems in Production of Khandsari Sugar

S. No.	Problems	MIM	IM	MIM	LIM	NIM	Total Score	Mean Score	Rank
1	Financial Problem	66(30.70)	88(40.93)	33(15.35)	15(6.98)	13(6.05)	824	3.83	VI
2	High wage rate	148(68.84)	22(10.23)	17(7.91)	10(4.65)	18(8.37)	917	4.27	II
3	Non availability of trained labourers	141(65.58)	34(15.81)	10(4.65)	19(8.84)	11(5.12)	920	4.28	I
4	High rental charge of machinery	25(11.63)	104(48.37)	40(18.60)	21(9.77)	25(11.63)	728	3.39	VII
5	High fluctuation of sugar prices	110(51.16)	48(22.33)	22(10.23)	21(9.77)	14(6.51)	864	4.02	IV
6	Problem in ratoon crops growth	145(67.44)	21(9.77)	11(5.12)	18(8.37)	20(9.30)	898	4.18	III
7	High cost of chemicals	5(2.33)	34(15.81)	141(65.58)	14(6.51)	21 (9.77)	633	2.94	VIII
8	Problems due to rainy seasons	100(46.51)	44(20.47)	42(19.53)	18(8.37)	11(5.12)	849	3.95	V

Source: Primary Data; MIM-Most Important, IM-Important, MIM–Medium Important, LIM-Less Important, NIM-Not Important (Figures in parentheses represents percentages)

Table 6.11 depicts that the non-availability of trained labourer is the primary problem in production of khandsari sugar with the highest mean score value of 4.28, followed by the high wage rate with the mean score value of 4.27, problem in ratoon crops growth (4.18), high fluctuation of sugar prices (4.02), problems due to rainy seasons (3.95), financial problem (3.83), high rental charge of machinery (3.39) and high cost of chemicals (2.94). Hence, it is concluded that the 'non-availability of trained labourer' is the primary problem in production of khandsari sugar with the highest mean score value of 4.28.

6.4. Problems in Marketing of Sugarcane and Khandsari Sugar

In this chapter to identify the problems in marketing of sugarcane and khandsari sugar. In order to identify the problems in marketing of sugarcane and khandsari sugar the rank based quotient has been applied. The quantification of data is done by first ranking the problems in marketing of sugarcane and khandsari sugar based on the responses obtained from the farmers and the Rank Based Quotient (RBQ) value is calculated. The formula for calculating RBQ is as follows:

$$R.B.Q. = \frac{\Sigma f_i (n+1-i)}{N \times n} \times 100$$

Where,

R.B.Q. = Rank Based Quotient

fi = Number of farmers are reporting a particular problem under i^{th} rank

N = Total number of Farmers

n = Number of problems identified

6.4.1. Problems in Marketing of Sugarcane to Factory

In the present study, out of 385 farmers, 313 farmers market their sugarcane to factory. In order to identify the most important problems in sugarcane marketing factory the rank based quotient has been applied. Five problems relating to marketing of sugarcane to factory are identified on the basis of outcome of pilot study and these are given in the final interview schedule. The results of RBQ analysis for problems in marketing of sugarcane to factory are presented in Table 6.12.

Table 6.12: Problems in Marketing of Sugarcane to Factory

S. NO	PROBLEMS	I	II	III	IV	V	RBQ	Overall Rank
1	Delay in harvesting	25	16	92	52	128	44.54	IV
2	High rate of cutting charge	12	27	102	168	4	52.01	III
3	Delay in payment	195	69	20	17	12	86.71	I
4	No transparency in weighing process	13	8	60	67	165	36.81	V
5	Fixed/low price of product	68	193	39	9	4	79.94	II

Source: Primary Data

Table 6.12 reveals that delay in payment is identified as the most significant problem in marketing of sugarcane to the factory with the highest RBQ value of 86.71, followed by fixed/low price of the product (79.94), high rate of cutting charge (52.01), delay in harvesting (44.54) and no transparency in weighing process (36.81).

Hence, it is concluded that delay in payment is the most significant problem in marketing of sugarcane to the factory with the highest RBQ value of 86.71.

6.4.2. Problems in Marketing of Sugarcane to Jaggery Producers

In the present study, out of 385 farmers, only 72 farmers market their sugarcane to jaggery producers. In order to identify the most important problems in sugarcane marketing to jaggery producers the rank based quotient has been applied. Five problems relating to marketing of sugarcane to jaggery producers are identified on the basis of outcome of pilot study and these are given in the final interview schedule. The results of RBQ analysis for problems in marketing of sugarcane to jaggery producers are presented in Table 6.13.

Table 6.13: Problems in Marketing of Sugarcane to Jaggery Producers

S. NO	PROBLEMS	I	II	III	IV	V	RBQ	Overall Rank
1	Non availability of crop insurance facility	5	8	8	21	30	42.50	V
2	Delay in harvesting	8	4	38	13	9	56.94	III
3	High wastage of sugarcane	30	26	12	0	4	81.67	I
4	Price flexibility	12	34	14	8	4	71.67	II
5	Delay in payment	17	0	0	30	25	47.22	IV

Source: Primary Data

Table 6.13 indicates that high wastage of sugarcane is identified as the major problem in marketing of sugarcane to jaggery producers with the highest value of RBQ (81.67), followed by price flexibility (71.67), the delay in harvesting (56.94), delay in payment (47.22) and non-availability of crop insurance facility (42.50).

Hence, it is concluded that high wastage of sugarcane is identified as the major problem in marketing of sugarcane to jaggery producers with the highest value of RBQ (81.67).

6.4.3. *Problems in Marketing of Khandsari Sugar through Commission Agent*

In the present study, out of 215 farmers, only 130 farmers market their khandsari sugar through commission agent. In order to identify the most important problems in khandsari sugar marketing through commission agent the rank based quotient has been applied. Nine problems relating to marketing of khandsari sugar through commission agent are identified on the basis of outcome of pilot study and these are given in the final interview schedule. The results of RBQ analysis for problems in marketing of khandsari sugar through commission agent are presented in Table 6.14.

Table 6.14: Problems in Marketing of Khandsari Sugar through Commission Agent

S. NO	PROBLEMS	I	II	III	IV	V	VI	VII	VIII	IX	RBQ	Overall Rank
1	High fluctuation in prices	20	50	28	0	4	20	0	0	8	73.16	III
2	High commission charge	60	33	5	5	4	10	0	5	8	80.94	I
3	Problem in grading and analysing	41	25	14	13	12	0	9	8	8	75.56	II
4	Non availability of crop insurance facility	0	8	61	33	5	0	9	9	5	65.30	IV
5	Delay in payment	5	5	5	60	47	4	4	0	0	63.50	V
6	Malpractices in weighment	0	5	12	5	24	46	25	13	0	47.78	VI
7	Can market only on Market day	4	0	5	0	21	4	13	69	14	32.74	VIII
8	High cost of loading, transport & rental charges	0	0	0	5	9	14	37	12	53	27.26	IX
9	Lack of market information	0	4	0	9	4	32	33	14	34	33.76	VII

Source: Primary Data

Table 6.14 exhibits that high commission charge is identified as the significant problem in marketing of khandsari sugar through commission agent with the highest RBQ value of 80.94, followed by problem in grading and analysing (75.56), high fluctuation in prices (73.14), non-availability of crop insurance facility (65.30), delay in payment (63.50), malpractices in weigh ment (47.78), lack of market information (33.76), can market only on market day (32.74) and high cost of loading, transport & rental charges (27.26).

Hence, it is concluded that high commission charge is identified as the significant problem in marketing of khandsari sugar through commission agent with the highest RBQ value of 80.94.

6.4.4. *Problems in Marketing of Khandsari Sugar through Regulated Market*

In the present study, out of 215 farmers, only 85 farmers market their khandsari sugar through regulated market. In order to identify the most important problem in khandsari sugar marketing through regulated market the rank based quotient has been applied. Nine problems relating to marketing of khandsari sugar through regulated market are identified on the basis of outcome of pilot study and these are given in the final interview schedule. The results of RBQ analysis for problems in marketing of khandsari sugar through regulated market are presented in Table 6.15.

Table 6.15: Problems in Marketing of Khandsari Sugar through Regulated Market

S. No	Problems	I	II	III	IV	V	VI	VII	VIII	IX	RBQ	Overall Rank
1	No advance money	35	5	20	0	4	4	12	0	5	74.77	I
2	Problem in grading & analysing	26	0	0	5	20	20	5	9	0	62.35	III
3	High cost of loading & transport charge	0	0	0	20	9	0	34	18	4	40.13	IX
4	Malpractices in weighment	4	22	5	5	16	29	4	0	0	63.40	II
5	Lack of packing materials	0	20	32	0	0	0	20	5	8	60.39	V
6	Lack of storage facility	0	4	16	9	13	0	0	25	18	43.27	VII
7	Lack of transport facility	0	4	4	37	14	5	5	0	16	52.68	VI
8	Time consuming	0	16	4	0	9	9	5	20	22	41.05	VIII
9	High rate of interest on loan	20	14	4	9	0	18	0	8	12	61.96	IV

Source: Primary Data

Table 6.15 displays that 'No advance money' is identified as the most important problem with the highest RBQ value of 74.77 in marketing of khandsari sugar through regulated market, followed by malpractices in weighment (63.40), the problem in grading & analysing (62.35), high rate of interest on loan (61.96), lack of packing materials (60.39), lack of transport facility (52.68), lack of storage facility (43.27), time consuming (41.05) and high cost of loading & transport charge (40.13). Hence, it is concluded that 'no advance money' is identified as the most important problem with the highest RBQ value of 74.77 in marketing of khandsari sugar through regulated market.

6.5. Summary

In this chapter, Problems in Cultivation and Marketing of Sugarcane farmers have been analysed. The major findings of this chapter are:

- By applying simple ranking technique, it is found that 'shortage and high wages of labourers' is the most important cultivation problem faced by the sugarcane farmers in this area. Further, it is found that the 'non-availability of trained labourers' are the major problem faced by the sugarcane farmers who produce khandsari sugar.

- By applying Rank Based Quotient technique, it is found that 'delay in payment' is the most significant problem in marketing of sugarcane to sugar factory. Further, it is found that 'high wastage of sugarcane' is the major problem in marketing of sugarcane to jaggery producers.
- It is also found that 'high commission charge' is the significant problem in marketing of khandsari sugar through commission agent and it is found that 'no advance money' is the most important problem in marketing of khandsari sugar through regulated market.

CHAPTER VII

A SUMMARY OF FINDINGS, SUGGESTIONS AND CONCLUSION

Keywords

Findings – Suggestions - Suggestions for further research - Conclusion

7.1.   Introduction

Agriculture is one of the strongholds of the Indian economy, draws its significance from the fact that it has vital supply and demand links with the manufacturing sector and is a source of livelihood for the rural population of India and it represents the backbone of rural livelihood security system. Agriculture is the mainstay of Indian economy because of its high share in employment and livelihood creation notwithstanding its reduced contribution to the nation's GDP. India is a large producer and consumer of agricultural commodities by world standards. Successful agricultural sector is the key to all the developmental processes in the country.

In the field of agriculture, the role played by sugarcane is a vital one. Today, sugarcane cultivation and sugar industry stands as supporting pillars of Indian economy and contributes for seven per cent of the total value of agricultural output. Sugarcane crop has a wider adaptability. It is predominantly grown in tropical and subtropical belt in India. Tamil Nadu is a large producer of sugarcane. Though Tamil Nadu is one of the leading producers in sugar production, it has various problems in cultivation and also in marketing. In order to modernise the cultivation and marketing practices of sugarcane, it is necessary to identify the functioning of marketing channels. Hence, this book has been undertaken.

In this chapter, an attempt has been made to bring together all the findings that have emerged from the present study along with various suggestive measures to improve the sugarcane cultivation and marketing practices in this area.

7.2.   Findings

The following are the findings:

Chapter II: Growth in Area, Production and Productivity of Sugarcane

In this chapter, an attempt has been made to analyse growth in area, production and productivity of sugarcane in Country-Wise, State-wise, District-wise and Sugar Export and Import in India. This study is based on the secondary data collected from various sources such as websites of Sugarcane Breeding Institution, Food and Agricultural Organisation Cooperative

Sugar Journal, Cane Info, Records of District Statistical office and Statistical year book published by Government of India.

From the analysis, it is found that India is in the second place in area used and production of sugarcane but the productivity of sugarcane in India is average among the countries. Compound growth rate is also revealed that Brazil, Indonesia, China, Argentina, India and Mexico have recorded positive and significant at 1 and 10 per cent level of significance in area used for sugarcane production. Brazil, China, India and Argentina have recorded positive and significant compound growth rate at 1 and 5 per cent level of significance in production of sugarcane. Thailand, South Africa and India have recorded positive and significant compound growth rate at 5 and 10 per cent level of significance in productivity of sugarcane in overall Period.

In State-wise analysis, it is found that Tamil Nadu is the first in productivity of sugarcane in India for all the period even though area used for sugarcane production and volume of sugarcane production in Tamil Nadu is in third place for the overall period. In Compound growth rate analysis, it is found that Bihar, Karnataka, Maharashtra and Tamil Nadu have positive and statistically significant at 1, 5 and 10 per cent level of significance in area used for sugarcane production, volume of sugarcane production and productivity of sugarcane for the period of ten years.

In District-wise analysis, it is found that Erode district stands third place in area used for sugarcane production, volume of sugarcane production but productivity of sugarcane is in second place for the period of ten years. Compound growth rate also exposed that Namakkal, Salem, Villupuram and Pudukkotai have recorded positive and statistically significant at 1 and 10 per cent level of significance in area used for sugarcane production for ten years. Tiruvannmalai, Pudukkotai and Villupuram have recorded positive and significant compound growth rate at 5 and 10 per cent level of significance in production of sugarcane. Tiruvannmalai and Thanjavur have recorded positive and significant compound growth rate at 1 per cent level of significance in productivity of sugarcane.

Erode district has recorded positive and insignificant compound growth rate in area used for sugarcane production and volume of sugarcane production but the productivity of sugarcane has recorded negative and insignificant compound growth rate for the overall periods. In India, the export and import of sugar, in terms of volume and value are increased during the Period II. Compound growth rate revealed that the sugar export and import in India in terms of volume and values are positive and insignificant in all periods.

Chapter III: Cultivation Practices of Sugarcane Farmers

In this chapter, cultivation practices of sugarcane in this area have been highlighted. Further, factors influencing the farmers to cultivate sugarcane, cost and returns from sugarcane have been examined.

Factors influencing the farmers to cultivate sugarcane have been examined with the help of factor analysis. The most important factors influencing the farmers to cultivate sugarcane are 'Crop orientation factor' and 'Economic factor' since their Eigen values are 4.171 and 4.147 respectively. The Crop orientation factor consists of four variables with the variation explained by 20.857 per cent. The Economic factor consists of three variables with the variation explained by 20.733 per cent. The third and fourth factors are 'Maintenance factor' and 'General factor' since their respective Eigen values are 2.071 and 2.070. These two factors consist of three and four variables respectively and the per cent of variation explained by these two factors are 10.354 and 10.352 respectively. The fifth and sixth factors are 'Natural factor' and 'Technology factor' since their respective Eigen values are 2.055 and 1.342. These two factors consist of three variables and the per cent of variation explained by these two factors are 10.276 and 6.710 respectively.

The highly correlated variable of the Crop orientation factor is 'One year crop' with the factor loading of 0.896. The variable 'To get lump sum amount' is the highly correlated variable of the Economic factor since it has the highest factor loading of 0.911. 'Minimum risk' variable of the Maintenance factor has the highest factor loading of 0.816. In General factor, the variable 'provision of fertilizer by sugar factory' has the highest factor loading of 0.810. The highly correlated variable of the Natural factor is 'Suitability of Land and Soil' which has the factor loading of 0.869. Regarding the Technology factor, higher correlation is noticed in the case of variable 'Easy to adopt Drip irrigation', since it has the highest factor loading of 0.780.

It is found that majority of the farmers (92.33 per cent) are not cultivating intercrops in sugarcane cultivation. In order to find the reason for not following intercropping in sugarcane cultivation, Garrett ranking technique has been used. It is found that the 'High Input Price' is identified as the most important reason for not following intercropping in sugarcane cultivation with the highest mean score value of 62.49.

It is found that 50.67 percent of the farmers are used borrowed fund for cultivation of sugarcane. Further, it is found that 57.33 per cent of the farmers purchase setts from factory and also found 54.17 per cent of the farmers use upto 20000 setts per acre for sugarcane cultivation.

It is found that majority of farmers (93.67 percent) are cultivating Co 86032 variety in sugarcane cultivation. The Garrett ranking technique revealed that 'High yielding' variety is identified as the most significant reason for using a particular variety in sugarcane cultivation.

It is found that the cost of cultivation per acre incurred for small farm is ₹ 59,314.20, for medium farm is ₹ 65,442.90 and for large farm is ₹ 70,560.60 to planted sugarcane and the cost of cultivation per acre incurred for ratoon sugarcane for small farm is ₹ 51,659.30, for medium farm is ₹ 57,507.50 and large farm is ₹ 60,392.50.

The F-test revealed that there is a significant relationship in the average total cost among three sizes of farms. Further, there is a significant relationship found as regard to overall average returns per acre from cultivation of sugarcane and khandsari sugar. The Post Hoc test revealed that large farms are spending more amount the small and medium farms. As regard to returns from cultivation of sugarcane and khandsari sugar, small farms get more returns than that of medium and large farms.

The influence of input factor to increase the cultivation of sugarcane has been analysed with Cobb-Douglas production function analysis. It is found that the regression co-efficient for manure & fertilizers (-2.62), irrigation operation (-3.90) and setts (-0.168) are negative and regression co-efficient of manure & fertilizers and setts are showing significant at 10 per cent level of significance but the contribution of irrigation operation is significant at 1 per cent level of significance. The manure and fertilizers (3.36) is highly significant at 1 per cent level of significance followed by intercultural operation (3.02), land preparation (2.91) and sowing (2.31) also significant at 1 and 5 per cent level of significance. This means increase in yield level of sugarcane is directly proportional to increase in use of these inputs. The elasticity of production variable manure & fertilizer is 0.140which means one per cent increase in manure & fertilizer leads to increase the yield of sugarcane by 0.140 per cent. Similarly 1 per cent increase in intercultural operation, land preparation and sowing leads to increase the sugarcane yield by 0.266, 0.536 and 0.661 per cent respectively.

It is found that the regression co-efficient for manure & fertilizer (-0.348), labour for crushing (-0.025), irrigation operation (-0.020) and intercultural operation (-0.270) are negative and statistically significant at 1, 5 and 10 per cent level of significance. The land preparation (2.53) is highly significant at 5 per cent level of significance followed by setts (1.78) significant at 1 per cent level. This means increase in yield level of sugarcane and return of khandsari sugar are directly proportional to increase in use of these inputs. In ratoon crop, land preparation (3.10) is highly significant at 1 per cent level of significance. The manure &

fertilizers (-0.098) is negative and regression co-efficient shows significant at 5 per cent level of significance.

Chapter IV: Adoption of Drip Irrigation System in Sugarcane Cultivation

In this chapter, the factors influencing the farmers to adopt the drip irrigation system in sugarcane cultivation has been analysed with the help of factor analysis. Satisfaction of the farmers about the adoption of drip irrigation system in sugarcane cultivation has been analysed with help of chi-square test, F-test, Z-test and multiple regression analysis. The problems faced by the farmers in adoption of drip irrigation system and reasons for non-adoption of drip irrigation system in sugarcane cultivation have been analysed with help of Garrett Ranking Technique.

Factors Influencing the Farmers to Adopt Drip Irrigation System under Sugarcane Cultivation

The most important factors influencing the farmers to cultivate sugarcane under drip irrigation system are 'Irrigation factor' and 'Maintenance factor' since their Eigen values are 7.944 and 5.629 respectively. The Irrigation factor consists of five variables with the variation explained by 37.827 per cent. The Maintenance factor consists of seven variables with the variation explained by 26.805 per cent. The third factor is 'Yield factor' since its Eigen value is 3.744 and it also consists of five variables with the per cent of variation explained by this factor is 17.827.

The highly correlated variable of the Irrigation factor is 'Efficient and uniform irrigation' with the factor loading of 0.944. The variable 'Reduction in weeds' is the highly correlated variable of the Maintenance factor since it has the highest factor loading of 0.842. 'High yielding' variable of the Yield factor has the highest factor loading of 0.942.

Satisfaction of Farmers in Adoption of Drip Irrigation System in Sugarcane Cultivation

In this chapter, an attempt has been made to analyse the relationship between socio-economic variables and level of satisfaction of farmers about the adoption of drip irrigation system in sugarcane cultivation.

Significance of the relationship of all identified socio-economic variables with the satisfaction of farmers about the adoption of drip irrigation system in sugarcane cultivation has been analysed by applying the statistical techniques such as Chi-square test, F test and Z test.

Out of 123 farmers, 79 (64.23%) have high level of satisfaction about the adoption of drip irrigation system in sugarcane cultivation whereas 44 (35.77%) have low level of satisfaction about the adoption of drip irrigation system in sugarcane cultivation. The average score of 123 farmers are 70.31.

In age group analysis, a high percentage (70.8%) of middle aged group (between 31 and 50 years) farmers have high level of satisfaction about the adoption of drip irrigation system in sugarcane cultivation as compared to old aged group (above 50 years) and young aged (upto 30 years) group. The average score of middle aged group farmers (73.40) is higher than the other two groups.

In Educational level analysis, a high percentage (81.50%) of school level educated farmers have high level of satisfaction on adoption of drip irrigation system in sugarcane cultivation as compared to other groups. The average score of school level education farmers (76.33) is higher than the farmers in other levels of education.

In occupation of the farmers, a high percentage (68.30%) of the farmers belonging to 'agriculture & others' group has high level of satisfaction on adoption of drip irrigation system in sugarcane cultivation as compared to 'agriculture only' group farmers. The average score of the farmers belonging to 'agriculture only' (70.71) is higher than the farmers belonging to 'agriculture& others'.

In nature of the family, a high percentage (77.20%) of the farmers belonging to nuclear family group have high level of satisfaction on adoption of drip irrigation system in sugarcane cultivation as compared to joint family group. The average score of the farmers belonging to nuclear family (71.65) is higher than the farmers belonging to joint family group.

In size of the family, a high percentage (84.80%) of the farmers who belongs to small family have high level of satisfaction on adoption of drip irrigation system in sugarcane cultivation as compared to other two groups. The average score (73.80) of the farmers belonging to small family is higher than the other two groups.

In number of members involved in agriculture, a high percentage (79.40%) of the farmers belonging to above 3 members involved in agriculture group have high level of satisfaction on adoption of drip irrigation system in sugarcane cultivation as compared to upto 3 members groups. The average score (74.24) of the farmers with above 3members involved in agriculture is higher than the other group of farmers.

In annual income of the family, a high percentage (87.10%) of the farmers belonging to medium income group of the farmers have high level of satisfaction on adoption of drip irrigation system in sugarcane cultivation as compared to other two groups. The average score (76.29) of medium income group farmers is higher than the other two groups.

In annual expenditure of the family, a high percentage (78.40%) of the farmers belonging to medium expenditure group have high level of satisfaction on adoption of drip irrigation system in sugarcane cultivation as compared to other two groups. The average score (75.43) of medium expenditure group of farmers is higher than the other two expenditure groups.

In case of experience in agriculture, a high percentage (65.60%) of the farmers who belong to medium experience group (10-20 years) have high level of satisfaction on adoption of drip irrigation system in sugarcane cultivation as compared to other two experience groups. The average score (71.27) of high experience group of farmers is higher than the other two experience groups.

In case of experience in sugarcane cultivation, a high percentage (83.90%) of the farmers who belong to medium experience group have high level of satisfaction on adoption of drip irrigation system in sugarcane cultivation as compared to other two experience groups. The average score (77.65) of medium experience farmers is higher than the other two experience groups.

In sources of water for drip irrigation, a high percentage (65.30%) of the farmers who use bore well are having high level of satisfaction about the adoption of drip irrigation system in sugarcane cultivation as compared to other group of farmers. The average score (70.70) of the farmers with bore well in source of water for drip irrigation is higher than the other group of farmers.

In methods of drip irrigation, a high percentage (69.90%) of the farmers who follow surface irrigation have high level of satisfaction on adoption of drip irrigation system in sugarcane cultivation as compared to other methods of drip irrigation. The average score (70.51) of the farmers who use surface irrigation is higher than the other group of farmers.

In Chi-square test analysis, it is found that there exists a significant relationship between independent variables such as Age, Educational level, Nature of the family, Size of the family, Number of Members involved in Agriculture, Annual income, Annual Expenditure, Experience in Sugarcane cultivation, Methods of drip irrigation and the level of satisfaction of farmers about the adoption of drip irrigation system in sugarcane cultivation. Whereas an insignificant relationship between variables such as Occupation, Experience in Agriculture and Sources of water for drip irrigation and the level of satisfaction of farmers about the adoption of drip irrigation system in sugarcane cultivation.

The F-test applied has revealed that there is no significant relationship between the experience in agriculture and average score of the farmers. Whereas, there is a significant relationship between age, educational level, size of the family, annual income, annual expenditure and experience in sugarcane cultivation and average satisfaction score of the farmers.

The Z-test applied has revealed that there is a significant relationship between Nature of the family, Number of members involved in agriculture and methods of drip irrigation. Whereas, there is no significant relationship between occupation, experience in agriculture and sources of water for drip irrigation and average satisfaction score of the farmers.

Multiple Regression Analysis (Step-wise Model)

The present study investigates the relationship between the farmers' satisfaction and independent variables. For this research two sets of variables are selected. The independent variables considered are Age, Educational level, Nature of the Family, Size of the Family, Number of Members involved in Agriculture, Experience in Sugarcane Cultivation, Earning members in the family, Annual Income and Annual Expenditure. It is found that the model fit increases from 0.289 to 0.742 by adding more variables such as Number of members involved in Agriculture, Size of the Family, Experience in Sugarcane Cultivation, Age, Educational level, Annual Income, Nature of the Family, Earning members in the family, Annual Expenditure to the independent variable in a step-by-step process. The adjusted R square also shows an increase from 0.076 to 0.515. This indicates that the increasing trend of nine independent variables is significant in affecting satisfaction level of drip irrigation system in sugarcane cultivation.

Problems Faced by the Farmers in Adoption of Drip Irrigation System in Sugarcane Cultivation

To identify the problems in adoption of drip irrigation system in sugarcane cultivation, the Garrett Ranking Technique has been applied. The ten problems analysed are viz., Improper after sales service, Risk in application of fertilizer, Used only for one crop, Not suitable for small land holding, Problems in getting subsidies, Rat, rodent, insect & human damage to drip lines, Problems in drip equipment, High maintenance charges, Risk during the period of harvest and Need of acid treatment. As per the Garrett Ranking Technique, it is found that 'Risk during the period of harvest' is identified as the most significant problem in adoption of drip irrigation system in sugarcane cultivation with the highest mean score value of 66.39.

Reasons for Non-Adoption of Drip Irrigation System in Sugarcane Cultivation

The reasons for non-adoption of drip irrigation system in sugarcane cultivation are the availability of adequate water, high risk in sugarcane crop, high initial investment, high cost of maintenance, reduce soil fertility and imbalanced land. In order to identify the significant reason for non-adoption of drip irrigation system in sugarcane cultivation, Garrett Ranking Technique has been applied. As per the Garrett Ranking Technique, it is found that 'high initial investment' is identified as the most significant reason for non-adoption of drip irrigation system in sugarcane cultivation with the highest mean score value of 59.32.

Chapter V: Marketing Practices of Sugarcane Farmers

This chapter is dealt with marketing of sugarcane and marketing of khandsari sugar. In this chapter, the factors which motivates the farmers to market their sugarcane and khandsari sugar, to study the marketing cost, price spread and level of satisfaction of farmers about the functioning of sugarcane and khandsari sugar marketing channels have been identified.

Factors Motivating the Farmers to Market their Sugarcane

Out 600 farmers, 385 farmers (64.17 per cent) are marketing their sugarcane. Regarding reasons for marketing of sugarcane, it is found that the 'fixed price' is the vital factor which motivates the farmers with the highest mean score value of 4.44 to market their sugarcane. Further, it is found that majority of the farmers 313 (81.30 per cent) prefer channel-I to market their sugarcane. It is found that 'fixed price' is the significant factor which motivates the farmers to market their sugarcane to factory.

The study revealed that 72 farmers (18.70 per cent) prefer channel-II to market their sugarcane. It is also found that 'flexibility in harvesting' is the significant factor which motivates the farmers to market their sugarcane to jaggery producers.

Satisfaction of Farmers about the Functioning of Sugarcane Marketing Channels

It is found that the sugarcane farmers have high level of satisfaction on the 'arrangement of finance' by the sugar factory. Among 313 farmers, 275 (87.84 per cent) farmers have high level of satisfaction about the functioning of sugarcane marketing to factory.

The logistic regression model has also been applied to find out the relationship between personal and socio-economic factor that influenced the farmers' level of satisfaction about the functioning of sugarcane marketing channel-I. It is revealed that among the nine independent variables Age (χ_1), Size of the family (χ_4), Experience in agriculture (χ_7) and Experience in sugarcane cultivation (χ_8) are significantly related to the level of satisfaction of farmers about the functioning of sugarcane marketing channel-I. The co-efficient of $\chi_4, \chi_5, \chi_6, \chi_7$ and χ_8, are negative. This tells us an increase in the independent variable will result in a decrease in the probability of the event.

Further, it is revealed that the sugarcane farmers have high level of satisfaction on 'reasonable price' provided by the marketing channel-II. Among 72 farmers, 47 (64.71 per cent) farmers have low level of satisfaction about the functioning of sugarcane marketing to jaggery producers. The logistic regression model revealed that among the nine independent variables Occupation (χ_3) and Earnings members (χ_5) are significantly related to level of satisfaction of farmers about the functioning of sugarcane marketing channel-II. The co-efficient of $\chi_4, \chi_5, \chi_6, \chi_7$ and χ_9, are negative. This tells us an increase in the independent variable will result in a decrease in the probability of the event.

Marketing Cost and Price Spread of Sugarcane

It is found that cutting charge (₹ 535.95) is the marketing cost incurred by the farmers to market their sugarcane to sugar factory. In price spread analysis, it is observed that the farmers received the maximum price (net) of ₹ 1912.94 in channel-II for marketing of sugarcane.

Factors Motivating the Farmers to Produce of Khandsari Sugar

It is found that 'remunerative price for sugar' is the main factor which motivates the farmers to produce khandsari sugar. It also reveals that 130 (60.47 per cent) farmers prefer to market their khandsari sugar through commission agent. Regarding reasons to prefer a particular channel, it is found that 'to get advance money' is the most significant factor which motivates the farmers to market their khandsari sugar through channel-I (through commission agent) and it is found that 'immediate cash payment' is the important factor which motivates the farmers to market their khandsari sugar through channel-II (through regulated market).

Satisfaction of Farmers about the Functioning of Khandsari Sugar Marketing Channels

Regarding the satisfaction level of farmers about the functioning of khandsari sugar marketing channels, it is found that 118 (54.90 per cent) farmers have low level of satisfaction. The logistic regression model revealed that among the nine independent variables insignificantly related to level of satisfaction of farmers about the functioning of khandsari sugar marketing channels. The co-efficient of χ_1, χ_2, χ_3 and χ_9, are negative. This tells us an increase in the independent variable will result in a decrease in the probability of the event.

Marketing Cost and Price Spread of Khandsari Sugar

It is found that transport cost and packing cost are the major costs incurred by farmers to market their khandsari sugar. Price paid by consumer ₹ 2276.78 in channel-I and the producers' share in consumer rupee is 81.17. Hence, it is concluded that price spread is ₹ 428.80 for marketing of khandsari sugar through commission agent. Price paid by consumer ₹ 1957.28 in channel-II and the producers' share in consumer rupee is 97.64. Hence, it is concluded that price spread is ₹ 46.25 for marketing of khandsari sugar through regulated market.

Chapter VI: Cultivation and Marketing Problems of Sugarcane Farmers

In this chapter, Problems in Cultivation and Marketing of Sugarcane farmers have been identified.

Problems in Cultivation of Sugarcane

In the present study, it is found that cultivation of sugarcane in Erode district is declining. In this regard, it is found that shortage and high wages of labourers (4.44) is identified as the most important problem in cultivation of sugarcane. The result of cronbach's reliability analysis (0.651) is the significant reliability between the variables tested.

Problems in cultivation of sugarcane farmers have been analysed with the help of factor analysis. It is found that the most important problem in cultivation of sugarcane is 'Shortage and high cost of fertilizer and pesticides' with the factor loading of 0.877. The variable 'Low yield in ratoon crop' is the highly correlated variable since it has the highest factor loading of 0.804. 'Severity of diseases and new diseases' variable has the highest factor loading of 0.788. In case of maintenance orientation, the variable 'Low awareness among farmers to use improved cultivation practices' has the highest factor loading of 0.796. The highly correlated variable of the input orientation is 'Poor quality of fertilizer & pesticides' which has the factor loading of 0.625. Regarding the general problems, higher correlation is noticed in the variable 'Frequent power failure', since it has the highest factor loading of 0.888.

It is found that discriminant function is significant at 1 per cent level as chi-square test value (22.965) and wilk's lambda value (0.844) are significant at 1 per cent level. It further reveals that the correlation is 0.396. This shows that there is a moderate level of correlation between the grouping variable and the independent variables.

It is found that the group means for the discriminant functions are 0.282 for low problem group farmers and -0.649 for high problem group farmers and shows that the prior probabilities of low problem group farmers are 0.697 and high problem group farmers are 0.303. It is revealed that the variable 'Age' is the maximum discriminating variable i.e. 28.62 per cent between low and high problem group farmers in cultivation of sugarcane.

Problems in Production of Khandsari Sugar

It is identified that the 'non-availability of trained labourers' is the primary problem in the production of khandsari sugar with the highest mean score value of 4.28, followed by high wage rate, problem in ratoon crops growth, high fluctuation of sugar prices, problems due to rainy seasons, financial problem, high rental charge of machinery and high cost of chemicals.

Problems in Marketing of Sugarcane

In order to find the marketing problems faced by sugarcane farmers, Rank Based Quotient has been adopted. It is revealed that 'delay in payment' is the most significant problem in marketing of sugarcane to the factory with the highest RBQ value of 86.71and it is found that 'high wastage of sugarcane' is identified as the major problem in marketing of sugarcane to jaggery producers with the highest value of RBQ (81.67).

Problems in Marketing of Khandsari Sugar

In order to find the marketing problems faced by khandsari sugar farmers, Rank Based Quotient has been adopted. It is found that 'high commission charge' is identified as the significant problem in marketing of khandsari sugar through commission agent with the highest RBQ value of 80.94 and it is found that 'no advance money' is identified as the most important problem in marketing of khandsari sugar to regulated market with the highest RBQ value of 74.77.

7.3. Suggestions

On the basis of the findings of the present study, the following practicable and fruitful suggestions are offered:

1. It is found out that Erode district occupies the third position in area of cultivation and production of sugarcane in Tamil Nadu. In terms of sugarcane productivity Erode district occupied a second position during the entire past ten years (vide Table No. 2.13, 2.15 and 2.17). In compound growth rate analysis, it is found that Erode district has a negative and insignificant growth rate for a period of ten years due to decrease in productivity of sugarcane during the Period II (vide Table No.2.18). Hence, it is suggested that the Government should take up necessary steps to improve the

productivity of sugarcane in Erode district by introducing high yielding varieties which will be suitable for all seasons; training to farmers about the cultivation practices and adoption of modern methods & technologies in sugarcane cultivation. In order to increase the area of cultivation of sugarcane, the Government should increase the Fair and Remunerative Price and State Advisory Price.

2. It is found that the majority of farmers (92.33 per cent) are not cultivating intercrops during sugarcane cultivation (vide Table No. 3.4). The high input price is the major reason for not following intercropping in sugarcane cultivation (vide Table No. 3.5). Hence, it is suggested that the Government and the sugar factories should provide inputs to farmers at concessional or subsidised rates in order to motivate them to cultivate intercrops.

3. It is found from the production function analysis that the regression co-efficient for manure & fertilizers (-2.62), irrigation operation (-3.90) and setts (-0.168) are negative (vide Table No.3.32). This shows that the farmers have not utilised these resources to the fullest capacity. Hence, it is suggested that the farmers should use these resources in an efficient manner to increase the productivity of sugarcane. It is also suggested that the Government and sugar factories should take efforts to develop the pace of research in cultivation of sugarcane through Tamil Nadu Agricultural University. Periodical meets should be arranged by sugar factories to improve the cultivation practices and make the farmers aware of the utilisation of resources in an efficient manner which in turn will lead to the increase in the productivity of sugarcane.

4. Through production function analysis, it is found that the regression co-efficient for manure & fertilizer (-0.348), labour for crushing (-0.025), irrigation operation (-0.020) and intercultural operation (-0.270) are negative (vide Table No. 3.33). This indicates that the sugarcane farmers who produce khandsari sugar have not fully utilised these resources through proper and efficient way. Hence, it is suggested that they have to use these resources in an efficient manner which will help them to increase the productivity of sugarcane and output of khandsari sugar. For this purpose, the Government should help the farmers by conducting awareness programmes about using the inputs in a balanced manner.

5. It is found that the 'risk during the period of harvest' and 'the high maintenance charges' are the most important problems in adopting drip irrigation system in sugarcane cultivation (vide Table No. 4.30). Hence, it is suggested to the dripping companies that they should demonstrate clearly and effectively through qualified

extension officers about the maintenance of drip irrigation system in a cost effective manner. It is also suggested that the dripping companies may also provide training and service facilities for maintaining drip irrigation system.

6. It is found that majority of the sugarcane farmers (79.50 per cent) do not adopt drip irrigation system in sugarcane cultivation. It is also found that the 'high initial investment' is the major reason for non-adoption of drip irrigation system in sugarcane cultivation (vide Table No. 4.31). Hence, it is suggested that the Government should extend the period of subsidy to the large farmers to adopt drip irrigation system. Private sector commercial banks should also come forward to provide agricultural loans to the sugarcane farmers for adopting drip irrigation system.

7. It is found that out of 385 farmers, who market their sugarcane to sugar factories and jaggery producers, only 18.70 per cent of the farmers prefer to market their sugarcane to jaggery producers (vide Table No.5.2). This may be due to price instability. Hence, it is suggested that the Government should regulate the pricing of jaggery through Fair and Remunerative Price (FRP) and State Advisory Price (SAP) systems which in turn may ensure price stability.

8. It is found that 'shortage and high wages of labourers' is the most important problem in cultivation of sugarcane (vide Table No. 6.1). Farm mechanisation is the viable solution to overcome this problem. Hence, it is suggested that the Government should take steps to provide loans at subsidised rates to purchase farm equipment needed for sugarcane cultivation. Further, it is suggested that the Government may take all possible steps to impart adequate training for the farmers to use of equipment in an efficient manner. The small size of the land holding, limits the use of machines for harvesting. Therefore, there is also a need for research towards evolving suitable machinery to facilitate harvesting of sugarcane particularly in small land holdings.

9. The present study shows that, out of 600 sugarcane farmers, 215 farmers (35.83 per cent) produce khandsari sugar. It is found that the non-availability of trained labourers is the major problem faced by the khandsari sugar producing farmers (vide Table No. 6.11). Hence, it is suggested to the Agricultural department and other concerned authorities to provide special training for labourers to improve their skills.

10. In the present study, out of 600 sugarcane farmers, 313 sugarcane farmers (52.17 per cent) market their sugarcane to sugar factories. It is found that delay in payment and fixed/low price are the major problems in marketing of sugarcane to sugar factories (vide Table No.6.12). It is suggested to the sugar factories that they may come forward

to settle the payment due to the farmers within a reasonable time by considering the economic status of sugarcane farmers. Further, it is suggested that the Government should regulate the payment mechanism of sugar factories. For solving the problem of fixed/low price for sugarcane, the government and sugar factories should fix reasonable price for sugarcane by considering the cost of cultivation of sugarcane.

11. It is found that 'no advance money' is identified as the most important problem in marketing of khandsari sugar through regulated market (vide Table No.6.15). Hence, it is suggested to the market committee of regulated markets or state government that regulate markets may extend the facility of payment of advance money to the farmers producing and marketing khandsari sugar through regulated markets which in turn may increase the number of sugarcane farmers to market their khandsari sugar through regulated market.

General Suggestions

1. Continuous usage of excessive water by farmers has led to depletion of soil fertility. Since water is often used in excess of requirement in sugarcane fields, there is a need for educating farmers to follow irrigation schedules properly.

2. The frequent power failure is another cultivation problem faced by the sugarcane farmers. It affects the sugarcane production. Government should ensure uninterrupted power supply to agricultural sector. This will lead to increased output.

3. Sugarcane, being a long term crop, the farmers are making it as sole crop, as they are not aware of intercrops in sugarcane. It is suggested that the agricultural department and sugar factories may direct their efforts to educate the farmers regarding intercrops that can be taken up along with sugarcane cultivation which not only increases the total income but also the intercrops can be used as natural manure.

7.4. Suggestions for Further Research

The following are suggested for further research:

1. Seasonality Index analysis can be made for the price arrivals of white sugar & khandsari sugar in markets and month wise production and export & import of sugar in India compared with other countries.

2. Compound growth rate of the productivity of sugarcane in Erode district has recorded negative and insignificant. Hence, a research can be made to find out the reasons for the reduction in productivity of sugarcane in Erode district.

3. Separate studies could be undertaken on cultivation and marketing of Khandsari sugar and Jaggery and value added product of khandsari sugar.

4. A study of this nature can be extended to all the districts of Tamil Nadu where sugarcane is a major crop so as to get a complete picture about the problem of sugarcane farmers of Tamil Nadu.

5. Separate studies could be undertaken for identifying the problems in the adoption of drip irrigation system in sugarcane cultivation.

6. A comparative study on profitability of sugarcane with other crops can be made.

7. Separate studies could be undertaken on cultivation problems in a sustainable sugarcane initiative and mechanisation of cultivation practices of sugarcane.

8. Further research on the role of sugarcane marketing in rural economy may be undertaken.

7.5.   Conclusion

Agriculture is an important sector in our Indian economy. Drastic changes are required to develop agriculture in India on par with advanced countries. The Government must initiate steps to improve agriculture in India through proper and well-defined strategies, to make the agricultural sector more flourishing in future. It is the pious duty of the government to bring the smile, back to our farmers and crucial measures are necessary to make agriculture a profitable activity. In fact, agriculture sector needs a thorough overhauling and a new deal including increasing investment in irrigation and rural infrastructure, credit delivery, increase the use of modern science &technologies, the diversification of the cropping pattern, educating the farmers, improving rural connectivity and access to information etc. to make agriculture a sustainable and globally competitive. The purpose of regulation of agricultural markets is to protect the farmers from exploitation of intermediaries &traders and also to ensure better prices and timely payment for their produce.

The results of the present study revealed the area, production, productivity of sugarcane in this area. The various constraints faced by the sugarcane farmers in adopting drip irrigation has also been studied. The various problems faced by the sugarcane farmers in the cultivation and marketing of sugarcane have also been identified. Several suggestions have been offered in relation to the finding. If the Government, Research Institutes, Sugar Factories, Agricultural department, Farmers and other concerned authorities are able to implement these suggestions, the life of the farmers and the sugarcane cultivation and marketing in this area would really be a shining one.

BIBLIOGRAPHY

Books

1. S.S. Acharya and N.L. Agarwal, "Agricultural Marketing In India", Oxford & IBH Publishing Company Private Limited, New Delhi, 2005.

2. H.S. Anitha, "Agricultural Marketing-A case study of Areca Nut Marketing", Mangaldeep Publications, Jaipur, India, 2000.

3. G.C. Beri, "Marketing Research", Tata McGraw-Hill Publishing Company Ltd., New Delhi, 2006.

4. H. Buntin, "A Change in Agriculture", Gerald Duckworth and Company Limited, London, 1970.

5. A. David, Aaker, V. Kumar, George and S. Day, "Marketing Research", Wiley India (P) Limited, New Delhi, 2006.

6. K. Dhanasekaran, "Computer Applications in Economics", Vrinda Publications (P) Limited, New Delhi, 2010.

7. I.C. Dhingra, "Indian Economy", Sultan Chand & Sons, New Delhi, 1999.

8. Gerald Keller, "Statistical for Management and Economics", Seventh edition, Cengage Learning, New Delhi, 2008.

9. S.P. Gupta, "Statistical Methods", Sultan Chand & Sons, New Delhi, 2007.

10. Jagdish Prasad, "Encyclopaedia of Agricultural Marketing",Mittal Publications, 1999.

11. Jonathan Anderson, Berry H. Durston and Millicent Poole, "Thesis and Assignment Writing", Oxford & IBH Publishing Company Private Limited, New Delhi, 1970.

12. C.R. Kothari, "Research Methodology: Methods &Techniques", New Age International Private Limited, New Delhi, 2007.

13. C.B. Mamoria and Satish Mamoria, "Marketing Management", Kitab Mahal publications, New Delhi, 1991.

14. Mohd Iqbal Ali and G. Bhaskar, "WTO, Globalization and Indian Agriculture", flew Century Publications, New Delhi, India, 2011.

15. Naresh K. Malhotra and Sathyabughan Desh, "Marketing Research-An Applied Orientation", Pearson Education, New Delhi, 2009.

16. K. Padmanabhan, "Economic Analysis of Marketing", Print well, Jaipur, 1993.

17. R.S.N. Pillai and V. Bagavathi, "Modern Marketing", Sultan Chand & Company Ltd., New Delhi, 2007.

18. Pranav K. Desai, "Agricultural Economics", Biotech Books, New Delhi, 2010.

19. H.R. Racer, "India Agriculture", Oxford and IBH Publishing Company, New Delhi, 1982.

20. Rajan Kumar Sahoo, "Agricultural Marketing Problems and Prospects", Doninant Publishers and Distributors Pvt. Ltd., New Delhi, 2011.

21. Ramesh Chand, "Agricultural Marketing", Educational publishers & Distributors, Delhi, 2011.

22. K.P. Ruddar Datt and M. Sundharam, "Indian Economy", S. Chand & Company Ltd., New Delhi, 2007.

23. S. Sankaran, "Agricultural Economy of India", Margham Publications, Chennai, 2006.

24. S. Sankaran, "Indian Economy", Margham Publication, Chennai, 2000.

25. A. Singh and A.N. Sadhu, "Agricultural problems in India", Himalaya Publishing, Mumbai, 1986.

26. S. SureshBabu, "Cocount Production and Marketing", Abhijeet publications, Delhi, 2010.

27. S.R. Takle and V.B. Bhise, "Behaviour of market prices of Agricultural Commodities", Serials Publications, New Delhi, 2007.

28. B.P. Tyagi, "Agricultural Economics and Rural Development", Jai Prakash Nath & Co., Neerut, India, 2005.

Journals

1. African Crop Science Journal

2. African Journal of Agricultural Research

3. Agricultural Banker

4. Agricultural Economics

5. Agricultural Economics Research Review

6. Agricultural Financing

7. Agricultural Marketing

8. Agricultural Situation in India

9. Agriculture Update

10. Asian Economic Review

11. Bihar Journal of Agricultural Marketing

12. Continental Journal of Agricultural Economics

13. Cooperative Sugar

14. Economic Affairs

15. Facts for you

16. Financing Agriculture

17. Independent Journal of a Management & Production (IJM&P)

18. Indian Journal of Agricultural Economics

19. Indian Journal of Agricultural Marketing

20. Indian Journal of Agricultural Research

21. International Journal of Advanced Computer and Mathematical Sciences

22. International Journal of Agricultural Science

23. International Journal of Commerce and Business Management

24. International Journal of Economics and Research

25. International Research Journal of Finance and Economics

26. Indian Sugar

27. Journal of International Agricultural Trade and Development

28. Journal of Sustainable Development in Agriculture & Environment

29. Karnataka Journal of Agricultural Sciences

30. Kisan World

31. Marketology

32. Research Methodology in Social Science

33. S.E. Golden Jubilee Year

34. Southern Economist

35. The IUP Journal of Marketing Management

36. World Journal of Agricultural Sciences

Magazines

1. Naveena Velanmai (Tamil)

2. KarumbuOru Kaiyadu (Tamil)

3. Pasumai Vigadan (Tamil)

News Papers

1. Dhina Thanthi

2. The Economies Times

3. The Hindu

4. The New Indian Express

Websites

1. www.agmarknet.nic.in

2. www.agriculture.com

3. www.apeda.gov.in

4. www.caneinfo.nic.in

5. www.dacnet.com

6. www.erode.tn.nic.in

7. www.fao.org

8. www.icar.org.in

9. www.iisr.nic.in

10. www.india.gov.in

11. www.indiansugar.com

12. www.indiastat.com

13. www.isosugar.org

14. www.jains.com

15. www.krishiworld.com

16. www.nabard.org

17. www.sissta.org

18. www.sugar.org

19. www.sugarcane.res.in

20. www.tn.gov.in